AMONG THE RIGHTEOUS

AMONG THE
RIGHTEOUS

Lost Stories from the Holocaust's

Long Reach into Arab Lands

ROBERT SATLOFF

PUBLICAFFAIRS
New York

The maps on pages 62 and 140 are taken from Martin Gilbert's *The Routledge Atlas of the Holocaust*, 3rd edition. London: Routledge, 2002. Reproduced by permission of Taylor and Francis Books, UK.

The poem on pages 193–195, Catherine Tihanyi, "Once upon a time, on the sparkling shores of the Mediterranean," originally appeared in *Anthropology and Humanism Quarterly*, 1988, 13(3), pp. 73–74.

Published in the United States by PublicAffairs™, a member of the Perseus Books Group.

Library of Congress Cataloging-in-Publication Data

Satloff, Robert B. (Robert Barry)
    Among the righteous : lost stories from the Holocaust's long reach into Arab lands / Robert Satloff. — 1st ed.
        p.   cm.
    Includes bibliographical references and index.
    ISBN-13: 978-1-58648-399-9 (alk. paper)
    ISBN-10: 1-58648-399-4
    1. Jews—Persecutions—Arab countries. 2. Jews—Arab countries—History—20th century. 3. Holocaust, Jewish (1939-1945)—Arab countries. 4. Arab countries—Ethnic relations. I. Title.
DS135.A68S28 2006
940.53'180961—dc22

2006020968

First Edition
10 9 8 7 6 5 4 3 2 1

To
Mom and Dad,
Benji and William,
and Jennie

We were educated from childhood that the Holocaust is a big lie.

—**Muhammad Al-Zurqani,** editor-in-chief of the Egyptian government newspaper *Al-Liwaa Al-Islami,* which published a July 2004 article, "The Lie About the Burning of the Jews," alleging that the extermination of Jews during World War II was a lie invented by Zionists

We all condemn the policies of Hitler and the Holocaust, but enough is enough. There is a moment of saturation and, let me be very blunt on this, world Jewry is in danger because of the very irresponsible policies of the government of Israel, supported by some unaware leaders of the Jewish community in the United States. I hate to see a day where there is an unleashing of dormant general anti-Semitism, in Europe, particularly, and maybe in the United States. But we Arabs are not part of it. We are not part of the Holocaust. We never persecuted Jews.

—**Kamal Abul Magd,** prominent Muslim theologian and political moderate, speaking at the American University in Cairo, September 2003

There are many admirable, high-minded intellectuals in the Arab world fighting and risking their lives for issues like human rights, liberty, democracy, justice, and so on, but it is amazing that no one has thought of why and how these issues are pertinent to the Holocaust, nor of why and how reflection on the Holocaust is essential to them.

—**Anwar Chemseddine,** pseudonym of a professor of English literature at a university in North Africa, from his Internet essay "The Arabs' View of the Holocaust Is Indeed Troubled"

This memorial stands in memory of history's most revolting events. I am disgusted and outraged by what I saw today. The evil and hatred used by mankind in that period is truly disgusting. These events must make us stand together to promote peace and teach tolerance to ensure that such brutality is never repeated. What we saw today must help us change evil into good and hate to love and war into peace.

—**A young prince from an Arab Gulf state,** after visiting the U.S. Holocaust Memorial Museum, February 2004

CONTENTS

MAPS AND INSERTS

MAPS

INSERTS

Introduction

Casablanca's Lost Story

T HE CENTRAL QUESTION OF THIS BOOK is "Did any Arabs save any Jews during the Holocaust?" Trite as it sounds, the idea behind that question came to me as I walked along the white stripe painted in the middle of Fifth Avenue in the eerie emptiness of the afternoon of September 11, 2001. Although this book was originally motivated by the awful events of that day, one of the conclusions I reached in the course of my research was that it could—and should—have been written much earlier.

I am, by training, an historian of the modern Middle East, schooled at Oxford, Harvard, and Duke, and, by profession, an analyst of the politics of the countries and peoples of that region. Almost everything I have ever written has been about Arabs. To do this, I have learned their language, studied their culture, and lived among them. Throughout, I have tried, with great empathy, to understand who they are, where they come from, and what makes them tick.

I am also a Jew—a fact that, I am sure, was responsible for my career choice. I am loyal to my country, America, and proud of my connection to the Jewish homeland, Israel. I came of age, intellectually and politically, in the late 1970s and early 1980s, the era of Anwar el-Sadat, the journey to Jerusalem, and Israel's peace with Egypt, a hopeful moment when, to many Americans—and certainly to most American Jews—Arabs stopped being caricatures and started being flesh-and-blood, three-dimensional figures. This was also the time when Islamic extremists, including Sadat's killers, began to set their sights on America as the Great Satan, with Israel relegated to

1

the lesser role of devil's helper. In one of those unspoken decisions that determine one's life, I decided that understanding Arabs was important to my being Jewish. And because of the many ties that bind America and Israel, and because of the rising sense of direct clash between the United States and the Middle East, I decided that understanding Arabs was also an important part of my being American. I have lived my life at the point where those four—America and Israel, Jews and Arabs—intersect.

In the twenty-five years since I started studying Arabic and traveling to the Middle East, two ideas stand out.

First is the fact that "Arab culture" is really many cultures, that "Arab people" are really many peoples, and that "Arab countries" are filled with a combustible mix of ethnicity, religion, nationalism, and race that produces the entire range of human passions. That insight alone, I believe, makes comprehensible much of the seemingly impenetrable politics of the Middle East.

Second is an observation about the role of history in the lives of Arabs and Jews. For both groups, the past is a powerful source of motivation, grievance, and legitimacy. From God's covenant with Abraham to his promise to Muhammad, from the Balfour Declaration to the Sykes-Picot Agreement, from Israel's War of Independence to the Nakba, which is the Arabic term for "catastrophe" commonly used for Israel's birth, the role of history as narrative resonates deeply among both Arabs and Jews.

Jews, both in Israel and the Diaspora, are steeped in the details of history. The United States alone boasts more than fifty separate local Jewish historical associations and another fifty local Jewish genealogical societies, plus all the national Jewish organizations;[1] Israel, a country of just 6 million, has more than 215 museums, with more opening every year.[2] The intra-Israeli clash between traditional historians and "new historians"—between mainstream Zionists and their "post-Zionist" critics—is the stuff of great national debate.

Similarly, in Arab countries, as throughout most Muslim societies, history excites, inspires, and animates civic life. "The Muslim peoples, like everyone else in the world, are shaped by their history, but, unlike some others, they are keenly aware of it," writes the eminent historian Bernard Lewis. "Middle Easterners' perception of history is nourished from the pulpit, by the schools, and by the media. [It is] vivid and powerfully resonant."[3] Across

Arab lands, historical allusions more than a millennium old—such as the names of Muslim battlefield victories from the seventh century—adorn freshly built universities (such as Yarmouk and Mu'tah, in Jordan) and even an inter-Arab consortium of satellites (Badr).[4]

But there is a difference: Jews live predominantly in democracies, where history, like politics, is alive with bustle, debate, and disorder. Most Arabs, by contrast, live in closed societies, where rulers fear uncertainty and spend their nation's wealth controlling it. Although Arab peoples may revere the study, writing, and teaching of history, their leaders are more likely to view a clash of historians as a source of threat, rather than a source of strength.

The result is that historians in most Arab countries are more like the court chroniclers of long-dead dynasties, and the hollow or distorted history they write and teach reflects the difference between intellectual and government employee.[5] This phenomenon has produced a generation of Arabs that knows little about the details and texture of their own history, especially the modern history of the republics, monarchies, and principalities in which they live today. I recall that many Jordanians who read a book I wrote on their country's politics in the 1950s, an especially turbulent time for the Hashemite royal family, told me it had filled in an historical black hole for them, telling stories of people and events that no Jordanian had ever done. Western scholars may chafe at rules that control access to official government documents, but they are nothing compared to the restrictions on information that exist in the Middle East. When I was doing doctoral research in the late 1980s, the University of Jordan housed a massive collection of books in what was then called the "forbidden room" of the school's library. Through political connections, I gained access to the room, which contained some hard-to-find volumes written by and about people out of royal favor but certainly nothing that was worthy of labeling secret. Indeed, the very act of writing history in many Arab countries can be risky business. In this part of the world, it is not uncommon for new leaders to airbrush their predecessors out of history—such is the fate, for example, of Egypt's Sadat and Tunisia's Habib Bourghuiba. Woe unto the historian who has already immortalized the ancien régime in print!

But none of this was actually in my mind as I walked down the middle of Fifth Avenue that sunny Tuesday afternoon. I had practical matters to think about—like contacting my wife, who I later learned had been evacuated from her office two blocks from the White House, deciding where I was going to sleep that night, and figuring how I was going to get back home, to Washington. But I also thought a lot about the audacity of the people who took down the towers that day.

Killing, as Cain learned, is an audacious act, and killing on a grand scale is even more so. As genocides have become frequent occurrences, we know that the potential for such killing is always there, from the knives drawn in Rwanda to the death pits of Bosnia. The worst genocide of all, the Holocaust, stands out because it was the most audacious—Germans employed the most scientifically advanced means of the day in the most culturally advanced society in the world to kill the greatest number of people as quickly and efficiently as possible. On a much smaller scale, the killers of 9/11 did just that. Using the most modern of technologies, they exceeded—if just for a couple of hours—the deadly output of Auschwitz, and were the terrorists able to do so, they would have multiplied the killing many times over. To my mind, the plume of smoke rising over the wounded towers conjured to me the chimneys of the death camps, two examples of killers audaciously perfecting murder on an industrial scale.

None of that would have occurred to the perpetrators of the attacks, of course. But that is as much because of the culture that shaped them as the ideology that motivated them. Virtually alone among peoples of the world, Arabs have effectively claimed—and won—exemption from the global campaign to remember the most audacious crime in history. Soon after 9/11, I surveyed Holocaust and tolerance-related institutions and found that not a single module, text, or program for Holocaust education existed in an Arab country, even within the context of studying twentieth-century history, modern genocides, or tolerance education.[6]

At one level, this phenomenon is easy to explain. Arabs—even many modern, moderate, and enlightened Arabs—opt out of discussions about the Holocaust because of its special relevance to Jews and its role in the creation of Israel. A review of documents at the U.S. Holocaust Memorial Museum, for example, shows that only one Arab at or near the highest level of government—a young prince from a Gulf state—ever left a record of an official visit to the museum in its history.[7] In the eyes of many Arabs, the catastrophe of Israel's founding would not have occurred if the catastrophe of the Holocaust had not occurred first; accepting the uniqueness and enormity of the latter therefore runs the risk of accepting the validity and legitimacy of the former. As an historian, it is important to recognize the critical role that the Holocaust did play in the founding of Israel—as source of tragic clarity to Jews about the need for independent Jewish sovereignty, as source of cruel stimulus for Jewish immigration to Palestine, and as source of international sympathy for the Jewish people's claim to self-determination. At the same time, it is necessary to point out that the Holocaust provides neither the first, nor the primary, nor the only rationale for the establishment of a Jewish state. By the time German panzers rolled into Poland, modern Zionism was already more than forty years old and the Zionists had attracted so many Jews to Palestine that the British, who governed the territory under a post–World War I mandate, had already proposed to partition the land to accommodate two states for two peoples, one Jewish and one Arab. For most Arabs I have met, that history muddies the image of European colonialists paying with Arab land to atone for their guilt over the fate of the Jews during World War II. To them, the creation of Israel was the world's indulgence to Jews as compensation for the destruction of the Holocaust; validating the latter can only validate the former.

However easy to explain, this phenomenon is not so easy to excuse. In the weeks that followed the 9/11 attacks, as my focus moved from Manhattan to the Middle East, it dawned on me that we do no favors to Arabs to exempt them from this history, whatever connection the Holocaust may have to their political dispute with Israel. To borrow a phrase from another context, sparing Arabs the responsibility of Holocaust remembrance actually exposes the soft bigotry of our own low expectations. And, as the events of 9/11 made clear, it certainly does us no favor either.

At that early date, I decided that the most useful response I could offer to 9/11 was to combat Arab ignorance of the Holocaust.[8] The question was how to do it. An adversarial approach, I soon realized, was the wrong way to engage Arabs if I truly wanted to change attitudes on a taboo topic. To do that, I needed to make the Holocaust accessible to Arabs; I needed to make the Holocaust an Arab story.

The answer came to me one autumn evening in 2001. "Whoever saves one life, saves the entire world," says the Qur'an, an echo of the Talmud's injunction "If you save one life, it is as if you have saved the world." If I could tell the story of a single Arab who saved a single Jew during the Holocaust, then perhaps I could make Arabs see the Holocaust as a source of pride, worthy of remembering, not just something to avoid or deny. It was, I thought, the most positive solution I could imagine.

When that idea first came to me, I figured my work was half done. I am not an expert on the history of the Holocaust, and my assumption was that stories of Arabs who saved Jews already circulated among the cognoscenti but were not widely known. In the context I know best—modern Middle East history—such was the case, for example, in 1929, when a few brave Arabs saved the lives of dozens of Jews from an Arab massacre in the biblical city of Hebron. Surely, I thought, the Holocaust had its share of these stories, too. I would only have to find them, mine them, and popularize them.

I was wrong. After a flurry of e-mails—to Sir Martin Gilbert, the renowned historian; to Walter Reich, the former director of the U.S. Holocaust Memorial Museum; and, ultimately, to Mordechai Paldiel, the widely respected head of the Department of the Righteous at Israel's national memorial to the Holocaust, Yad Vashem—reality set in: Nearly sixty years after the war, no Arab had ever been officially recognized as a rescuer of Jews. "What an interesting topic," a distinguished scholar wrote in reply to a query from me. "Good luck in your work."[9]

Two months after 9/11, my wife and I decided to move to Rabat, the capital of the North African kingdom of Morocco. My first encounter with North Africa was as a child, when my father told fascinating, if unnerving, tales from his wartime stops in Casablanca, Algiers, and Oran in 1943, courtesy of the U.S. Air Force, but I had never been there myself. For Jennie and me, the decision to move there broke a pattern. Throughout our eleven years of marriage, we had kept our professional lives apart; she, an economist at the World Bank, worked previously on Vietnam, Russia, and sub-Saharan Africa, but never an Arab country. When Jennie received an offer to relocate to the field office in Rabat, we decided not to pass up the one opportunity to live in a country where our interests might overlap. In April 2002, we left Washington with our two young boys and settled into our new home in Morocco.

Over the next two and a half years, my tiny office on the second floor of our white stucco house at 1 Oulad Fares Street became the world headquarters of a far-flung effort to find Arabs who had saved Jews during the Holocaust. My research extended to a dozen countries on four continents; I drew on the skills of a small army of archivists, translators, interviewers, and researchers as well as the advice and counsel of many experts far more knowledgeable than I in the history of the Holocaust. Early on, I realized that it made no sense to focus solely on a narrow search for Arabs who saved Jews. Context matters. Without understanding the Nazi, Fascist, and Vichy efforts to extend their Holocaust-era persecution of Jews to Arab lands, without understanding how the half-million Jews of Europe's Arab possessions fared under this threat, and without understanding the many different roles that Arab populations of these lands played during this experience, there could be no real meaning to specific stories of Arabs who saved Jews—if they existed, at all. What started as a small, boutique effort to find one Arab who saved one Jew mushroomed into the most complex mega-project of my life.

This book contains what I found. It is, I admit at the outset, not the comprehensive account of any of the concentric circles I just described. That mammoth task awaits a team of graduate students who will make their careers combing over each of the more than 100 sites of German, French, and Italian forced labor set up in Arab countries, sketching the personal tales of the thousands of Jews—both Ashkenazim and Sephardim—interned at "punishment camps" in the Sahara, or assessing the way scores of Arab leaders and officials dealt with the competing tugs of their public responsibilities, on the one hand, and their private friendships with Jews, on the other hand. This book is a more modest undertaking. It is part history, part travelogue, part memoir. It is the story of *my* search for an Arab who saved a Jew during the Holocaust—the "Righteous" of the title—and what I found along the way: the discoveries I made, the personalities I encountered, the lessons I learned.

One of those lessons is that the Holocaust experience of Jews and others persecuted in Arab lands are not "untold stories" but rather "lost stories." Recall, for example, this scene from the movie *Casablanca*, in which a Gestapo officer urges the devoted wife of the Czech underground leader to convince her husband to return to Paris under German protection.

MAJOR STRASSER: There are only two other alternatives for him.
ILSE: What are they?
MAJOR STRASSER: It is possible the French authorities will find a reason
to put him in the concentration camp here.
ILSE: And the other alternative?
MAJOR STRASSER: My dear Mademoiselle, perhaps you have observed
that in Casablanca, human life is cheap. Good night, Mademoiselle.

When Warner Bros. released the movie, in December 1942, filmgoers did
not scratch their heads at this passing reference to French "concentration
camps" in Morocco. The existence of these camps—much like the terrible
fate of Jews more generally—was known, certainly among those who were
interested in knowing. Somehow, over the last sixty years, those stories have
been lost. There were even brief accounts of Arab rescuers mentioned in
well-known books and memoirs of the period; historians never picked up on
these, either, and they were also lost. One of the goals of this book is to recapture those stories and revive them; another is to explain how they were lost
and why.

Along the way, I include relevant statistics—how many were killed, how
many were interned, and so on—but I try not to fixate on them. Based solely
on a numerical comparison with the enormity of the horror in Europe, the
experience of Jews in Arab lands during the war barely deserves mention
and the frequent recitation of statistics inevitably invites such judgment.
Such an emphasis on numbers, however, has the effect of ripping these stories from their historical, cultural, and geographic roots and distorting the
narrative of the people—both Jews and Arabs—whose lives were touched
by the long reach of the Holocaust. This book represents the distillation of
years of research, but it is ultimately about stories and the people who lived
them; the comprehensive, authoritative account of what transpired in Arab
lands during World War II awaits a future volume.

I expect this book to provoke controversy. Over two generations, most
Arabs and most Jews have settled into a comfortable pattern of how to view
each other's role *in* history and each other's understanding *of* history. The
stories I tell—both of what happened between Jews and Arabs sixty years
ago and how each of them relate to that history today—challenge conven-

tion within each community. The lessons I derive from my research are not likely to go down easily with either.

No one who knows me or reads what I have written over the past two decades can accuse me of romanticizing the politics or peoples of the Middle East. The gruesome accounts of torture, betrayal, and death I recount in this book will only confirm that reputation. But, in fact, this is the most hopeful story I have ever told. Recapturing these lost stories from the Holocaust's long reach into Arab lands offers people of goodwill among each community—Arab and Jewish—a way to look through the lens of one of the most powerful narratives in history and see each other differently. It is the most positive response I could offer to the events of that Tuesday morning in September.

———— ∞ ————

EARLY IN THIS INTRODUCTION, I wrote that understanding the complex ethnic, religious, national, and racial makeup of Arab societies makes comprehensible much of the Middle East's seemingly impenetrable politics. In order to make this book accessible to nonspecialists, I have taken the risk of disregarding that prime directive. Throughout, I use the shorthand term "Arab" to refer to the Muslim population of the countries in question. Many of these people were not, in fact, ethnic Arabs; a large proportion, for example, were Berbers, native peoples of northwest Africa whose culture and languages predate the Arab Muslim conquests. Similarly, the distinction between Jews and Arabs fails to take account of the variety of Jewish communities in Arab lands at this time. Most Jews in these countries spoke Arabic as their first language; in a sense they were "Arab Jews." There were also large groups of Jews of recent (and not so recent) European origin—Italian, Maltese, Greek, and so forth—who maintained linguistic, cultural, and sometimes even political ties to their countries of origin. Dissecting the different wartime experiences of these various ethnic and national subgroups will, someday, make an excellent dissertation (or two). Because the stories I tell in this book are complicated enough as they are, I decided that the limitation of using the shorthand terms was worth the risk.

In the same vein, I have also tried to make the many names of Arabs mentioned in the book as accessible to the nonspecialist as I could. Therefore, I opted not to apply academic standards of transliteration, which have a way of making Arabic names even more distant and unattainable to a Western reader. Instead, wherever possible (and with a few exceptions), I used the spelling actually preferred by the person in question. So, for example, "Muhammad" often becomes "Mohamed," the way Tunisians in the 1940s tended to spell the name.

Chapter 1

From Tunis to Dachau

I N LATE OCTOBER 2005, on a beautiful Indian summer day in Paris, I pressed the security code on a panel outside a stately residence on fashionable Avenue Kléber, not far from the Arc de Triomphe, pushed open the massive front door, and went inside. After identifying myself on the intercom, I pressed the buttons on another security code inside an elevator and went up to the third floor. There, I was met by Frédéric Gasquet, a trim, silver-haired man whose youthful looks belied his sixty-four years. My host, whom I had never met before, greeted me as though we were old friends. An intense, precise man with a warm, welcoming smile, Mr. Gasquet was attired in that sort of casual elegance that sophisticated Parisian men carry off so well. He led me to a comfortable sofa and brewed me a cup of coffee. I could tell that he was anxious about what I had come to discuss, but he masked it well.

I had come to talk with Mr. Gasquet about our common interest in what happened six decades ago to a Tunisian Jewish family named Scemla. In the closing weeks of 1942, thousands of German troops fanned out throughout the eastern third of Tunisia, a small Arab country under French colonial rule. Few Tunisians were as agitated by the German occupation as the fifty-four-year-old Joseph Scemla. Jo, as he was known to his family and friends, was married with two children, a prosperous businessman who had made his comfortable living as a wholesale fabric merchant and textile importer.

He believed he owed his good fortune to the enlightened politics of liberal France, which had opened the door of opportunity to Jews all across its North African possessions. In the 1920s, as soon as Tunisian law permitted Jews to acquire French nationality, Jo had jumped at the chance. He worked hard to give his eldest son, Gilbert, the opportunity to study at the elite École Polytechnique in Paris, where generations of French business and government leaders were schooled for success. For Gilbert, the call of France was even more powerful than it was for his father. When war drums rumbled in 1939, Gilbert left school to volunteer in the French army and served with distinction as a junior artillery officer at the Battle of the Somme, during the French military collapse of spring 1940. Jo's younger son, Jean (nicknamed Dadi), was preparing his own entrance examinations for the Polytechnique when war broke out.

After the armistice, Gilbert was demobilized and managed to make his way back to Tunis to rejoin his family. For the Scemla family, as for all Tunisians, the shortages and rationing that followed the French defeat made life difficult and trying. Jews suffered special hardship because of the legal persecution and condoned harassment imposed specifically on them by the new collaborationist government at Vichy, established under Field Marshal Henri-Philippe Pétain in the wake of the French collapse. But after sixteen months of Vichy rule, a bad situation for Tunisian Jews turned much worse. On November 7–8, 1942, American and British troops launched Operation Torch, the amphibious invasion of Morocco and Algeria. Germany responded by building up its defenses in Tunisia, where it decided to hold the line against Allied advances. On November 9, 1942, German airplanes landed at Tunisia's airports. So began the German occupation of Tunisia.

From the beginning, the Germans had more on their minds than just military strategy. Very soon after their arrival, they began to put together the building blocks of their master plan for Tunisia's Jews. This included arbitrary arrests, confiscations, forced labor, deportations, the yellow star.

The Scemla boys decided they had to fight back. They told their father they wanted to escape German-held territory to join Allied forces in western Tunisia. From there, they could join in the battle to expel the invaders and reclaim their country.

Jo supported his sons. Together, they developed a plan to cross German lines near the mountainous region of Zaghouan, south of Tunis. To help them devise a way to evade German patrols, Gilbert and Jean confided in a trusted business associate of their father's, an Arab named Hassen Ferjani. With German soldiers in every corner of the capital, Ferjani suggested that it would be best to leave Tunis and launch their plan from the sleepy seaside resort town of Hammamet. He offered to put them up in a house he owned there until the right moment for their escape. The Scemlas accepted and Jo moved his entire family to Hammamet, where he rented a small vacation cottage near Ferjani's home for his wife, Claire, and Gilbert's own young bride, Lila.

For weeks, they debated the details of various escape plans. On Ferjani's advice, the Scemlas eventually decided on a scheme whereby Gilbert and Jean would travel through Hammamet and on to Zaghouan, hidden inside an inconspicuous horse-drawn wagon. Jo would follow unobtrusively behind in another wagon, to make sure they got away safely. To set the plan in motion, the Scemlas advanced Ferjani 20,000 francs to hire a local man named Jeb Farjallah to handle the transport. Farjallah traveled the route frequently, Ferjani said; the German guards along the way knew him, so he would not arouse suspicion. During this time, the Scemlas relied heavily on Ferjani for help and advice and freely showed their gratitude. When Ferjani asked Jo to extend him a line of credit to buy a stock of merchandise for his own small clothing store, Jo readily said yes.

On the morning of March 10, 1943, the Scemla boys donned the clothes of local Arab workers and hid themselves inside the wagon. Ferjani and Farjallah rode atop as they set off through the center of Hammamet village. Soon after passing in front of German headquarters, 200 yards from the main road in the Villa Sebastian, a whitewashed waterfront mansion, German soldiers stopped the wagon. The Scemla brothers were discovered and arrested; their father, a short distance behind, was also arrested. Several hours later, Ferjani showed up at the cottage where Jo's wife and daughter-in-law lived and told them the terrible news. Then, as they were reeling from shock, he warned them that the Germans were likely to show up any minute to confiscate whatever money or jewels they could find. "Let me hold them for you," he offered. "They will be safe." Claire knew how much her husband trusted Ferjani, so she handed over all the valuables she had in the house.

News soon reached Claire and Lila that their men had been sent to the military prison in Tunis, where they were to be brought before a German military tribunal. The women rushed to the office of the highest French official in Tunis, the resident-general, to demand that he do something. The arrested men were French citizens, after all, and one of them—Gilbert—had nearly died fighting in a French uniform just a few months earlier. The senior diplomat who met them could only wring his hands: There was nothing he could do, he said. Then they appealed to Arab notables they knew, including friends and ministers of the traditional ruler, called the "bey." To no avail. Still, Claire was not deterred. A determined, even headstrong Jewish mother, she headed straight to German headquarters to beg for mercy from whoever would listen. Perhaps as a way to amuse himself, a German officer graciously heard her story before he smashed her hopes once more. "Madame, I am sorry," he said, "but you should not have married a Jew!"

On April 5, 1943, with the Allies only days away from breaking through German lines in central Tunisia, these three Jewish men—not an active soldier or foreign agent among them—were deported, by air, to Germany. By the time the Free French marched into Tunis in early May, the Scemlas had been locked up in a special section of Dachau. The Germans kept the Scemlas in Dachau for a year and then transferred them to the infamous German military prison Fort Zinna, in Torgau, on the Elbe River. Finally, in May 1944, the trio was brought before a German court-martial.

At their trial, the key piece of evidence against them was a deposition by German officials in Tunisia citing the testimony of Jo's old friend, Hassen Ferjani. As it turned out, Ferjani was not such a good old friend after all. He was an informer. Everything had been a ruse—the 20,000 francs to pay Farjallah, the merchandise purchased on credit, the offer to safeguard the Scemla family jewels. The Scemlas had trusted Ferjani with their lives and he betrayed them. His statement accusing the Scemlas of espionage sealed their fate. The three were found guilty and promptly sentenced to death.

Two days later, not knowing when the end might come, Gilbert penned his parting words to Lila from his prison cell, number 53. After expressing his undying love, he asked her to focus her energies on their son, Freddy, now three years old. "This child will be for you a consolation and a support," he wrote. "Teach him that to give is better than to receive, that friendship is the greatest blessing in the world ... Teach him to live." Then, he begged her to do one more thing for him and for their son. "Lila, you must remarry," he wrote. "Choose well and love him."

Two months later, the Scemlas were executed. The manner of execution was particularly gruesome. The Germans beheaded first Gilbert, by axe, and then his younger brother, Jean. Their father was forced to watch the grisly murder of his two children before he was himself beheaded. After the war, a fellow prisoner of the Scemlas who survived Fort Zinna, a vice admiral in the French navy, sent a letter to Claire to explain exactly what had happened to her husband and two sons. "They were condemned only because they were Jews," he wrote.

Meanwhile, back in Tunisia, history had caught up with Ferjani. On May 14, 1943, just days after the triumphant Allied entry into Tunis, he and Farjallah were arrested by French gendarmes and sent to the local prison in Nabeul, the provincial capital up the road from Hammamet. Evidently, once the Germans had been chased from Tunis and the Free French were in charge, Claire had rushed to file a complaint against Ferjani. Although she did not know all the details of the plot, she knew that Ferjani had stolen her family heirlooms as well as a warehouse full of merchandise.

After twelve days in Nabeul, Ferjani was sent to the military prison in Tunis—ironically, the same prison in which Germans had held the Scemlas before they were deported to Germany. (Farjallah, who by all accounts was in the dark about Ferjani's scheme, was released.) After several months, Ferjani appeared before the French military tribunal in Tunis. For his role in informing on the Scemlas, Ferjani was found guilty of conspiracy and collaboration with the enemy. In a twist of fate, the French tribunal sentenced him to death six months before the Germans gave the same sentence to the Scemlas. In four years of research for this book, spanning four continents, he was the only Arab I ever found who was convicted by an Allied court specifically for actions that led to the deaths of Jews during World War II.

But unlike his victims, Ferjani escaped execution. Back in Hammamet he was known as an ardent Tunisian patriot, a member in good standing of a clandestine nationalist cell, and his case became a minor cause célèbre. A

prominent local attorney took the case, lost a round in Tunis, and then appealed the verdict to the military appeals court in Algiers. Evidently, his
strategy was to play on the political currents of the day. Here, we see the
complications of colonial politics in North Africa. Members of a Tunisian
Jewish family that had chosen French citizenship were blaming a good
Tunisian nationalist for whatever tragedy befell them. I could not find evidence that the Algiers court ever formally ruled on Ferjani's appeal—such
documents, I was told, are closed for 100 years—but Ferjani's death sentence
was soon commuted to life in prison.

Even that sentence was not served in full. On March 19, 1957, one year after Tunisia received its independence from France, the new republican government released him. All told, Ferjani spent just fourteen years behind
bars. He returned to his life in Hammamet, where he reopened his small
fabric shop and then eventually became a chauffeur. He died in 1981.

I came to Frédéric Gasquet's chic apartment in Paris that autumn morning because sixty-four years earlier he had been born Frédéric Scemla, the
son of Gilbert and Lila. When he was four, his widowed mother married an
engineer named Louis Gasquet. The elder Gasquet—who still lives in
Tunisia, well into his nineties, and talks to his son almost every day on
Skype—was a kind, loving father who wanted to adopt Freddy as his own.
The Gasquets were Catholic, and after all the cruelty that Gilbert and his
family suffered for being Jewish in Tunisia, Lila decided to raise her son in
her new husband's faith. Freddy grew up knowing little of his family's origins and nothing of how his father, uncle, and grandfather had died. Then,
late in life, curiosity about his roots turned into an obsessive quest to piece together every detail of his family's story, especially his father's tragic tale. I
tracked down Frédéric Gasquet to learn everything about the Scemlas. For
his part, he was interested to meet me because I had done something in the
course of my own research that he could never bring himself to do: I had
tracked down the oldest living relative of Hassen Ferjani to learn the Arab
side of the story. "I could never go to Tunisia to do what you did," he told
me. "Only in the last few years could I bring myself to even contemplate the
enormity of the crime and the disaster that befell my family." Together,
Frédéric Gasquet and I spent a late autumn morning telling each other what
we had learned about the Holocaust's long reach into Arab lands.[1]

By February 1943, after the Red Army had finally turned back the Germans at Stalingrad, the main front of the European theater of war was not in Europe at all. It was in Tunisia, an Arab land with ancient roots on the northernmost point of Africa.

Just twelve weeks earlier, U.S. and British troops had launched the largest amphibious assault in history, landing tens of thousands of troops along a wide swath of territory from Safi, south of Casablanca, to Cap Matifou, east of Algiers. Three days of often fierce fighting against Vichy forces—the first major American engagement since entering the conflict eleven months earlier—ended with the second French surrender of the war. General Eisenhower quickly moved his headquarters from the underground bunkers of Gibraltar to the whitewashed villas of Algiers and began to execute plans for the 560-mile march eastward, to Tunis. His goal was to expel Axis forces from the African continent and to begin a methodical march northward, through Italy and into the heart of Nazi-controlled Europe.

Germany had another plan. After defeating France in 1940, Berlin decided not to dispatch its own troops to rule French possessions in North Africa. Instead, Hitler permitted France, now under the compliant Vichy regime, to continue governing the region and contented himself with supervising the French through the several hundred officers of local German Armistice Commissions. But the Anglo-American invasion and the opening of a North African front compelled a change in strategy. "To give up Africa means to give up the Mediterranean," Hitler declared. "[It] would mean not only the ruin of our revolutions, but also the ruin of our people's future."[2] When Berlin dispatched squadrons of airplanes into airstrips in Bizerte, the strategic port along Tunisia's northern shore, and at el-Aouina, outside Tunis, the local French commanders did not know what to do: fire on the Germans, welcome them, or stand aside. Higher-ups in Algiers and Vichy sent conflicting orders that created chaos. As the French naval commander at Bizerte, Admiral Louis Derrien, wrote in his diary: "November 8, we fight everybody. November 9, we fight the Germans. November 10, we fight nobody. November 10 (noon), we fight the Germans. November 11 (night), we fight nobody."[3] Eventually, Pétain, head of the Vichy regime, stepped in to impose order. Support the Axis powers, he decreed. Within days, elite German paratroopers established a forward base in Tunis and began to prepare for an eventual deployment of a vast army of German soldiers, sailors, and airmen—SS officers included. Hitler's order was crystal clear: "North Africa, being the approach to Europe, must be held at all costs." That sentence, wrote one historian, "condemned a million men from both sides to seven months of torment."[4] But soldiers were not the only ones to suffer torment because Europe's war took a detour through Arab lands. The people of Tunisia suffered, too. And the Jews of Tunisia suffered most.

———————

THE HOLOCAUST was almost exclusively a European ordeal. Both its perpetrators and its victims were principally, predominantly, overwhelmingly European. Europe was, in the 1930s, home to the bulk of world Jewry. Europe was the nesting ground for the ideology of hate that brought devastation to the Jewish people. Europe manufactured the guns, gas, ovens, and other machinery of death that exterminated 6 million innocent Jews. Europe was the place where one-third of the world's Jews were killed in the most systematic, organized, methodical mass murder in history. Comparing calamities across time and space is a gruesome task, but the attempt by Germany and its allies to annihilate the Jewish people during World War II remains without parallel. Our lexicon includes two words used uniquely for identifying this crime—"Holocaust," from the Greek, and "Shoah," a term from biblical Hebrew.

But even so, the Holocaust was not *solely* a European story. From the outset, German plans to persecute and eventually to exterminate Jews extended throughout all lands Germany and its allies hoped to conquer, which included a great Arab expanse, extending from Casablanca to Tripoli and onward to Cairo. This region was home to more than a half-million Jews.

Evidence of German ambition to target the Jews of these Arab lands can be found in the country-by-country plan for the extermination of Jews approved by Nazi leaders who gathered at the infamous Wannsee Conference in Berlin in January 1942. This gathering of Nazi planners and technicians, including Adolf Eichmann, debated and then formulated the systematic plan for the execution of the "final solution." Decisions on the logistical complications of exterminating the Jewish population of the thirty-one countries the Third Reich either already controlled or had its sights on were based on a master list of Jewish populations in those countries. That list added up to 11 million people, and the Nazis planned to kill them all.

Of those countries, however, one stands out for the wildly inaccurate figure of its Jewish population: unoccupied France, the southern part of France that was left under the nominal control of the collaborationist Vichy regime. According to the Wannsee list, unoccupied France had 700,000 Jews.[5] In reality, there were fewer than 200,000. How could the exacting, meticulous Nazi planners—who concerned themselves with the most minute logistical problems of transporting millions to their death, disposing of their remains, and hiding this hideous crime from the world—make such a huge error? Could the Germans have simply made a mistake? No. The hugely inflated Wannsee number for the Jews of unoccupied France was no mistake, because it included the hundreds of thousands of Jews who lived in France's North African possessions: the colony of Algeria and the two protectorates that bordered it, the sultanate of Morocco to the west and the principality of Tunisia to the east.[6]

During the three years from the fall of France in June 1940 to the expulsion of German troops from Tunisia in May 1943, these Arab lands—along with Libya, an Italian colony that did not appear on the Wannsee list—shared a largely common fate. In the brief period when they had a chance, the French Vichyites, the German Nazis, and the Italian Fascists applied in these countries many of the same methods that would be used to devastating effect against the much larger Jewish populations of Europe, often at the same time and pace as they were being used in Europe. These included not only statutes depriving Jews of citizenship, property, education, livelihood, and residence, but also forced labor, confiscations, deportations, and executions. The goal was to isolate Jews, to persecute them, and—in Tunisia, at least—to lay the foundation for their eventual extermination.

Virtually no Jew in North Africa was left untouched. Thousands suffered in more than 100 forced labor camps set up throughout the region. Many thousands more lost homes, farms, jobs, professions, savings, and years of education. Still more lived in a state of perpetual fear and daily privation, victims of a ration system that gave them the least and gave it to them last.[7] By a stroke of fortune, relatively few perished directly as a result of Fascist rule, with estimates ranging between 4,000 and 5,000 people.[8] Some, like the

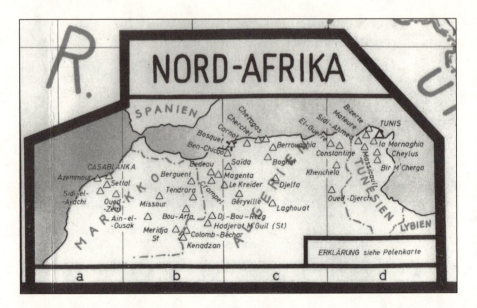

MAP 1.1   German map of labor camps in North Africa, excerpted from a larger map originally printed in Edward Kossoy, *Handbuch zum Entschädigungsverfahren*, Munich, 1958.

Scemlas, were deported by Germans and Italians to their deaths in Europe. About 1,200 North African Jews, trapped in metropolitan France, were sent by the Vichy regime to Nazi death camps in Poland and elsewhere. The youngest was a three-month-old infant, Abraham Taieb of Bône; the oldest, eighty-five-year-old Isaac Adda of Algiers.[9] Some were killed in cold blood, others died of hunger or torture or disease in desert "punishment camps" in the Sahara. Many were killed in the almost-daily American and British bombings of Tunisia's air and seaports in the early months of 1943, when the Germans compelled Jewish laborers to work through the attacks at their hazardous jobs clearing rubble.

The low death count—just about 1 percent of the Jewish population in French North Africa, compared to more than half of all the Jews numbered on the Wannsee list—is as much testament to the fortunes of war as to the lesser threat faced by these Jews. The Mediterranean complicated the logistics of transport; Germany and its partners could not just stuff North African Jews into trains and send them to death camps in Central and Eastern Europe. But, as we shall see, the Tunisian experience suggests that the Nazis would have found alternatives, if they had had the time. That factor—time—was responsible for saving North African Jewry, most of all. If Allied troops had not driven the Germans from the African continent in 1943, two years before the fall of Berlin, then the 2,000-year-old Jewish communities of Morocco, Algeria, Tunisia, Libya, and perhaps Egypt and Palestine, too, would almost certainly have met the fate of their brethren in Europe.

Chapter 2

The Holocaust's
Long Reach into Arab Lands

A s the Greatest Generation passes from the scene, Americans know less and less about World War II. A quarter century ago, national assessments showed that most high schoolers studied the war but knew little of what happened during it. Only half could name Joseph Stalin as the leader of the Soviet Union, and fewer than two in five put D-day in the correct four-year period.[1] Fifteen years ago, when the Harris polling firm found that the vast majority of Americans knew that Pearl Harbor triggered America's entry into the war and that Japan was the aggressor, it was so surprised it headlined its press release "Congratulations, America! You DO Know Something About Pearl Harbor."[2] In 2001, tests of high school seniors showed that half believed one of Germany, Japan, or Italy was a U.S. ally during the war.[3] In 2003, the chairman of the National Endowment of the Humanities bemoaned the fact that just 37 percent of university students knew that the Battle of the Bulge occurred during World War II.[4]

Knowledge of the Holocaust isn't much better. On the one hand, most Americans display an almost instinctive understanding for the fact that Jews suffered a terrible fate during the war, and they overwhelmingly endorse the idea that it is important to remember the Nazi-era extermination of Jews. On the other hand, however, Americans know very little of what actually occurred. The same 2005 poll that highlighted abiding American sympathy for the wartime suffering of Jews, for example, also showed that fewer than half of the respondents could identify Auschwitz, Dachau, or Treblinka as concentration camps.[5]

So, before telling the stories of Arabs who saved Jews and Arabs who collaborated with Europeans who came to persecute the Jews, it is important to tell the wider story of what happened to Jews in Arab countries that fell under Vichy, Nazi, or Fascist rule. In this context, Rick Atkinson's Pulitzer Prize–winning 2002 book, *An Army at Dawn: The War in North Africa, 1942–1943*, did wonders to fill a knowledge gap about American understanding of the events of the war on the southern side of the Mediterranean. But with only five references to Jews in a 681-page tome, even this magisterial account barely touched on the fate of North African Jewish communities during the war.

From the Atlantic Ocean to the Persian Gulf, the lives of Jews in Arab lands were touched by the Holocaust. It is a complex story. The persecution of the region's Jews cannot be disentangled from the politics of colonial rule and the ambitions of the Jews' European tormentors. But proximity was paramount. The closer to Europe, the more intense and pervasive was the persecution.

Syria and Lebanon, located on the eastern shore of the Mediterranean, were controlled by France under the mandate system set up by the victorious allies after World War I. There, Jews faced severe shortages of food and fuel in the difficult winter of 1940–1941, but so did the entire urban population. In the mayhem of war, local commanders had little time to implement anti-Semitic edicts from Vichy before Free French forces captured Damascus in June 1941.[6]

Iraq was a different case. A formally independent kingdom since 1932, when Britain terminated its mandate over the land, Iraq was ruled by the Hashemite clan, British allies from the Great Arab Revolt against the Turks during World War I. On April 1, 1941, a Nazi sympathizer named Rashid Ali al-Gaylani led a coup that forced the pro-British regent, Abdul Ilah, to flee Baghdad. Al-Gaylani was a devotee of the mufti of Jerusalem, Haj Amin al-Husseini, whose anti-Jewish tirades were a staple of Baghdad radio during the eight weeks the usurpers were in power. By the end of May, British and royalist forces succeeded in retaking Baghdad, opening the way for Abdul Ilah's return. At this point, British troops left the city so it would not appear as though Abdul Ilah was an imperialist stooge. When he arrived at Baghdad airport, Jews were prominent among the crowd that came to welcome him home. To a mob of enraged Iraqis, the sight of treacherous Jews celebrating the return of Britain's Arab quisling was enough to trigger a rapacious campaign of violence, the worst pogrom in the country's history. In just two bloody days, June 1–2, 1941, Arabs rampaged through Baghdad's Jewish neighborhoods, killing 179 Jews. The extent of the damage to the Jewish community was devastating—the rioters orphaned 242 Jewish children, looted 586 Jewish-owned buildings, and destroyed the homes of more than 12,000 people.[7] Jewish life in Iraq would never be the same.

But despite this wanton destruction, I choose not to include the events of Baghdad as part of the larger drama of the Holocaust. The Germans certainly inspired the local actors and even delivered them some material support, but neither the Germans nor their other European partners were pivotal players in the Iraqi drama. Indeed, the al-Gaylani coup was quashed by British troops before German forces had time to intervene. (The British bear responsibility for waiting two days before sending their soldiers to suppress the anti-Jewish rioting.) The carnage inflicted upon the Jews of Baghdad, which is known to history by the Arabic term *farhud,* was a lurid, animal bloodletting. On balance, however, I consider it more appropriate to view it as one—perhaps the worst—of the periodic spasms of violence by Arabs against Jews that regrettably dot the history of Jewish life in Arab-ruled lands, rather than as part of the European-spawned campaign to persecute and annihilate Jews that eventually came to be known as the Holocaust.[8]

In my view, the long reach of the Holocaust had its greatest impact on the southern shore of the Mediterranean, in lands whose close encounters with the Europeans on the opposite side of the sea harkened back to the days of Carthage and Rome. The story of Europe's wartime persecution of Jews in this region has three main parts: the application by Vichy France of its policy of "state anti-Semitism" to its North African possessions; the imposition by Mussolini's Italy of an increasingly harsh regime of anti-Jewish laws, arrests, and mass incarcerations in the colony of Libya; and Germany's six-month occupation of Tunisia.

Arab Lands in World War II: Events in a Wider Context

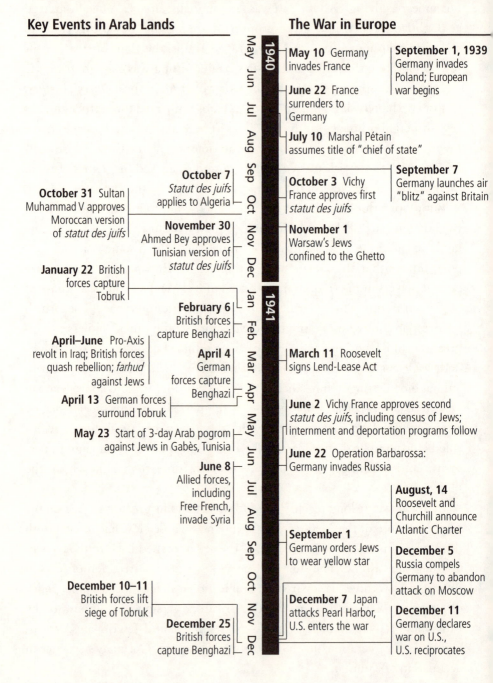

Key Events in Arab Lands

October 31 Sultan Muhammad V approves Moroccan version of *statut des juifs*	**October 7** *Statut des juifs* applies to Algeria
	November 30 Ahmed Bey approves Tunisian version of *statut des juifs*
January 22 British forces capture Tobruk	
	February 6 British forces capture Benghazi
April–June Pro-Axis revolt in Iraq; British forces quash rebellion; *farhud* against Jews	**April 4** German forces capture Benghazi
April 13 German forces surround Tobruk	
May 23 Start of 3-day Arab pogrom against Jews in Gabès, Tunisia	
	June 8 Allied forces, including Free French, invade Syria
December 10–11 British forces lift siege of Tobruk	
	December 25 British forces capture Benghazi

The War in Europe

1940
May 10 Germany invades France
June 22 France surrenders to Germany
July 10 Marshal Pétain assumes title of "chief of state"

September 1, 1939 Germany invades Poland; European war begins

October 3 Vichy France approves first *statut des juifs*
September 7 Germany launches air "blitz" against Britain

November 1 Warsaw's Jews confined to the Ghetto

1941
March 11 Roosevelt signs Lend-Lease Act

June 2 Vichy France approves second *statut des juifs*, including census of Jews; internment and deportation programs follow

June 22 Operation Barbarossa: Germany invades Russia

September 1 Germany orders Jews to wear yellow star

August, 14 Roosevelt and Churchill announce Atlantic Charter

December 5 Russia compels Germany to abandon attack on Moscow

December 7 Japan attacks Pearl Harbor, U.S. enters the war

December 11 Germany declares war on U.S., U.S. reciprocates

Timeline months (center column): May, Jun, Jul, Aug, Sep, Oct, Nov, Dec, Jan, Feb, Mar, Apr, May, Jun, Jul, Aug, Sep, Oct, Nov, Dec

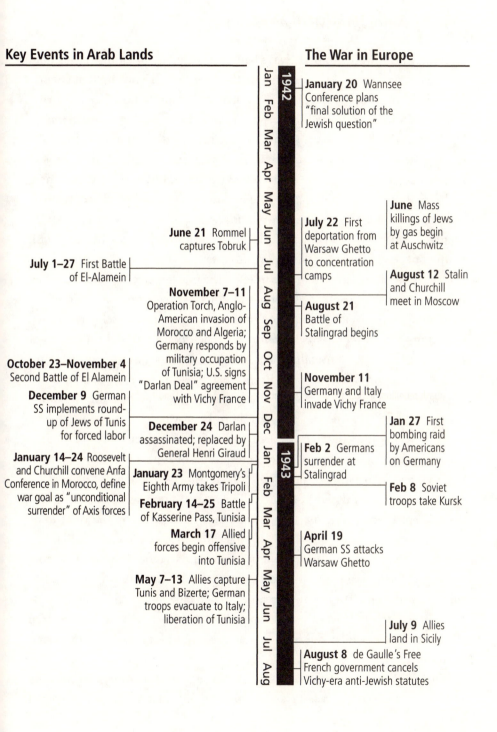

Key Events in Arab Lands

June 21 Rommel captures Tobruk

July 1–27 First Battle of El-Alamein

November 7–11 Operation Torch, Anglo-American invasion of Morocco and Algeria; Germany responds by military occupation of Tunisia; U.S. signs "Darlan Deal" agreement with Vichy France

October 23–November 4 Second Battle of El Alamein

December 9 German SS implements round-up of Jews of Tunis for forced labor

December 24 Darlan assassinated; replaced by General Henri Giraud

January 14–24 Roosevelt and Churchill convene Anfa Conference in Morocco, define war goal as "unconditional surrender" of Axis forces

January 23 Montgomery's Eighth Army takes Tripoli

February 14–25 Battle of Kasserine Pass, Tunisia

March 17 Allied forces begin offensive into Tunisia

May 7–13 Allies capture Tunis and Bizerte; German troops evacuate to Italy; liberation of Tunisia

The War in Europe

1942

Jan Feb Mar Apr May Jun Jul Aug Sep Oct Nov Dec

January 20 Wannsee Conference plans "final solution of the Jewish question"

June Mass killings of Jews by gas begin at Auschwitz

July 22 First deportation from Warsaw Ghetto to concentration camps

August 12 Stalin and Churchill meet in Moscow

August 21 Battle of Stalingrad begins

November 11 Germany and Italy invade Vichy France

1943

Jan Feb Mar Apr May Jun Jul Aug

Jan 27 First bombing raid by Americans on Germany

Feb 2 Germans surrender at Stalingrad

Feb 8 Soviet troops take Kursk

April 19 German SS attacks Warsaw Ghetto

July 9 Allies land in Sicily

August 8 de Gaulle's Free French government cancels Vichy-era anti-Jewish statutes

Vichy Across the Mediterranean

Although Jews were almost always better off ruled by Muslims rather than Christians, it is a mistake to exaggerate the amity and friendship that characterized relations between rulers and ruled in Muslim lands. For centuries, Jews in North Africa, as elsewhere under Muslim rule, lived as *dhimmis,* a legal status defined by Muslim law in which Jews, as monotheists from the pre-Qur'anic era, paid for the privilege of protection from arbitrary attack. In practice, *dhimmi* status left Jews heavily taxed, physically quarantined, and socially reviled. The Golden Age of Andalusia, fondly recalled as a halcyon moment for Jewish-Muslim relations, was, at most, only that—a moment—dwarfed in both historical and geographical terms by the harsh realities of Jewish life as second-class subjects.

This millenium-old system was upset in the mid-nineteenth century, when France established itself in Algeria and emerged over time as the region's dominant power. With its tradition of emancipation and its self-proclaimed civilizing mission *(la mission civilatrice),* French policy offered thousands of Jews a cultural and eventually a political escape route from their lives of predestined inferiority. For a time, France extended to Jews a warm and full welcome. In 1870, France's socialist minister of the interior, Adolphe Crémieux—a Sephardic Jew, who was born Isaac Moïse Crémieux—issued a decree offering Jews in Algeria the option of full French citizenship. (Unlike Morocco and Tunisia, which were protectorates of France, Algeria had been annexed and incorporated into France; its territory—though not its population—was an integral part of France.) The sole proviso was that aspiring citizens accept French civil law. For Jews, that meant giving up the right to be governed by tribunals of rabbinical judges under Jewish communal law, as had long been local tradition. In the 1920s, a similar, though somewhat more restricted, offer was made to Tunisian Jews.[9] All told, tens of thousands jumped at the opportunity and became French citizens. In so doing, they effectively leapfrogged over the Muslim majority—which had not been offered the option of French citizenship—to join the ranks of the colonialists, at least in the legal sense.

The early decades of the new century were a heady moment in the long history of North African Jewry. Many filled their lungs with the fresh air of *liberté, égalité, fraternité* for the first time in their lives. These freshly minted citizens repaid French generosity by volunteering in droves to fight in the Great War. Among Algerian Jews alone, 1,353 died on the battlefield during World War I; thirty-nine were awarded the prestigious Croix de la Légion d'Honneur. In 1939, when war again broke out, Jews across North Africa flocked to volunteer, donate money, buy war bonds, hold prayer vigils, and pledge support. "It is Israel as a whole rather than each Jew as an individual that must help France and its allies in gaining victory over the common enemy," editorialized the Casablanca Jewish newspaper *L'Avenir Illustré* in December 1939.[10]

Given the fierce loyalty many Jews expressed toward France, it is a great irony that—among the three European powers that brought the Holocaust to Arab lands—France was the most eager to persecute Jews in North Africa. But by onset of World War II, France had rolled up its welcome mat for Jews. Earlier, the fin de siècle Dreyfus affair, in which a Jewish army captain was arrested and convicted of false charges of treason, had polarized the nation and sparked a nationalist wave of rabid anti-Semitism. By the 1930s, Frenchmen increasingly viewed the Jews in France—from the throngs of immigrants from Central and Eastern Europe fleeing from the spread of Nazism to citizens whose roots in France dated back centuries—as pollutants; they considered Jews to be the source of national weakness, the cause of France's economic depression, and the vehicle through which foreign ideologies took hold of the country through flaccid, often socialist governments. Speaking from the floor of the Chamber of Deputies, France's parliament, in 1936, Xavier Vallat bemoaned the rise to power of the Jewish prime minister Léon Blum: "To govern a peasant nation such as France, it is better to have someone whose origins, however modest, are deep in our soil, than to have a subtle Talmudist."[11] A more guttural reflection of these sentiments was the popular right-wing motto "Better Hitler than Blum."[12] In metropolitan France, even liberal governments had, throughout the 1930s, begun to impose severe restrictions on the growth and movement of the swelling numbers of refugees, largely Jews. France imposed harsh restrictions on newcomers who wanted to practice their profession or start a business, subjected both naturalized citizens and foreign refugees to close surveillance, and set up a central system of identity cards to monitor them. Even before

France fell to the Germans, its government interned foreigners without valid residence or work permits in detention centers, where thousands— again, largely Jews—languished. In France's North African possessions, the situation was even more acute. Anti-Semitism was a unifying force among the communities of European colonialists, who feared that offering indulgences to local Jews was the first step toward extending political rights to a vast sea of Arabs. Odd as it sounds, German anti-Jewish propaganda made inroads both among the Europeans living in North Africa and among some segments of the Muslim intelligentsia, who reviled the Europeans (and who were reviled by them, too). Taken together, this potent mix left Jews in a grave and precarious situation.

The fateful months of May and June 1940 saw the rapid collapse of what remained of France as a haven for Central European Jews, North African Jews, even long-standing French Jews. France's ignominious defeat on the battlefield, the decision to seek a collaborationist armistice rather than to carry on the fight from the colonies, and the swift discarding of the republic and the subsequent elevation of Marshal Pétain to serve as *chef d'état* of the rump French state headquartered at Vichy all came in speedy succession. Disgraced at their rapid loss of honor, pride, and confidence, the French sought a scapegoat and the Jews were a ready candidate. When Pétain unveiled a "national revolution" to revive French spirits and build the country anew, anti-Semitism was formally adopted as state policy.[13]

One of the first official acts of the new regime was to annul the Crémieux decree, the edict that gave Jews the opportunity to become French citizens. Abrogating the decree was an easy way to appease the powerful settler community, which had always fought against enfranchising any part of the local population, because it feared the eventual collapse of its own privileged system of command and control. Overnight, more than 105,000 Algerian Jews who had enjoyed French citizenship for up to three generations suddenly found themselves relegated to a netherworld status—no longer citizens, though still subject to French civil code.[14]

With this act, France earned the dubious distinction of joining Hitler's Germany as the only two countries in the world officially to strip Jews of their citizenship.[15] As Michael Marrus and Robert Paxton observe ruefully, "Algerian Jews found themselves in exactly the same situation as German

Jews after the passage of the Nuremberg Laws: having previously been citizens, they were reduced to subjects."[16] Moreover, the decision to cancel the Crémieux decree—as with most other anti-Semitic acts undertaken by Vichy—was not made in response to German pressure, German request, or even German suggestion. It was, as Pétainists were proud to point out, a wholly French affair. After the war, when he could have blamed Vichy policy on German pressure, Pétain's own chief of staff insisted that France deserved full credit: "Germany was not at the origin of the anti-Jewish legislation of Vichy. That legislation was spontaneous and autonomous."[17]

At almost exactly the same moment that they lost their French citizenship, Jews in Algeria and elsewhere in French North Africa also lost most of their civil, legal, and personal rights, which was precisely the objective of Vichy's Law of the Jews *(statut des juifs),* issued in October 1940. This law, which affected all Jews in French-controlled territories—citizens, subjects, and foreigners alike—applied almost immediately to Algeria and was before long approved, with modest amendment and no substantial dissent, by the sultan of Morocco and the bey of Tunis.

The purpose of the *statut des juifs* was to define "Jewishness" and then to deny virtually all those so defined of most of their legal and civil rights. According to the law, a "Jew" was "any individual issued from three grandparents of the Jewish race; any individual issued from two grandparents of the Jewish race if his/her spouse is also Jewish." This definition focused solely on parentage and marriage; it offered no leeway to Jews who had converted to other religions or even to the children of Jews whose parents had converted. As such, it was an especially rigid formula, even less forgiving in its approach to defining Jewishness than the laws the Nazis themselves implemented in the occupied zone of France.[18]

Under this law, Jews were barred from almost every public function. They were prohibited from holding political office or appointments; from any administrative post except at the very lowest levels; from all diplomatic positions; from all teaching posts; from all governmental or military positions; and even from employment in businesses of "public interest" and in any business or company that received benefits (contracts, concessions, subventions, and the like) from public bodies. In addition, whole professions were closed to Jews, including journalism, theater, film, and radio broadcasting.

In Morocco and Tunisia, local variants of the law were looser, but only marginally so. Jews in these protectorates could retain jobs in Jewish communal schools, for example. Also, in Morocco, the sultan—who reigned in both his temporal capacity and, in the religious sense, as "commander of the faithful"—did not accept the idea that Jews who converted to Islam should still be considered Jews, under the law. Otherwise, there were few exemptions, and even these were severely limited. In Tunisia, only two Jews received special dispensation from the statute.[19] In Morocco, the local version of the law offered privileged treatment to Jews who had received a military distinction in the Moroccan armed forces. But this was a Potemkin loophole, because so few Jews chose—or, more accurately, were allowed to choose—a career in the army.[20]

Severe as these laws were, they were evidently not severe enough. In June 1941, Vichy issued a second and even more restrictive *statut des juifs;* before long, it was extended to France's North African possessions, too. This law was designed to narrow or even close some of the loopholes in the first. For example, to win an exemption, Jews who had served in the French army needed to earn a special decoration for valor, not just show that they had served and been discharged honorably. The law extended the list of professions from which Jews were barred to include advertising, banking, insurance, stockbroking, real estate, trade in grain and livestock, trade in antiquities or art or painting, publishing, and all managerial and executive positions in businesses and corporations. In essence, any position that involved handling items of value or sums of money was closed to Jews.

Especially painful were stringent quotas (called *numerus clausus*) on the number of Jews allowed to practice certain professions. Jews were permitted to compose just 2 percent of all lawyers, doctors, midwives, notary publics, and dentists.[21] Only when one considers the prominence of Jews in these professions does the severity of these quotas become real. At the onset of war, Algeria had only 938 doctors providing health care to a total population of between 7 million and 8 million people. Of those, about 100—more than 10 percent—were Jews. The Vichy-mandated quota cut this number to just sixteen. The result was to deprive thousands of Algerians of medical care, a fact that meant little to the anti-Semites of Vichy. As a further absurdity, Jewish doctors in Algeria did not even have the right to minister to other Jews. Although some did so clandestinely, many had to find other work, such as removing unwanted hair from Muslim women.[22]

Once Vichy banned Jews from working as teachers in France's Arab possessions, it only made sense to restrict the number of Jewish students, too. A June 1941 decree that limited Jewish matriculation at universities to 3 percent resulted in the expulsion of 80 percent of Jewish students. Urged on by rabid anti-Semites in the Algerian education system, another decree even capped the number of Jewish pupils in public primary and secondary schools. This measure applied uniquely to Algeria; it was so draconian that Vichy did not try to impose it inside that part of metropolitan France under its control. Limits on Jewish enrollment meant that half of all Jewish public school students in Algeria—19,000 students—were denied entry in 1942–1943.[23]

Vichy also targeted Jewish assets. In October 1941, Vichy issued a decree giving Jews in Algeria less than one month to sell, transfer, or liquidate all businesses and property, in a manner subject to the state's approval. If the Jewish property owner failed to meet the deadline, the state would assign the asset to a temporary trustee who would liquidate it in the owner's name. According to the law, local prefects had the right to "impose internment in a special camp" for property owners who protested.[24] Then, in November 1941, another Vichy decree gave the governor-general of Algeria the right to assign a temporary trustee to any industrial, commercial, real estate, or craft enterprise, to any building (except personal lodging or residence), to any kind of lease, or to any kind of movable property, belonging in whole or in part to Jews. The governor-general alone had the power to appoint trustees. These were lucrative positions, which gave the incumbent the right to draw up to six months' salary as he prepared the sale of the business or property.

The purpose of all this, as one of the anti-Jewish statutes baldly stated, was to "eliminate all Jewish influence from the national economy." To a substantial degree, these laws and decrees achieved their objective. Jews throughout French North Africa lost jobs, property, businesses, and livelihoods; not a single Jewish family was untouched. In Algeria alone, the government fired more than 80 percent of Jewish civil servants.[25] As a precursor to more drastic measures to strip Jews of their assets, Vichy initiated a painstaking census of all Jewish persons and property in its possessions. "No stone was left unturned in the hunt for Jews to count, control and deprive of their property," wrote historians Marrus and Paxton.[26]

In the period before the Anglo-American invasion, Algeria's Jews suffered the most. They were the target of both Vichy's most zealous anti-Semites in the bureaucracy and the most venal Jew haters among French settlers. The situation in France's other North African possessions was marginally less severe—a fact born not of tolerance but of necessity. In Tunisia, for example, the medical profession was so dependent on Jews that both the French and Muslim communities all clamored for the quota of Jewish doctors to be raised to 5 percent. And in certain places, what seemed to be an easing of the law actually just reflected the personal tactical preferences of local governors. In Morocco, for instance, the French resident-general preferred to allow local business groups and professional guilds to implement restrictions on Jewish participation in private enterprise, rather than to sully his own hands with the task.[27]

Sometimes the human factor played a role as well. On occasion, French officials were lax in enforcing Vichy statutes because they could not abide the fact that Pétain's "national revolution" had taken a turn into such fanatical anti-Semitism. Case in point: Tunisia's resident-general, Admiral Jean Estéva. An ascetic man and devout Catholic, the diminutive Estéva was torn between his loyalty to Pétain and his sense, inspired by his faith, that persecuting Jews was wrong. He sought practical, often ingenious, ways to balance Vichy's anti-Jewish statutes with compassion toward the Jews. When pressed to speed up the confiscation and auction of real estate owned by Tunisian Jews, for example, he appealed to his superiors' Gallic pride. Italians, who outnumbered the French in Tunisia, were likely to buy the land, he argued, and that would further erode France's hold on the protectorate. It was better, therefore, to let French-speaking Jews keep their property than to let it fall into the hands of the Romans. For acts such as this, Estéva was even once denounced by a German propaganda mouthpiece, Radio Stuttgart, for his alleged friendship toward Jews.[28]

But the relative leniency of the persecution of Jews in the protectorates had its limits. In Morocco, for instance, Jews bore the brunt of a special decree that was imposed nowhere else in North Africa: All Jews who lived in the new, modern neighborhoods of large cities had to give up their homes and relocate back to the narrow alleys and crowded lanes of the traditional Jewish quarter *(mellah)*. To add insult to injury, the date by which all Jews had to fulfill the requirements of this decree fell on Yom Kippur, 1941, the holiest day on the Jewish calendar. By that day, one-fifth of Casablanca's 50,000 Jews, along with comparably sized groups in the imperial cities of Rabat-Salé and Fez, had to find new lodgings. One result, noted an historian, was to hasten the spread of disease in the already cramped quarters of the old Jewish quarters.[29] Unlike Tunisia's Estéva, the resident-general in Rabat, General August Paul Noguès, implemented Vichy's anti-Jewish statutes with zeal and efficiency. His enthusiasm may have been spurred by his desire to cover up the fact that he was married to a woman of Jewish descent.[30]

For many Jews, survival itself in Vichy–held North Africa was often a daily battle. Although Jews filled the ranks of the region's lawyers, doctors, and businessmen, the vast majority of them lived at or near the poverty line. More than half of Tunisia's Jews were described as being "poor, illiterate, living off the community or of very modest means."[31] Everyone—European, Arab, and Jew alike—engaged in the daily scramble to overcome shortages of basic foodstuffs and essential products, but Jews carried a bureaucratic penalty greater than everyone else. In Morocco, for example, Jews were allotted rations of key goods, such as cooking oil and sugar, which were much smaller than those allotted to Arabs. Rations for both were smaller than for Europeans.[32]

For Jews, who had lived for centuries in the netherworld between being a protected people and a persecuted one, the most menacing threats to life, limb, and property came from the fact that the state changed from being defender to tormentor. The removal of state protection opened the floodgates for the region's anti-Semites. Anti-Jewish propaganda moved from fringe pamphleteers to the mainstream press—newspapers, journals, radio, and theater. In Algeria, violent, proto-Fascist organizations whose members would otherwise be marginalized as hooligans and misfits—groups such as the Légion des Combattants and the Parti Populaire Français—received a wink and a nod from Vichy officialdom to taunt, threaten, bully, and harass Jews. They constituted the "gangster wing" of French settler society, about which insightful American journalist A. J. Liebling sardonically wrote, "They had not really collaborated with the Nazis; the Nazis had come along belatedly and collaborated with them."[33]

Daily life for many Jews was a marathon of fear. Wherever they went, whomever they spoke to, whatever they wrote, Jews were afraid that they were being watched, listened to, spied upon. This was not misplaced paranoia. Even before the arrival of German troops in November 1942, Tunisian Jews composed 10 percent of all Tunisians interned or placed under house arrest by Vichy—more than three times their share of the population.[34]

Even so, the Vichyites were still not satisfied with their handiwork. Whenever Jews showed the slightest sign of banding together in the face of their harsh treatment, Vichy and its local agents would pounce.

Faced with a debilitating assault on their lives and livelihoods, many Jews in French-held Arab lands responded by creating or strengthening communal self-help mechanisms. Foremost among these was a vast shadow-education system that sprang up in Algeria to provide for the thousands of students expelled from state schools. In an intense flurry of activity, the Jews of Algiers set up a network of seventy schools that were operational by the start of the 1942–1943 school year. These schools spanned the entire educational spectrum, from elementary schools up to university classes, and provided daily education to nearly 20,000 students. This was a remarkable achievement, especially given the daily hardships many individual Jews had to overcome just to provide for their families. To Vichy, however, communal self-reliance was both a political threat and a cultural affront, a Jewish ploy to subvert the intent of "state anti-Semitism." Its response was to expand its control of lives and fortunes of individual Jews by establishing control over the lives and fortunes of Jewish communities as well.

At first, Vichy tried to put a stop to private Jewish education. The government imposed new regulations that prohibited the teaching of college-level courses without official permission and required state approval to open all schools, purchase books, and define curricula. In a cruel, catch-22 twist on the decree revoking the citizenship of Jews, Vichy even issued an edict requiring all teachers in Algerian schools to be French citizens, even teachers in private Jewish schools.

After reining in any expression of Jewish independence in education, Vichy set its sights on the independence of the Jewish community itself. In March 1942, it established the Union Général des Israélites d'Algérie, an institution whose express purpose was to implement Vichy edicts on and policy toward Jews. All existing Jewish organizations were, according to this law, supposed to come under the UGIA umbrella; all Algerian Jews, as defined by law, were supposed to affiliate with the UGIA and would be represented by it. Its fifteen-person leadership was to be appointed by the governor-general, replacing the elected groups, known as *consistoires,* that had traditionally governed Algerian Jewish communities.

The UGIA was, in essence, a pale, North African version of the Judenrat, Jewish communal councils that the Nazis created and then compelled to do their bidding throughout Europe. Thankfully, the administrative process of forming the UGIA and appointing its members moved slowly, and the organization itself was in existence for only six weeks before the Allied invasion of North Africa. If Vichy French plans had not been so interrupted, the situation of Algerian Jewry—totally without exhortation by or intercession of the Germans—almost surely would have worsened and become perilous. Indeed, just a few days before the Allied landings, Algeria's governor-general, the efficient and unscrupulous Jew hater Yves Châtel, gave a hint of things to come when he ordered the manufacture of yellow Star of David armbands for all Algerian Jews. This was an innovation that even the most ardent anti-Semites of Vichy were never able to impose on the Jews of the Unoccupied Zone of France.[35]

The arrival of Allied troops blocked the distribution of yellow stars. Tragically, though, it did not end Vichy's persecution of Jews in the "liberated" Arab lands of Algeria and Morocco.

Operation Torch, the massive U.S.-led invasion of North Africa in November 1942, was one of the war's pivotal moments. It not only marked the first major military setback for Hitler but opened a critical new southern front from which the Allies could launch their long, grinding campaign across North Africa and through the underbelly of German-held Europe. Protecting Jews from Vichy's predations, however, was not on the Anglo-American agenda.

Ten days after the invasion, on November 17, 1942, President Franklin D. Roosevelt delivered a broadcast statement, cheered by anti-Fascists throughout the world, saying he wanted "the abrogation of all laws and decrees inspired by Nazi governments." Roosevelt's words were powerful. In practice, though, they meant little. That is because American officials in North

Africa—headed by General Eisenhower and Roosevelt's personal emissary to the area, diplomat Robert Murphy—opted instead to defer to the defeated Vichy officers in virtually all local matters. This was in line with an agreement reached soon after the landing with the Vichy leadership in Algiers, headed by Admiral Jean François Darlan, which gave the Anglo-American forces free passage through French-controlled territory in exchange for continued recognition of Vichy French sovereignty over France's North African possessions.[36] In his November 17 address, Roosevelt called the accord a "temporary expedient," and despite the withering criticism of British and American media, it probably did save the lives of some American soldiers. But the agreement came at a stiff price, paid in both the abstract coin of American honor and the real-life suffering of Moroccan and Algerian Jews.

Thanks to this agreement—and under the watchful but disinterested gaze of U.S. forces—Vichy's most zealous bureaucrats in North Africa stayed firmly ensconced in powerful posts. These included vicious Jew haters like Châtel and Noguès. The anti-Jewish statutes they had championed under Pétain's rule remained in force under Eisenhower's. Jews who had been barred from schools, jobs, housing, and property remained so. Jews who had been stripped of their French citizenship remained so. Jewish rights would not be reestablished, Darlan said, "in the interests of the Jews first, who would certainly be attacked and massacred by the Muslims."[37] (When the Free French eventually restored Jewish rights, in late 1943, the Muslims did not protest; there were no massacres.) Vichy generals prevented Jewish men called up to do military service from joining regular army units and instead relegated them to work gangs, where all the Jews could do was dig ditches and tend farmland. The reason—as a French general admitted plainly enough in a circular to his officers—was to deny any Jew the right eventually to claim French citizenship based on his wartime active-duty service. "Out of all of Vichy's legacy, the maintenance of anti-Jewish legislation was to become the most eloquent symbol of the Algiers regime's independence from the Allies and at the same time the best proof, the most telling sign, of its Pétainist legitimacy," historian Michel Abitbol noted.[38]

In some ways, life for Jews in Morocco and Algeria was even worse in the weeks after "liberation" than it was before. Embarrassed by their second swift and sudden surrender in thirty months, French officials and soldiers were incensed at the warm welcome local Jews extended to the conquering Anglo-American forces. When Moroccan Jews rejoiced at the arrival of U.S. and British troops, French prefects closed the gates of Jewish quarters in many cities, effectively jailing an entire population for up to three weeks.[39] Jews were thrown in prison or sent to labor camps for the felonious act of receiving an American into their home or waving to a GI on the street.[40] In the wake of Operation Torch, Jews suffered attacks in the *mellah* of Casablanca, riots in Rabat and Salé, and new discriminatory measures in Meknès and Fez. In the Moroccan town of Beni-Mellal, a new decree invited any European who wanted to settle there to choose a Jewish home, whereupon the residents would have just forty-eight hours to evacuate.[41]

Jews who sought employment with the U.S. troops as clerks, translators, drivers, fix-it men, or just gofers—whether European refugees or local Moroccans who had lost their own jobs due to Vichy laws—were a special target for the frustrations of French officers. American archives relate the sad tale of Peter Winkler, a German Jewish escapee from Nazi Europe who made his way to Morocco, survived refugee internment camps, and found work during the Vichy years in a photographer's shop. When the Americans arrived, Winkler got a job with U.S. Army engineers in Casablanca. In January 1943, however, he was arrested by French officials and charged with having had contact with the German Armistice Commission in the months prior to the Anglo-American invasion. Winkler's crime: He had worked in a photography shop that sometimes developed photos for visiting German officers. As the official U.S. account of the episode noted, fraternization with German officers was "a rather preposterous charge for an ex-German Jew." U.S. army supervisors who knew Winkler appealed to the French on his behalf, to no avail. The French jailed Winkler and tortured him.[42]

The story of the anti-Fascist underground resistance group in Algiers was especially tragic. Just days before U.S. forces came ashore, American emissaries had promised to supply these courageous partisans with weapons and ammunition so that they could sabotage essential services of the Vichy government, for example, by cutting telephone lines, intercepting messages, and even forcibly detaining Vichy commanders. At the last minute, the Americans reneged and sent no weapons, no ammunition, and no money. Nevertheless, the

Algerians were undeterred. They went ahead with their plan, and armed with knives, hunting rifles, and relics from World War I, they carried out one of the war's greatest—and least recognized—exploits in sabotage. Thanks to their courage and cunning, they helped prepare the way for the successful Allied landing and, in the process, saved the lives of many American and British soldiers. Of the 377 members of the underground who participated in the events of November 7–8, 315 were Jews.[43]

Given such bravery in the face of overwhelming odds, those 315 Jews had every right to believe that the arrival of American troops would mean the end to Vichy's anti-Jewish policies in their homeland. In fact, the opposite occurred.[44] Under cover of "the Darlan Deal," as the American agreement with Vichy was derisively called, Vichy police promptly proceeded to arrest these patriotic Jews. As one of them explained to A. J. Liebling,

> The army brass hats and the people of the Prefecture, whom we arrested, hate us. They hate us because we know what cowards they are. You should have seen how miserably they acted [the night we captured them] when they saw [us waving] the tommy guns [at them], the brave Jew-baiters. The chief of the secret police, who has been, of course, restored to his position, kneeled on the floor and wept, begging one of my friends to spare his life. Imagine his feeling toward the man who spared him! Another friend, a doctor, is to be mobilized—in a labor camp, of course—under the military jurisdiction of a general HE arrested.[45]

Vichy's reprisal against the Jews provoked little protest from the victorious Yanks and Brits. To my mind, the most outrageous case of all is that of Dr. Henri Aboulker, a seventy-eight-year-old decorated World War I veteran whose wartime injury made it nearly impossible for him to walk unassisted. Aboulker's son, José, was the intrepid leader of the main group of Jewish activists, called the Géo Gras. The night of the fateful Torch landings, Aboulker père's apartment served as the nerve center of the underground's operation; even Roosevelt's envoy, Robert Murphy, spent part of the night there. Several days later, after Vichy was restored to power, Aboulker was arrested by Vichy police. In an account dripping with sarcasm, an

American war correspondent related the story of the arrest through the eyes and mouth of Aboulker's daughter, Colette:

> She was alone in the apartment with her father and her two children, aged three and eight. She had answered the door and a plain-clothes man had pushed a tommy gun into her stomach while another had pointed his submachine gun at her 8-year-old boy and ordered him to put his hands up. The brave Fascists were taking no chances. Then a dozen detectives had searched the apartment for weapons. [None were there.] They dragged her father from his electric cabinet, where he was treating his injured leg, not allowed him to dress, and hauled him off to jail without his trousers. "They would not let him take his cane and without it he cannot stand upright, which amused them," she said. "They dragged him down the stairs. I haven't been allowed to see him in prison."

Colette then recalled that Murphy had raced out of the apartment on the night of Torch, leaving his Homburg hat behind. "He left it here that evening of the landing. He said, 'I will be right back,' and went out. He hasn't been here since."[46]

Not until 1943, when news of the arrest of the Jewish ringleaders of the underground made headlines in the American and British media, did Allied representatives eventually press the French to release them. By then, a French monarchist had assassinated Darlan and General Henri Giraud was installed in his place. Although he was a committed nationalist and anti-German, Giraud shared much of Vichy's anti-Semitism. Under him, the dismantling of Vichy's legal regime of "state anti-Semitism" proceeded at a glacial pace. It was not until August 8, 1943, that the National Committee of French Liberation—by then under the full control of General Charles de Gaulle—canceled all Vichy-era anti-Jewish statutes. And not until December 21, 1943, did the NCFL formally dismiss from government posts all high-level officials who were members of Fascist organizations.[47] This was more than thirteen months after the arrival of American troops in North Africa. During that time, Vichy's anti-Jewish handiwork enjoyed the tacit endorsement of the U.S. government.

Libya's Fascist Moment

France was not the only colonial power in North Africa, and the Vichyites were not the only Europeans to impose an official policy of anti-Semitism on the Jews of Arab lands. East of Tunisia is the huge expanse of Libya, an area larger than Alaska. There, ambitious Italians had long claimed an imperial foothold and, in 1931, Mussolini finally wrested full control.

In the early years of Italian rule, there was little anti-Semitic content to Fascist colonial policy, and Libya's 30,000-strong Jewish community—about 4 percent of the population—survived more or less undisturbed. That began to change in 1938, when Mussolini's rapprochement with Hitler spurred Italy to adopt its own anti-Jewish racial legislation. This included laws calling for the expulsion of Jewish students and teachers from Italian schools; the confiscation of most Jewish-owned real estate; a prohibition on Jews working as doctors or lawyers or in other professional occupations; and a ban on the ownership by Jews of factories, stores, and other business concerns. Virtually overnight, Italian Jews—some of whom had been loyal members of the Fascist Party—became hounded targets of the state.

Libyan Jews feared that the full weight of these laws would be imposed on them, too, but in the beginning, they were spared. Italo Balbo, the local governor, was a loyal party man and a zealous Italian nationalist, but he never supported the turn to rabid anti-Semitism that marked Italy's alliance with Nazi Germany. He believed that the racial laws against Jews were not only distasteful and odious but counterproductive, in that they undermined the critical role that Jews played in the economic and financial life of Italy's vast colonial possessions. Balancing between his commitment to the success of Italy's colonial enterprise and his loyalty to his Fascist superiors, Balbo found clever ways to slow the pace of implementation of Rome's anti-Semitic decrees.

In a remarkable exchange of letters with Mussolini, Balbo had the courage to urge Il Duce himself to tread carefully in applying the harsh strictures of racial laws on Libyan Jews. Appealing to his leader's sense of order, he wrote, "If the Jews suddenly stopped participating in the economy before they could be replaced by a group of Catholic merchants and industrialists, there would be economic imbalances in Libya." Then, in a subtle reference to the potential for racial laws to upset the policy of divide and rule, he took a different tack: "The Jews are already a dead people; there is no need to oppress them cruelly, especially since the Arabs, the traditional enemies of the Jews, now show signs of feeling sorry for them." In reply, Mussolini acceded to some of Balbo's requests to suspend application of anti-Jewish laws in specific situations—saving the jobs of Jewish midwives, Jewish women employed in cigarette factories, and Jews who served as government translators, for example. But on the fundamental principle of squeezing the Jews, the Italian leader would not budge. "The Jews may seem to be dead," he replied to Balbo in a terse telegraph. "[T]hey never really are."[48]

In June 1940, just days after France fell to the Germans and Italy entered the war in earnest, Balbo was killed when his airplane was mistakenly shot down in a friendly fire episode by Italian antiaircraft gunners. That confluence of events marked the beginning of a new, darker period for Libya's Jews. As shortages of basic goods worsened and Allied air raids on major cities began to wreak widespread death and devastation, Jews became the target of increasingly violent reprisals. "In the chaos and confusion, there were many racial attacks against Jews," wrote one Tripoli Jew, Roberto Arbib. "The Fascists could not stand the sight of a single Jew."[49]

In spring 1941, the shifting fortunes of war raised and then dashed the hopes of Libyan Jews, leaving them worse off than they were before. In February of that year, British troops temporarily took control of the eastern region of Libya, called Cyrenaica, home to the city of Benghazi. Many local Jews naturally looked to the Brits as liberators and celebrated their arrival. Some even took the opportunity to take revenge against Italian interests for Italy's persecution of Jews. In April, the Italians retook the area, and their retaliation against "treasonous Jews" was swift and harsh. In the back-and-forth of war, Cyrenaica was again occupied by British troops at year's end, only to be retaken once more by the Italians several weeks later. This time, the Italians imposed an even more zealous wave of repression against Jews who showed any sympathy with the Allies.[50] Most severe of all the new Italian policies was internment. The second recapture of Cyrenaica triggered a violent outburst of anti-Jewish sentiment that culminated in an order by Mussolini to round up all the region's Jews and imprison them in internment camps. More than 2,500 Jews of all ages were, in the local terminology, "cleared out" and dispatched to camps, such as Giado and Gharyan, south of Tripoli.

Conditions were perilous. Broria Dadosh, who arrived pregnant, gave birth at Giado. Her newborn daughter died there. "All the time I think of the child," she told an interviewer decades later. "There was hunger, famine and typhus," another Giado survivor, Rafael Dadosh, remembered. "I looked to one side, one died; I looked to the other side, another died." More than one-fourth of the internees—562 in total—perished there, mainly from typhus. More died at this one Libyan internment camp in just six months than at all other North African labor camps combined. Another decree ordering the forced labor of Jewish adult males under age forty-five led to the dispatch of another 3,000 Jews to a chaotic and ill-managed labor camp at Sidi Azaz. Eventually, one-third of these men were sent to join work gangs at labor sites near the border with Egypt. "There was no mercy, to shoot a person was like today to kill a fly. To take a stick and hit a Jew and break his shoulder they didn't care, not one," recalled one forced laborer, Shalom Arviv of Tripoli.[51]

Twice, Libyan Jews smelled the whiff of liberation from Fascist persecution and twice they suffered from the experience. Finally, the third time provided relief. When the Allies came ashore in Morocco and Algeria in November 1942, the Afrika Korps was reeling from the debacle at El Alamein only three days earlier. Field Marshal Erwin Rommel, the German commander, urged a quick retreat across Libya to shore up the Axis hold on Tunisia, which he rightly saw as the key strategic prize. After several days of posturing, Hitler and Mussolini agreed. As the Germans and Italians fled westward across Libya, they took their anger and frustration out on the Jews. All along the coast, troops from the Afrika Korps plundered Jewish property. Only when a victorious General Montgomery strode into Tripoli on January 23, 1943, did the pillaging and persecution of Libyan Jews finally come to an end.

Nazis in an Arab Land

The Nazi occupation of Tunisia was a Hobbesian experience—nasty, brutish, and short. It lasted only six months, from November 1942 to May

1943. During that time, the Germans were under constant military threat, as Allied and Axis forces struggled back and forth for control of key slices of the country's territory. At no time did the Axis control the whole of Tunisia, and the situation was, from the very start, quite precarious for them. During the first month of the occupation, there were only 11,000 Axis troops—8,000 Italians and just 3,000 Germans—in the entire country, and the much larger Allied forces twice sought (and twice failed) to break through Axis lines to capture Tunis. The Germans and their Italian partners held their ground, fortified their presence, and eventually established a semblance of control over about one-third of the country. Still, they faced American and British bombing raids nearly every night, the numbing consistency of which took a steep toll on men, materiel, and confidence.[52]

Despite the fragility of their military situation, the Germans nevertheless found the time and wherewithal to persecute Tunisia's Jews. Over the course of their six-month occupation of the country, the Germans and their local collaborators borrowed many of the tactics they used to devastating effect in Europe: They took hostages, confiscated property, extorted millions of francs in gold, jewels, and money, sent thousands to labor camps, executed prisoners, and deported others.[53] They required thousands of Jews in the countryside to wear the Star of David, and they created special Judenrat-like committees of Jewish leaders to implement Nazi policies under threat of imprisonment or death. Geographic complications—the difficulty of transporting Jews across the sea in the midst of intensive Allied aerial bombardment—may have impeded Nazi plans for the eventual extermination of Tunisian Jewry, but the Germans certainly laid the groundwork for this. To execute and supervise their plans for Tunisia's Jews, the Nazi hierarchy dispatched to Tunisia some of its most ruthless and notorious killers. Leading the effort was SS Colonel Walter Rauff, a short, choleric-looking man who had invented the mobile death-gas van as an economical way to kill as many Jews as possible, as quickly as possible, during the German advance into the Soviet Union. For Rauff, Tunisia was evidently a consolation prize: German historians recently reported that he was poised to lead a special SS mobile death squad, called "Einsatzgruppe Egypt," charged with massacring the Jews of Palestine, when the plan fell apart with Rommel's defeat at El Alamein.[54]

Just two weeks after they arrived in Tunis, the Germans made their first official contact with the Jewish community, and it was a harbinger of things to come: They arrested Moïse Borgel, president of the Jewish community, along with Borgel's predecessor and the Finnish consul. (The consul was the son-in-law and brother-in-law, respectively, of the first two.) Three days later, after the French resident-general, Estéva, protested that the arrests violated French authority over civil affairs, Borgel was released on condition that he report twice daily to Rauff.[55] This pattern—arrests and hostage taking as leverage for political compliance—would become the Germans' standard operating procedure over the next five months.

By early December, the Germans' military situation looked somewhat less precarious than before. Axis forces had not only repulsed two Allied ground attacks, but they had begun to beef up defenses and to prepare for a long, protracted fight. Hitler appointed a new commander, Field Marshal Hans-Jurgen Von Arnim, on December 8 and ordered him to protect Tunisia at all costs. Von Arnim focused on the military defense of the country. Rauff dealt with the Jews.

On Sunday, December 6, Rauff summoned to his office Borgel and Haim Bellaïche, the chief rabbi of Tunis. In his hoarse, guttural voice, the SS officer read out a military decree ordering Jewish men to perform labor in support of Axis forces. Rauff told the stunned Jewish leaders that he would hold the Jewish community responsible both for ensuring that workers showed up on time for work and for providing them with the food, equipment, transportation, and supplies to do their jobs. Jews would themselves serve as foremen over other Jews; any foreman failing to implement orders would be treated as a hostage. Five thousand workers were needed, he said. They should all wear large yellow Stars of David on their chest and back so "that they could be recognized even from afar and shot in case of attempted escape." Rauff also announced that the occupation forces had abolished the governing council of the Jewish community and formed, in its place, a new committee, chaired by Rabbi Bellaïche and charged with implementing the forced labor edicts. The committee's first responsibility was to provide Rauff with the list of names of 2,000 Jewish men who would make up the initial installment of forced laborers. It had just twenty-four hours to comply. If there was any delay, he warned, the Germans themselves would round up the Jewish workers. By the time Rauff motioned that the meeting was over, Rabbi Bellaïche was crying.[56]

The Jewish leaders were in a panic. Thirty months of Vichy rule, during which the French imposed progressively more restrictive anti-Jewish decrees, had conditioned them to expect the worst. But the German demands were of a wholly different order of magnitude. Not only was the community itself expected to implement and enforce German plans for its own enslavement, but it had to do so with virtually no time to think, plan, or act.

Their first reaction was to gain time. Borgel hurried to the office of the French resident-general, where, over the previous two years, he had often found in Estéva a quiet ally who discovered one bureaucratic excuse after another to delay the full implementation of Vichy statutes. Borgel thought Estéva could win the Jews extra time with the Germans, too. After listening to Borgel's plea for help, Estéva agreed to intercede with Rauff but cautioned that the Jews should prepare themselves to be "resigned and compliant." In the end, Estéva did convince Rauff to extend the deadline—by one day. But the price of this concession was high: Instead of a list of 2,000 workers, Rauff demanded a list of 3,000. When the exhausted Jewish leaders presented him with a list of 2,500 names the next day, they hoped they had sated Rauff's appetite, at least temporarily. Instead, he stunned them again with a demand that 2,000 of those men should assemble at two meeting points the following morning, provisioned with food and tools, ready to start work. To the Jewish leaders, who thought they had performed a Herculean task just by creating a list of potential workers, the idea that they could actually identify and compel the men to show up for work the next day—fully supplied—was mind-boggling. This time, when the Jewish leaders once again turned to Estéva to intercede with the Germans, the Frenchman explained that there was nothing more he could do.[57]

That night, the Jewish leadership debated its options. In his memoir, Paul Ghez, a community leader and decorated French army veteran who eventually took charge of the thankless task of procuring Jewish laborers for work gangs, explained that only two solutions were possible. "The first: resistance. One does nothing; one abstains completely; one waits. It's heroic but absolutely in vain ... We must yield. We have to hold on until liberation which, without doubt, will not make us wait long."[58] The strategy of

Tunisian Jews was to accept their fate. "[The leadership] didn't have the right to condemn an entire population, and especially the poor people of the Hara [the Jewish ghetto], who had nowhere to hide," Borgel's son, Robert, later explained. "[T]o try to hold on without devastation, that was the decision."[59] And so, the leadership committee and its aides worked through the rain-soaked night of December 8 trying to arrange for Jewish volunteers to show up the following morning at the preassigned meeting points.[60]

For Tunisian Jews, December 9, 1942, was one of the darkest days of the calendar, their Kristallnacht. That morning, SS men with submachine guns circulated around the German headquarters on the Avenue de Paris, just down the road from where Jewish workers were to gather. At the appointed hour of 8:00 AM, Rauff arrived. He expected to see 2,000 laborers. When only 128 showed up, he became apoplectic. Ghez described the scene in his memoirs: "Colonel Rauff, foaming with anger, agitated like a madman . . . spit out a torrent of insults: 'Pigs, dogs, deaf-mutes . . . You will be shot within the hour, along with the Grand Rabbi who I am now searching for. You will see how the SS knows how to deal with the Jews.'"[61] But Rauff did not kill the rabbi, nor did he shoot the poor souls who had shown up. Precisely why is not clear—perhaps he was unsure of the reaction of local Arabs, including the bey; perhaps he thought the Jewish leadership could still be of use to him. In any case, his reaction was to launch a massive roundup of Tunisian Jews to fill the empty ranks of Jewish laborers.

German soldiers, machine guns in hand, broke into the Great Synagogue, where dozens of homeless families seeking refuge from Allied bombing raids filled the basement. There, the German troops brutalized women and children and dragged every man they could find outside in the pounding rain. Eyewitnesses reported a scene of indescribable panic. The Germans then proceeded to the Alliance Israelite school, swollen with refugees from bombed-out Bizerte. They grabbed still more men. Other Jews unlucky enough to be in the streets and byways of nearby neighborhoods were taken as well.

All told, more than 1,500 Jews—including the elderly, the sick, and teenagers as young as fifteen years old—were rounded up that day. Captives over fifty were sent to the military prison of Tunis. The rest were led on a forced march to a work site forty miles away. Along the route, a handicapped, eighteen-year-old named Gilbert Mazuz, who wore an orthopedic device on his leg, pushed himself to the limit and, when he could walk no more, was carried along by his healthier buddies. Just before they stopped for the night, Mazuz tried to walk again, tripped, and fell. As he lay on the ground, a German soldier came up to the helpless, writhing young man, removed his revolver, and shot him in cold blood. Not until the following day did Mazuz's comrades receive permission to bury him. He was the first Jew to be killed by the Germans on Arab soil.[62]

As this was happening, a detachment of SS troops descended upon the offices of the president of the Jewish community and arrested Borgel and everyone there. Another hundred of the most prominent leaders of the community were arrested, held as hostages, and threatened with execution.

If Rauff intended the SS roundup of December 9 to convince the Jewish community that it should not take lightly his demand to provide Jewish labor, it fulfilled its purpose. The responsibility for Jewish leadership effectively fell to Paul Ghez. His response was to try to convince Rauff to suspend further roundups in exchange for his commitment to do everything possible to deliver the Jewish laborers.

So began the work of the Committee for the Recruitment of Jewish Labor, Tunisia's version of a Judenrat.[63] It was an efficient, well-oiled operation, with offices for recruitment and records, quartering, and liaisons with individual work camps. Most controversial was the "summons and search office," which was tasked with the unhappy job of tracking down workers who escaped from labor camps or who failed to show up when they were drafted. (The committee instituted a system whereby Jewish men were drafted by the year of their birth.) Not surprisingly, leading the labor recruitment effort did not make Ghez a popular man. A large segment of Tunis's Jews detested Ghez and what even he called his "pseudo police," earning him the periodic toss of a homemade bomb through his window. ("I understand their complaints and forgive their insults," he wrote in his journal.)[64] Most common were accusations that sons of the rich and affluent were given preferential treatment at the expense of poorer Jews. On this charge, Ghez claimed complete innocence: "We have decided to stand our ground and to not grant any favor to anyone . . . I know I have made enemies, but that's unavoidable!"[65]

Finding and keeping the laborers was one problem. Feeding, clothing, outfitting, and providing medical care for them was an even more complicated, and costly, project. Here too, the Tunisian Jewish community benefited from the energies of a small group of resourceful, committed Jews, all of whom were driven by the idea that deliverance—in the form of Allied troops—was only days away. That prospect motivated the generosity that allowed the community to pay the Germans 25 francs per worker per day—and sometimes up to 40 francs per day—in exchange for rations that were supposed to be on par with soldiers'. In reality, the community had to arrange its own shipments of food to camps around Tunisia to ensure that their laborers received enough to survive.[66]

But generosity was not always enough, especially when the Germans imposed huge, multimillion-franc fines on the Jewish community as punishment for Allied bombings or when the Germans simply ordered the Jews to supply all manner of goods—jewels, furs, cameras, typewriters, radios, even hundreds of yards of cloth to camouflage the Wehrmacht café. So, to ensure that all Jews contributed fairly to communal needs, the leadership committee created an "office of requisition and furnishings," a body that—like the recruitment commitment—inspired fear and loathing in the eyes of many Jews. Even Robert Borgel, son of the community president, seemed to admit the justice of some its critics: "Perhaps our representatives were not always tactful enough, but in all fairness they were very much pressured by the flood of [German] requests to be satisfied." The Germans, who exploited the Judenrat system (and, as in Tunisia, its more limited local variant) as a way to force Jews to turn on other Jews for the benefit of the larger German plan of communal control, must have been pleased.[67]

All told, about 5,000 Jews were eventually sent to forced labor camps throughout Tunisia. Most came from the Tunis area, which was where the majority of Tunisian Jews lived, but smaller pockets of Jews could be found in just about every city and town under German occupation, and virtually all were required to provide workers. The approximately forty camps set up were divided into the German sector, the Italian sector, and the German-controlled Tunis area. In the first two sectors, the occupation forces set up full-fledged work camps. In the area around Tunis, Jewish workers assembled in the morning, hiked to work sites, returned home at night, and assembled again the next day. Work was long, brutal, backbreaking, and often dangerous. Sometimes the danger came from the setting, such as when the Germans forced Jewish workers to stay on their jobs clearing rubble and repairing the el-Aouina airfield and the seaports in Bizerte and Sousse, even as Allied bombers razed buildings and strafed streets. Other times, the danger came from the sadistic overseers and camp guards who enjoyed toying with the lives of laborers. And still other times, the nature of the work itself— transporting explosives or digging near minefields—was inherently dangerous. Even with the additional rations supplied by the Jewish community, food and supplies were often scarce, especially in the more remote work sites. In just one testimony of many, a man named Sion Raymond Uzan, a veteran of the December 9 roundup, said that all the food each worker received in his first four days of labor was a half loaf of bread and some jam.[68]

Of all the camps, the "inferno of Bizerte" stands out as the site where all the "worsts" came together—the most fearsome work, the most inhumane facilities, and the most sadistic guards. Workers were housed in the notorious Philibert barracks, where, as one inmate recounted, "lice and parasites became their most loyal companions." Here is the account of an inmate named Gilbert M. Taïeb:

> Recruited and placed in animal wagons, guarded by a German submachine gun controlled by a savage soldier, we arrived in Bizerte in an hour. We were led into a basement where [only] fifty people had enough [air] to breathe and we were 150 . . . In columns by threes, under the surveillance of a German soldier not less ferocious, his whip always in action, we were led to the camp where we were to spend the next six months . . . The slow ones received blows until they bled and were abandoned along the route . . . At the camp we were introduced to a German soldier named "Memento," who spoke a little Italian but who made himself understood with his whip. Quickly put to work, we helped with the distribution of munitions; every German had the right to hit us. Those of us who showed the most zeal were well-viewed by the chiefs. During work, those [guards] who spoke French would translate the conversations of their compatriots who would say: "As soon as the work is finished and we have no more need of you, we will do to you what we did to Jews in Germany and

Poland." The Germans were known to us only by their nicknames: Memento, Grandma, the Killer, etc.[69]

Another Bizerte veteran, a crew chief named Jacques Cacoub, offered this description of the camp's German guards:

> The soldier Walter, nicknamed "the Killer," is the perpetrator of the murder of my brother-in-law, Victor Lellouche. The soldier nicknamed "Grandma" is the murderer of Alfred Hababou and Elie Saadoun. The soldier nicknamed "Little Fella" beat the Jews with sticks and bones. The soldier "Memento," in addition to blows with sticks and whips, applied to certain workers the torture of freezing showers in the middle of winter. Lt. Elfess was a Nazi fanatic . . . It was he who gave the order and agreed to the murder of the three Jewish workers.

Jews lucky enough to be sent to the Italian zone usually received better treatment than those in the German zone. In general, Italian soldiers lacked the anti-Semitic zeal of their German allies, and this was especially the case in Tunisia, a country that had a large Italian Jewish population as well as an Italian expatriate population larger than the French one.[70] But even this rule had its exceptions. The remote, mountainous region around Zaghouan and Enfidaville, where the Italians were given about 1,000 workers in December 1942, was a notoriously harsh and unforgiving setting. After several weeks, even the Italian military leadership recognized this and dispersed many of the laborers sent there to other camps.[71]

As German military fortunes in Tunisia waned in late winter and early spring 1943, the morale of German guards sank and they became lax in their duties. Many Jewish workers took advantage of this opportunity to escape from labor camps. Visiting Jewish community liaisons bribed guards with liquor, cologne, silks, and other specialties to look the other way at escapees; sometimes visiting Jewish doctors spread rumors of infectious disease that enabled large groups of workers to return to Tunis for "medical care." By the end of April, through a combination of bribery, trickery, and German war weariness, the number of Jewish laborers left in all of Tunisia was down to 1,500.[72]

In the beginning, the Germans ordered roundups of additional Jews to compensate for the escapees. When that proved insufficient, they ordered a few thousand Muslims to form their own work gangs. Finally, in the days just before the fall of Tunis, the Germans even pressed local Europeans into forced labor. According to one account, up to 6,000 Tunis residents went into hiding in the days before the Allied entry into the city, trying to avoid labor roundups. By the end, the entire system collapsed. But along the way, German officers zealously inflicted harsh punishments—including summary execution—on attempted escapees or captured fugitives. In addition, they imposed huge fines on the Jewish communities of Tunis, Sousse, Sfax, Gabès, and Djerba to pay for the lost labor.[73]

Indeed, the Germans' appetite for Jewish money and goods was voracious and insatiable. Some of this was politically motivated, such as when the Nazis made a public relations display of demanding millions of francs from the Jewish community as payment for the Jews' "responsibility for the Anglo-American attack on North Africa" and then distributed the money to a collection of Muslim and European charities.[74] The fines were huge sums—20 million francs in Tunis (on top of the 31 million francs the Jewish community spent to feed and outfit Jewish laborers), 20 million francs and 20 kilos of gold in Sfax, 15 million francs in Sousse, 20 kilos of gold in Gabès. Local Jewish communities could sometimes only pay the fines after the French administration instructed local banks to loan them the money, at interest.[75]

Often, the German demand for Jewish money was old-fashioned extortion, done because the Germans had the power to extort. In Gabès, the Germans ordered the banks to open their vaults, which they then looted of all Jewish deposits.[76] In Sousse, according to a local community leader, "the pillaging was done by the Germans in a methodical and systematic manner."[77] On the island of Djerba, home to one of the world's oldest continuous communities of Jews, the Germans arrived on a Sabbath in mid-February and demanded 10 million francs to be paid in just two hours. When the stunned Jews instead offered 40 kilos of gold, the Germans accepted. To gather this fortune, the local rabbi and community leaders got in their cars—some, for the first time on a Sabbath in their lives—and collected rings, necklaces, bracelets, and other goldware from the island's Jewish families, poor and rich alike. All they could put together was 32 kilos, which the Germans took, promising to return for the rest. The occupation ended before they could.

On top of this communal extortion were the daily predations of German (and sometimes Italian) soldiers and pro-Fascist local groups and militias. At times, this degenerated into what contemporary observers called "violation" of Jewish women—sexual attacks.[78] The German high command in Tunis grew so alarmed at the extent of lawlessness among German troops—who seemed to be filling their kit bags with everything they could steal—that it banned soldiers from the Jewish quarter of Tunis.[79] None of this was done out of sympathy for the Jews, however; it was merely to stem grave breaches in discipline. At the same time, the Germans gave license to mini-pogroms regularly undertaken by armed gangs of Fascists, who prowled the streets ransacking Jewish homes and shops. Attacks on Jews—both their persons and property—were no less frequent in small towns and outlying villages. "The cities of Sousse and Sfax were destroyed," Ghez lamented.[80]

The Germans had grand plans for the Jews of Tunisia that were never fully realized. One concerned the yellow star. Although Rauff had originally ordered that all Jewish laborers wear the symbol, his subsequent command that Jews assemble on short notice gave the workers no time to prepare it. Those Jews trapped in the roundup of December 9 obviously went off to labor camps without stars on their clothes. Rauff soon left the Jewish file in the hands of his two deputies and did not return to the question of the yellow star until March, when he suddenly ordered the prefect of police to issue a directive demanding that all Jews in Tunisia wear the insignia. More than most other indiginities suffered by Jews, the star was viewed with special disgust because it so bluntly defined one's identity for all to see. Rauff's order mandating the star triggered surprisingly strong consternation in official French circles, not so much out of sympathy for Jews as Jews but because the Italians demanded an exemption for the 3,200 Jewish Italians living in Tunisia. After some diplomatic exchange, Berlin acceded to Rome's request and the requisite decrees were prepared. But the Americans and British finally broke through German lines before the plan was implemented.[81] Still, thousands of Jews in towns and villages outside Tunis were required to wear the star and did. (Photos of the era show that the star sometimes had five, rather than six, points.) In Sousse, where forced laborers were commanded by French thugs armed with whips and cudgels, the local SS commander ordered all Jews—male and female, aged six and older—to wear the star.[82]

Another element of German plans was the deportation and execution of Tunisia's Jews. Piecing together evidence from interviews and various sources, it appears that the Germans planned to arrest local Jewish leaders and deport them to concentration and death camps in Nazi-held Europe, as they had done earlier with about forty Jews, including anti-Fascist resistance leaders, prominent leftists, and even just troublesome laborers, seventeen of whom ultimately perished.[83] Once again, time proved to be on the side of the Jews: Many were warned about German intentions and went into hiding, where they evaded arrest until the Allies took the capital on May 7, 1943.[84] Meanwhile, in the port city of Sousse, the Germans evidently wanted to kill all the Jewish workers before evacuating the town ahead of Allied troops. Only a last-minute intervention by the local French police commissioner, combined with the sangfroid of a local Jewish community leader, averted this catastrophe.[85]

Perhaps the fear of what might have been is the most searing legacy of the German occupation. Tunis was rife with rumors, for example, that Djebel Djeloud, a hill outside the capital city, was the site where the Germans secretly started to build a crematorium. German archives make no reference to this, but given the few SS files for Tunisia that have ever been found, this is no surprise.[86] There is also no mention of a crematorium in French diplomatic archives. Indeed, a visit to Djebel Djeloud—exposed high ground surrounded by valleys—shows it to be an odd choice for what would have been a clandestine industrial complex. But still, the dark image of a German death factory hovering over Tunis remains deeply embedded in the psyche of ordinary Tunisian Jews. It is part of their "inherited memory," one Tunisian Jewish emigrant living in Paris told me.[87]

According to one accounting, a total of 2,575 Tunisian Jews were killed during the German occupation, most of whom died in Allied bombing raids.[88] A walk through the Jewish cemetery in Sousse, a port city that was largely destroyed by the Allies' nightly bomb attacks, reveals numerous graves dating to the six months of German rule. I recall a pair of headstones, side by side, whose epitaphs told the story of two lovers, engaged to be married, who were killed together in an air raid. Such was the capriciousness of

Jewish life under the Nazis. And yet, as difficult and tragic as the experience of Jews in Tunisia under German occupation was, the number of Tunisian Jews killed could have been much higher. If not for luck, chance, and the vagaries of time and space, Tunisia's Jews almost surely would have suffered the same fate of Jews just a few dozen miles away, on the other side of the Mediterranean.

In the small central Tunisian town of Kairouan, the local Jews welcomed their British liberators with the joy and relief that came from knowing just how close they had come to an even greater calamity. Journalist Philip Jordan, traveling with the troops, described the scene in his memoir:

No Arabs came to greet us but the Jews turned out in force, clapping and crying. The bolder among them tore the yellow stars from their lapels and set them on fire, with the matches we gave them. These book matches have a "V" printed on the cover; and these they tore off in a kind of hysterical frenzy and pinned them on their coats. The Jewish leader, an old gentleman with a great beard, stopped the car and from a piece of paper read a message to us. What was written there were these words: "I wish say you goott morning and goott nite."[89]

Chapter 3

Buchenwald in the Sahara

IN LATE 1937, a twenty-six-year-old Jewish tailor's apprentice named Morice Tondowski left his home in Kalish, a town in southwestern Poland, and set out for France, where he sought to escape the coming war. After living for several months in Paris, he drifted south, to the Mediterranean port of Nice, where he found steady work sewing ladies' coats. When war finally broke out in September 1939, Morice—like all male refugees in France—was ordered to register for military service. He joined the Foreign Legion, where he imagined himself sitting out the war in some obscure colonial outpost in North Africa.

After passing a medical examination in Marseille, Morice was sent for training to camps in the Algerian towns of Sidi Bel Abbès and Saïda. He was then transferred to a long-term posting in Meknès, Morocco, the once-grand capital of a medieval Arab dynasty. On his very first night in Meknès, his fellow Legionnaires covered him with a blanket and beat him with sticks and clubs. The ordeal, he later said, had been brutal but fair: All new enlisted men suffered the same initiation into Legion life, Jew and non-Jew alike.

In 1940, after Germany's lightning victory over France and the establishment of the collaborationist regime at Vichy, Morice's life changed abruptly. One day, without warning or explanation, he was stripped of his rifle by his French officers and transported by train to a transit camp. A week later, he was thrown into a crowded locomotive and taken to a desolate spot on the fringe of the Sahara Desert, about sixty miles south of the Mediterranean coast, not far from the Morocco-Algeria frontier. This was the hot spring oasis of Berguent.

After arriving at Berguent's tiny railroad station, he was marched with dozens of others to an empty expanse, five miles away, under the gun sights of French soldiers and Arab and Senegalese colonial troops. Along with Morice were other Legionnaires, regular army soldiers and illegal refugees—all Jews. When they arrived at nowhere, Morice and the other men were ordered to dig holes in the gravelly, hard-packed earth and told that was where they would sleep, with only a thin canvas tent to protect against the desert night frost. So began Morice's life as a prisoner at the only all-Jewish labor camp established by France in its Arab possessions.

THE WARTIME EXPERIENCES of two communities of Jews—the Jews of Christendom and the Jews of Islam—rarely crossed, and they had little to do with each other. But there were at least three exceptions. The first was a group of several dozen Jews, mostly Tunisians and Libyans, who were deported from their homeland by the Germans and Italians and sent to Auschwitz, Bergen-Belsen, and other concentration camps in Europe. The second included approximately 1,200 Jews from France's North African possessions who were trapped in Europe when the war broke out and killed, along with millions of European Jews, in Germany's effort to implement the "final solution." The third group headed in the opposite direction. This is the story of the 2,000 or so European Jews, like Morice Tondowski, interned by Vichy in labor camps in Arab lands. Whereas stories of the horror of the Holocaust in Europe are familiar, tales of Jews who suffered their Holocaust fate in the deserts and mountains of Morocco and Algeria are virtually unknown.

French internment camps originated in the 1930s, during the relatively liberal Third Republic, when France opened its doors and provided safe haven to thousands of Central European Jews who had read the Nazi and Fascist writing on the walls and fled their homelands while they still could. Many of these new arrivals showed their appreciation to their adopted homeland by promptly joining the French army. Indeed, fully half of the

60,000 Jews who had volunteered in 1939–1940 were foreign refugees.[1] But when France fell in May 1940, the fierce loyalty of France's Jews—both new and old—meant little. The new Pétainist regime transformed French Jews, both foreign and native born, into ready scapegoats for its swift and shameful collapse at the hands of the Germans. Several years earlier, the very same leftist governments that, under the Third Republic, had at one time welcomed Jews and other refugees, had also responded to a growing wave of xenophobia by setting up a program for the confinement of "undesirable aliens," most of whom were also Jews. Vichy raised this streak of nativist anti-Semitism to the level of official state policy. Eventually, French officers and troops herded thousands of French Jewish citizens into cattle cars, sent them to notorious transit stations like Drancy, and then on to death camps in "the east." It was, however, the foreign Jews living in France who first felt the brunt of the French defeat.

For Vichy, an especially thorny problem was presented by those who had honorably joined the army (or the Foreign Legion) and had been led to believe that their service to France would be repaid with legal residency and perhaps citizenship. Even the most zealous Jew haters blanched at the idea of discharging Jewish soldiers one day and consigning them to death the next. Once demobilized, many were sent directly to internment camps inside France, which often was their last stop on the road to Auschwitz.[2] For the practical men of Vichy, the deserts of French North Africa offered another practical solution.

One of the first acts of Pétain's government was to revive the old imperial idea of constructing a Trans-Sahara Railway: a thousand miles of track across the sands that would drastically cut the travel time from Niger to Nice and bring the riches of Africa to the glory of France.[3] To level the dunes, clear the rocks, lay the tracks, and mine the considerable deposits of coal and ore near the route, Vichy summarily dispatched more than 7,000 unwanteds to desolate corners of western Algeria and eastern Morocco. Most were political prisoners of various stripes: Spanish republicans, Communists, socialists, anti-Nazi Germans, Gaullists, a smattering of Arabs, and even one Japanese. Almost one-third of them, meaning more than 2,000, were Jews. Unlike the rest, the Jews were deported—or, like Morice, transferred from their Foreign Legion duty—because of their religion, not because of their politics. They earned their punishment simply for who they were, not for anything they thought, did, or said.[4]

Technically, Vichy demobilized these soldiers and Legionnaires and immediately compelled them to sign contracts classifying themselves as "wartime labor conscripts," a legal designation that kept them under the control of the French military. Though contracts stipulated the payment of wages—such as a few francs a day from the payroll of the Mediterranean-Niger Railway Company (Mer-Niger)—few ever received any money. They were, in fact, prisoners in all but name. Shipped southward in packed, overheated trains from the ports of Algiers and Oran, they were herded into harsh, desolate camps. They worked from dawn to dusk with little food, water, rest, or medical care, gathering, breaking, loading, and moving rocks. They built stone barracks for their French overseers, but were forced to sleep outside in tents. Pictures smuggled out of the camps and testimonies of survivors show forty people packed inside tents designed for eight. Their clothes and blankets were threadbare; often, they had no shoes. Some were killed trying to flee.[5]

One survivor called his camp a "French Buchenwald."[6] Torture was common and frequent. According to testimonies, the camp commandants and senior officers, mostly Legionnaires, were vicious, sadistic, often drunk anti-Semites. Many were of German origin or boasted of their Fascist sympathies.

One German Jew, Harry Alexander, gave a vivid, at times lurid account of his experience in an oral history for the U.S. Holocaust Memorial Museum.[7] After his father was taken to Sauchenhausen and brother to Buchenwald, Harry managed to escape to France, where he planned to join the French army. Instead, French authorities caught him and put him on a freight train to Djelfa, a Vichy labor camp in the Algerian desert.

> We never knew really what hell was but when we got into that camp and stayed there awhile, we really found out what hell was. If this wasn't hell, it sure came close to it, believe me. [When we arrived,] we stood on attention for the camp commander. And he came and said—and I've never forgotten what he said to me, to us, he said "You all came here to die. You are the scum of Europe. You are the garbage of the world. My job is to see that

you all die here. It's just a matter of time. If you behave yourselves and do as you're told, you may live a little longer. If not, you're going to die sooner. This is my job. And I'm good at what I'm doing."

Harry survived two years without adequate food, water, shelter, or medical care. "There were many ways to die" at Djelfa, he explained: "You had dysentery. You had malaria. A lack of food. A lack of water. Bitten by scorpions. Bitten by vipers . . . and you're dead in an hour." And that didn't include the torture. One form of torture that Harry suffered twice was called "the fort."

[The French soldiers and the Arab camp guards] would tie your arms in the back and hang you on your arms naked for about two, three days. You would hang on your arms and every night they would come in and, when it's the coldest, hose you down with ice water and beat you about. And that was fun for them. They would laugh when they did it. And when you got through hanging there, when they cut you down, you were not able to walk. In fact, you were lucky to be alive. I went there twice and I was lucky they didn't beat me that hard anymore. But after a while you don't feel the beatings anymore.

All told, Vichy established about sixty labor camps in Morocco and Algeria, where Jews—both deportees from Europe and local North Africans—toiled in the broiling African sun. It is difficult to come up with a precise number, because camps sometimes opened and closed, with larger ones frequently setting up their own satellite camps for mining, specialized work, or "punishment," the French euphemism for torture.[8]

———————— ∞ ————————

THE STORY OF THESE Vichy labor camps that I found in archives and testimonies was powerful, but I wanted to see for myself. I wanted irrefutable, tangible evidence of the Arab setting for the European persecution of Jews. So, in the first week of November 2003, my wife, our two children, and I loaded into our Land Rover and set out on a journey from our home, in Rabat, Morocco's Atlantic Coast capital, to hunt for

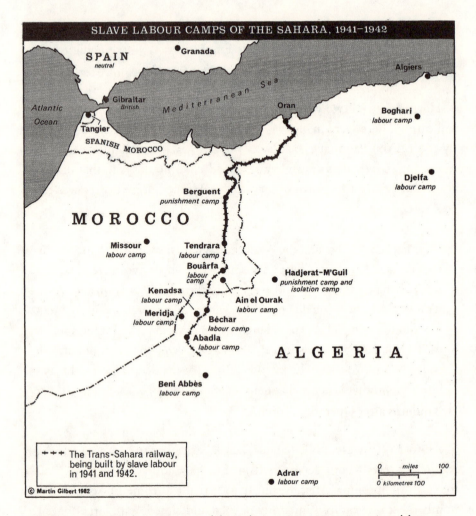

MAP 3.1 "Slave Labour Camps of the Sahara, 1941–1942," reprinted from Martin Gilbert, *The Routledge Atlas of the Holocaust,* 3rd edition (London: Routledge, 2002), p. 56.

physical artifacts of Berguent and other labor and punishment camps on the fringes of the Sahara.

Our first stop was 340 miles due east—the city of Oujda, Morocco's easternmost provincial capital and the last stop on the road to Algeria. Oujda had once been a prosperous frontier trading post, boasting fashionable shops and sophisticated cafés along its French colonial boulevards. Now the border with Algeria was closed, a victim of Algerian-Moroccan tension and mistrust, and like many Moroccan towns and villages along the eastern frontier, Oujda was suffering hard times. The black marketeers selling cheap Algerian gasoline provided only a trickle of the region's former cross-border commerce.

We set out the morning after our arrival to explore the 150-mile route south of Oujda to Bou Arfa. This road paralleled the route of the Chemins de Fer du Maroc Oriental (CMO), or Eastern Moroccan Railways, which formed the northern segment of the Trans-Sahara plan. Though most of the CMO had been built in the 1920s and 1930s, Vichy set up labor camps at stations along the route, where prisoners repaired the line, worked in nearby mines, and serviced the construction farther south of the next stage of the Trans-Sahara line toward the Algerian town of Colomb-Béchar (now called Béchar).

I knew from my research that the route also included some of French North Africa's most notorious wartime torture sites. There was no map to guide my way to them, only a sixty-year-old document from the British Foreign Office, titled "Barbaric Treatment of Jews and Aliens Interned in Morocco." The file contained composite stories of five Polish-Jewish camp survivors who had been interviewed by British intelligence in January 1943, two months after Operation Torch.[9]

Our first stop, about fifty miles south of Oujda, was Berguent, which was also the first stop on the railway heading south. After Morocco's independence in 1956, the town was renamed 'Ain Benimatthar, in honor of its hot springs oasis (*'ain* is Arabic for "spring"). Many locals, however, continue to refer to it by the name of the French colonel who, according to lore, "discovered" the springs; that is, he was the first European to cross the desert and stumble on them. Berguent was the site of the only all-Jewish Vichy-era work camp in North Africa. At one point, 400 Jews were reportedly interned there. When an International Red Cross official visited the camp in July 1942, he counted 155; 90 percent of them had been volunteers to the French army or, like Morice Tondowski, to the Foreign Legion.[10]

At a gas station at the edge of this languid town of a few thousand people, we chatted with a pump attendant and before long a lanky, talkative man in his late twenties came to join us. After I explained that I was looking for the site of a World War II camp of foreign laborers who worked on the railway, he told me his name was Omar, that he worked for the municipality, and that he knew the area well. He added that his father was a lifelong railroad employee. Omar said he would be happy to hop in the car and help us. I accepted. Omar rode shotgun, and off we went.

Our first stop was the deserted Berguent train station, which looked like a quaint Provence village depot plopped down into this desert hamlet. It had not been used in years; its doors were locked and windows boarded up. The freight train from the mines near Bou Arfa only passed through town once a week and there was no longer any passenger traffic to speak of.

For the next hour, we looked for the site of the labor camp. The Polish-Jews' testimony said the camp was five miles from town but did not mention which direction. We made a 270° arc around Berguent, cutting a swath of territory about three to six miles wide along the way; we presumed the camp was not to the north, as we had just passed that way. In the end, we could not find convincing evidence of the site. This was disappointing but not surprising. The desert is a harsh environment, a good place to bury a secret. There may well not have been anything permanent to survive all these years. According to the Polish-Jewish survivors' testimony:

> The camp consisted of holes in the ground or burrowed into the side of a hill. Each man had to provide his own shelter. All they found when they arrived were holes into which one man might wriggle on his stomach. They had to make larger caves in their own spare time.

Berguent, however, did reveal some of its secrets. In a clearing less than a mile southeast of the train station, near the base of foothills overlooking the town, we found a rectangular walled enclosure about forty by sixty yards. Omar explained that it was the local Jewish cemetery. Like scores of towns and villages throughout Morocco, Berguent at one time had a vibrant Jewish community, but thirty or forty years ago, they had all left. On the hunch that Berguent's Sephardic Jews might have looked after the burial of those strange Ashkenazim from faraway who died working at the local labor camp, we decided to look inside the cemetery walls. Later, when I checked an on-line registry of the world's Jewish cemeteries and found no mention of one in Berguent or 'Ain Benimatthar, I realized we may have been its first Jewish visitors in many years.[11]

With me at the wheel and Omar next to me, waving us forward, a little this way, a little that, we maneuvered the four-by-four around rocks and through irrigation gullies, until we could go no further. Then we left the car and crossed a small stone bridge toward the narrow entryway into the cemetery. Inside, we found a garbage dump. Grave after grave had been desecrated, the tombstones removed, defaced, or crushed to rubble. Sheep wool and guts, left over from a slaughter, littered the grave sites. In one corner, where the ground was dug up, something stuck out of the earth. It appeared to be a human jawbone.

All told, we found just five tombstones still in place. The earliest was dated 1939; the latest, 1961. Only one, that of a seven-year-old boy named Georges Katan who died February 15, 1942, was from the period when the Berguent labor camp was in operation. It was impossible to tell whether the despoiled graves contained the remains of Jewish inmates from the camp. Perhaps they did; we could not know for sure. But as we stood in the shadow of an old French church, whose cross still stood unmolested atop its steeple decades after the last Catholic left town, it was clear that the people of 'Ain Benimatthar had not dealt so benevolently with the memory of the Jews of Berguent.

Neither, it seemed, did the French. Five weeks after our visit to Berguent, I visited an animated, alert Morice Tondowski, then ninety-two years old, in the comfortable lodgings of a retirement complex in Ilford, England, a suburb of London. I showed Morice pictures of the site, and he, in turn, proudly displayed photos of himself in his smart Legionnaire uniform. He then handed me a letter he had received only eight months earlier from the French Ministry of Defense. For a small fee, it said, he could take possession of a commemorative medal that was waiting for him in Paris recognizing his wartime service as a Legionnaire more than six decades ago. There was no mention of his time at Berguent.

———— ∞ ————

OUR NEXT STOP, another sixty or so miles farther south, was the town of Tendrara, the second station stop on the route to Bou Arfa. With many sites left to inspect, we didn't expect to spend much time there. We found a wan, listless town that made 'Ain Benimatthar seem, by comparison, bubbling with action and decided to make a quick visit to the station house and be on our way.

A railroad map from the 1950s showed the station to be east of town, but we had no idea whether the town had itself migrated westward since then. We stopped two well-dressed men for directions along Tendrara's main boulevard, and they told us the station was about six miles east of town. One of them then dispatched a teenager on a bicycle to show us the beginning of the route that, he said, led toward the old station house. After a few hundred yards, the biker pointed to some ill-defined path that snaked around a hill, told me to always stay left, and waved good-bye. On the other side of that hill, we saw nothing but the empty expanse of the gravelly, hard-packed desert and a set of old, lonely tire tracks. No one had passed this way in a very long time.

After a few anxious minutes avoiding large rocks and scaling shallow wadis, we realized that we were lost. Turning 360°, we saw nothing but rock and sand. Suddenly, an ancient Ford truck appeared over a hill coming toward us from the southeast. I motioned for the truck to stop, exchanged Arabic greetings, and asked if we were on the correct road for the old Tendrara train station. The four sun-baked men in the cab who had gotten down from the truck to shake our hands nodded yes, pointed eastward, got back in their truck, and drove on. Only after we had traveled another half mile or so did I realize they were almost surely Algerian black marketeers and that, alone in the middle of nowhere, we were lucky they had not robbed us of everything we owned. Perhaps they saw William, then three years old, napping in the back seat.

Before long, we began to make out several structures on the horizon and drove up to a group of abandoned, deserted stone buildings located along the track of the CMO. All the buildings, save one, were on the west side of the railway, facing east. At the center was a station house heading toward collapse, its roof fallen in and beams balancing precariously. Behind the station were a couple of low-roofed buildings, each divided into small cubicles. Black charcoal markings rising to the top of the walls in the corner of the large rooms at the front of the building suggested they had once been kitchens. To the rear of the encampment were more primitive structures of larger, roughly hewn stone. These, too, were divided into small cubicles. About 200 yards to the south of the station stood a large, gabled house. Everywhere we looked, broken shards of red roofing tile, neatly stamped with the name of its manufacturer in Marseille, littered our path.

In the desert stillness, with not a living thing in sight, we had found what historian Sir Martin Gilbert, in his *Atlas of the Holocaust*, listed as the Tendrara "slave labour camp."[12] There were no artifacts left from the internees, but the buildings were clearly laid out for use either by soldiers or the military-like overseers of the CMO and Trans-Sahara Railways. The "posher" quarters closest to the tracks may have been set aside for the Europeans; the "steerage"-quality buildings farther back were probably for local Arab guards. The prisoners who labored there—Jews from Warsaw, Leipzig, Salzburg, and Bucharest as well as Spaniards and others—lived in tents.

Tendrara was the most perfectly preserved site we found on our trip. According to an official company history of Moroccan railroads, the Tendrara station was formally opened to service in 1945, but it had already been the scene of forced labor three years earlier.[13] By the time of our visit, the winds had washed away all the graffiti from the walls and blown bits of tile and glass throughout the grounds, but the foundation of the buildings stood firm. It was as though the desert had tried to cleanse the site but the camp's roots were just too deeply embedded in the rock and gravel to blow away.

<hr>

WE LEFT THE TENDRARA STATION at about 4:30 PM, as an autumn sunset approached. We had spent more than an hour and a half inspecting every inch of the site, walking up and down the track, roaming inside each of the buildings, taking photographs and video. But we realized we had better hurry to make even Bou Arfa before nightfall, let alone our original goal of the oasis town of Figuig, about eighty miles farther southeast.

For the next two hours, we raced south and southeast, sometimes topping 100 miles per hour. It was ineffably beautiful. In one part of the sky, the sun was a brilliant orange ball. As day gave way to night, orange gave way to the beaming whiteness of a full moon. We passed one of Bou Arfa's two prewar train stations at about 6:00 PM and decided to continue on, through the moonlight, to Figuig, for a night's rest. We planned to stop on the way back the next day to inspect the Vichy-era sites in the Bou Arfa environs.

Figuig is located at the end of a spit of land surrounded on three sides by Algeria, at the southeastern corner of Morocco. Despite its isolation, this town of 12,000 people has long been a bustling, enterprising place. It contributed more than its share to the Moroccan independence movement in the

1940s and 1950s and boasts numerous successful "favorite sons" who send back euros and dollars to pay for what the government in faraway Rabat does not provide. In the mid-1970s, when Morocco and Algeria sporadically fought each other over border disputes, the western Sahara, and bragging rights in northwest Africa, some of the fighting played itself out in the streets of Figuig. Now, with the border closed, Figuig has lost some of its entrepreneurial luster, but with a quarter million palm trees arranged in an ancient, well-irrigated palmerie, its romance and wonder are undiminished.

That night, we slept at Figuig's only hotel—a friendly, one-star place called the Figuig Hotel. By midmorning, we were on the road again, backtracking toward Bou Arfa, the terminus of the CMO and launching point for the great Trans-Sahara leap toward Central Africa. Bou Arfa was also a hub of southeastern Morocco's mining industry, with a train spur off the main track built to transport manganese northward to Mediterranean ports. For these reasons, Bou Arfa was home to the largest Vichy-era labor camp in Morocco, located near the main train station. According to the Red Cross, 818 people were interned there as of July 1942.[14]

Despite this, we decided not to devote our limited time to inspecting Bou Arfa itself. Our visit to pristine Tendrara had given us, we thought, a good idea of what a railroad labor camp probably looked like. Besides, we had a different mission to pursue—to track down the site of a Vichy "punishment" or "discipline" camp.

If workers led a harsh and severe life in forced labor camps, their existence in punishment camps was, as Harry Alexander said, pure hell. One of the Polish-Jewish survivors who passed through both Bou Arfa and its nearby punishment camps described the former as a "relative rest cure" compared with the latter. Indeed, the "discipline" meted out in these camps seems to have been designed for the sole purpose of inflicting pain and torture on the internees. According to the testimonies, virtually every worker at Bou Arfa was sentenced to "discipline" for some offense or another.

Bou Arfa had three satellite punishment camps. The first was at an old Foreign Legion post called Meridja, fifty-five miles from the town of Colomb-Béchar. The French abandoned that camp after a few months and relocated to 'Ain al-Ourak, near a mining outpost about twenty-five miles south of Bou Arfa. 'Ain al-Ourak does not appear on maps of Morocco—in fact, commercial maps show nothing at all south of Bou Arfa toward the Algerian border—but it served until May 1942 as the main "discipline" site for Bou Arfa laborers. When French officers sold the site to a local Arab notable for 100,000 francs, they moved the camp to a place called Foum Deflah, about nine miles east of Bou Arfa.

Like 'Ain al-Ourak, Foum Deflah does not exist on any map. However, along the Bou Arfa–Figuig road there is a sign marking the route of a meandering dry riverbed called Oued Deflah. When we reached this point on our drive west from Figuig, we stopped the car next to a man waiting for one of the infrequent inter-city buses to take him on to Bou Arfa. He was the quintessential "old Berber man," straight from central casting. Dressed in a drab-brown jellaba, he was anywhere between fifty and eighty years old, with dark leathery skin, wide piercing eyes, rotten multi-directional teeth, and a welcoming, twinkly smile. His name, he said, was Sa'id.

In French-spiced Arabic, Sa'id told me that he had lived in this valley his entire life. Foum Deflah, he said, referred to a parcel of land along the wadi, between the road and the foothills about a mile and a half north. The small stone structures that we could see in the distance were definitely relics of the French period, he said. Then, he proudly told us about his daughter, who lived in Belgium. From the emptiness of Foum Deflah to the capital of Europe in one generation is not an insignificant leap.

After bidding Sa'id farewell, we turned the car around and went off-road, along the edge of the wadi, toward those stone structures. The wartime report of a visiting Red Cross official stated that Foum Deflah's unfortunate inhabitants lived in tents and slept on straw mats; "the whole thing [was] reduced to most rudimentary terms," he wrote.[15] Perhaps those small primitive rock huts, arrayed in a rectangle a few hundred meters apart, could have served as guard outposts. Even if they were of later construction, the area they marked off almost certainly was the site of the Vichy-era "punishment camp" by that name.

Foum Deflah was the scene of some of the worst torture in Morocco. There, Jews were subjected to the *tombeau,* French for "tomb," a method of punishment in which camp overseers ordered prisoners to dig holes in the ground two meters long, fifty centimeters wide, and thirty-five centimeters deep and to lie in these faux graves for weeks on end. They stayed there day and night, exposed to blistering summer heat that could rise to more than 120°F and frigid winter nights that could dip to below freezing. They lay in their own waste, surviving only on bread and water. The slightest movement by prisoners would trigger, in the words of one witness, "a rain of stones or blows from rifles" from the camp guards.[16] According to the testimonies of the Polish-Jewish survivors,

> The routine at Lt. Thomas' "discipline" [at Foum Deflah] was even fiercer than that of Lt. Grunter at Ain el-Ourak . . . Thomas ordered that a man under *tombeau* sentence must continue to work flat out during the day and return to *tombeau* by night—but all the time on *tombeau* rations of bread and water—now reduced to one liter of water per day and 175 grams of bread.

After relating the story of how one of them tried to escape from Foum Deflah, was arrested in Bou Arfa, and tried unsuccessfully to commit suicide, the Polish Jews then told their British interviewers the following story about two Jews, one named Brenman, aged thirty-six, and the other, Kleinkoff, aged forty-one:

> Neither Brenman nor Kleinkoff were able to escape. After their first stint in the *tombeau*, they had not the strength to stand up. They therefore missed work the next morning. Lt. Thomas immediately reported to his chief at Bou Arfa, Commandant Kissler, that these two had gone on strike. He was then authorized to apply the anti-strike course of no work, no food. So Brenman and Kleinkoff just lay there in their open graves, broiling and burning by day and freezing by night. No food was given them and barely enough water to keep them alive. Brenman was seen licking and eating the swarms of flies that settled on his dying lips. By night, when the guard was not looking, he and Kleinkoff raised themselves up and drank their own urine out of their cupped hands.
>
> Kleinkoff lay in his open grave from September 3 [1942] till September 28. On September 28, he died. Brenman was dying. Commandant Kissler and Doctor Koeren came over from Bou Arfa and took Brenman with them. He then weighed 35 kilos, about half his normal weight. They took

him to the so-called hospital at Bou Arfa where he was thrown in a bed in the same room as [one of the five Polish-Jewish informants]. The bed was indescribably filthy. Brenman was given no special treatment or diet. They brought him exactly the same course of food as they had in the camps. When Doctor Koeren visited him he saw that Brenman had fouled the bed still further. He had no strength to do otherwise. Thereupon the doctor stormed and cursed and threatened Brenman with immediate return to Foum Defla. Fortunately for Brenman, he died on October 15, before this threat was implemented.

Brenman was Morice Tondowski's best friend. As Morice explained to me over tea in Ilford, he remained haunted with memories of Brenman for the next sixty years. "I think of him all the time," Morice said. Then, in an eerie echo of the motto that adorns the gate to Auschwitz—the infamous slogan "Arbeit Macht Frei"—he explained, "I told him he had to keep on working. 'Hitler will lose, the war will be over, and we will be free. But you have to live and to live you have to work,' I told him. But Brenman just couldn't."

Chapter 4

"Nobody Told Them to Do That"

A T EVERY STAGE OF THE NAZI, Vichy, and Fascist persecution of Jews in Arab lands, and in every place that it occurred, Arabs played a supporting role. At times, Arabs were essential to the process. At other times, the Arab role was passive yet still critical. And there were those occasions when certain Arabs did more than just collaborate—they made an already trying situation intolerable.

If there is one word to characterize the attitude of most Arabs toward Jews during the war years, it is "indifference." That word appears time and again in Jewish accounts of the period. A veteran of the Bizerte labor camp, for example, described in his memoirs how Arabs reacted when they saw Jewish workers filing through the streets, pail and shovel over their shoulders: "The Arabs regarded them indifferently," he wrote.[1] An historian of the period, writing in the early postwar years, observed that the "attitude of the great majority of the non-Jewish population of Tunis conformed to that of the [French] authorities: there were gestures of sympathy, but in large there was glacial indifference."[2]

Indifference has many shades. At one end of the spectrum, indifference could refer to a certain steely stoicism, a my-hands-are-tied inaction. As harrowing as life was for Jews in Arab lands during the war, the mass of Arabs suffered considerable hardships, too. Goods were scarce, food was rationed, and hunger and disease took a heavy toll. Politically, Arabs were not on sure ground, either. To many Germans and their European partners, Arabs were only marginally less inferior than Jews. As one German officer said ominously to an Arab enjoying the comeuppance of Jews near Tunis, "Your time will come. We will finish with the Jews and then we will take care of you."[3] If indifference meant that Arabs were primarily concerned with securing the means for their own survival—finding food, shelter, work, and so on—and could not spare the effort to act on their natural human sympathy toward their Jewish compatriots, then theirs was an understandable, even legitimate "indifference," born of necessity.

At the other end of the spectrum, indifference could also reflect a callous disregard for Jews that had lived—simultaneously protected, tolerated, and subordinate—within Arab societies for hundreds of years. If that is what contemporary observers meant when they used the term, then the indifferent were, in a sense, tacitly complicit in the crimes of the foreigners. It is clear that, whatever their attitude toward the fate of the Jews, many Arabs were not indifferent to the coming of the Jews' tormentors. "Go, go, I would wish to be with you, Hitler," were the lyrics of one popular Berber song of this period.[4] The head of the Vichy regime, Marshal Pétain, had a position of particular respect in the eyes of many Arabs, because of his age, his military exploits, his emphasis on family, his carefully crafted persona of personal modesty. As Algerian professor Ahmed Ibnou Zekri, a member of Vichy's National Council, said, "For us Muslims, Marshal Pétain is 'a sid' [an honored lord]."[5]

Clarity on this issue is important: By virtually all accounts, the mass of Arabs neither participated in nor actively supported the anti-Jewish campaign that European Fascists brought to North Africa. The preoccupation of most Arabs was survival; for those of the political class, the emerging challenge to colonial rule was a much greater concern than contributing to the persecution of Jews.[6] But if one can excuse those Arabs who took satisfaction at the collapse of the French republic before the forces of Nazi Germany, the general sense of welcome accorded to European persecutors of Jews bespoke an indifference to the fate of the Jews that was hardly benign. In the view of many Arabs, if the humbling of French colonialists brought with it the humbling of the Jews, too, then so be it.

A rung up the ladder of Arab complicity were those Arabs who not only watched as Europeans imported and then imposed major elements of their system of racial persecution on Jews but who also cheered what they saw. Though not lead actors in the anti-Jewish drama, they were, in a certain way, its Greek chorus.

Here are some excerpts from oral testimonies that tell this part of the story.

Gad Shahar, a veteran of Tunisia's Safsaf and Sedjanane work camps, recalled that local Arabs hailed German soldiers as they paraded Jews through the country's capital. "Muslims applauded the Nazi forces that arrested the Jews and made them march through Tunis," he told an interviewer. "Muslims smashed bottles at us, at the Mateur station, jugs from which [we planned] to quench the thirst of old and tired Jews."[7]

Yehoshua Duweib, another survivor of a Tunisian labor camp, testified that the "Arabs were gloating" when the Germans marched him and fellow Jews through town on the way to a work site. "They would say to us: 'Push the shovel, ya Shalom' [a common Jewish name]. They meant: 'Until now you were a merchant or a clerk, but now you'll work hard.'" Even Arab women, breaking local custom that kept them in their homes virtually all the time, came out to watch and laugh at the humbled Jewish workers, he said.[8]

Victor Cohen, also from Tunis, reported that when the Germans herded Jewish laborers through the streets, the "true nature" of the city's Arabs was finally revealed. "They were happy," he said. "They would mock and laugh: 'Take the shovel, pick up the shovel.'"[9]

Yehuda Chachmon, who lived under Italian rule in Benghazi, Libya, said Arab street gangs grew so brazen and powerful during the war years that Jews were too afraid to leave their homes after dark. "Arabs would throw oranges, tomatoes, stones at us," he said. "Every Jew would hide in his house after five in the evening. The houses were closed [i.e., locked up] with bars and you could not leave until the morning."[10]

Ernest-Yehoshua Ozan, a sales representative for his family's business, was ordered by the Germans to do his forced labor on a farm in Tunisia. He recalled the special pleasure some Arabs derived from the misfortune of Jews. "Near the farm where we worked were several Arab families [who would] always try to tell us things like: 'Your Tunis has been completely destroyed by bombings . . . No one was left alive in the city of Tunis.' They knew we were from Tunis. They always 'made sure' to tell us things like that," he said.[11]

These cheerleaders for the persecution were normally from the lower economic classes. They took a certain measure of satisfaction from the comeuppance of Jews, who, despite the large number of Jewish poor, were widely considered to be a wealthy community. Higher up the Arab social ladder were those who either applauded the imposition of anti-Jewish laws or complained that the new laws did not go far enough. Some Arab notables argued that anti-Jewish statutes contained too many loopholes and did not adequately benefit the local Arab community. In December 1940, an Arab newspaper in Algiers proposed that Vichy authorities take a page from the Germans and require Jews to wear special distinguishing clothes: "It is necessary to prohibit Jews from wearing the hats of Europeans and indigenous peoples . . . . We propose that the Government impose on Algerian Jews their particular headgear—the ancestral skullcap . . . ." One month earlier, the same newspaper suggested that Jews were so cunning that protecting the Arab majority from their schemes might require more extreme measures. "The only effective remedy may be to isolate them on a faraway island or in a distant desert under rigorous international control," ran an editorial in *el-Balagh*—a proposal that was *not* intended as an endorsement of Zionist aspirations.[12]

If some Arabs enjoyed seeing Jews made low, there were also those who took advantage of Jewish suffering for their own commercial gain. Although they did not inflict pain or anguish on Jews, they did reap direct financial benefit from the Jews' plight. They engaged in behavior typical of this kind of situation, such as profiteering. With the coming of war, there were severe shortages of many basic goods and foodstuffs in Morocco and Algeria, and the extra francs Arabs earned from Jews in trying circumstances no doubt softened the blow. Tunisians, for example, celebrated a plentiful Ramadan in early autumn 1942, and the country maintained a semblance of normalcy until the onset of the German occupation. By year's end, however, they faced bare store-shelves, a raging black market, and the early signs of hunger, so the fact that some Arabs took advantage of Jews by hiking up prices on food, rent, and other necessities seemed to be a reasonable solution for trying times. In the grand scheme of the war, this was petty profiteering. To the Jews in question, however, the exorbitant prices demanded for basic necessities and the larceny, corruption, and double-dealing that characterized the black market economy often determined who survived and who did not.

Testimonies provide numerous accounts of Jews victimized by Arab wartime profiteering. Miriam Levy, of Benghazi, explained that the havoc caused by aerial bombardments was often compounded by the looting of Jewish property that would follow immediately thereafter. "The Arabs, they would take advantage of us. Always wanting money, a bomb falls in the house of the Jews, all the property is lost. Stealing and robbing, doing want they want . . . ."[13] According to Isaac Jacques Smadja of La Marsa, an upscale seaside suburb of Tunis, looting sometimes assumed gruesome proportions: "At the end of the bombings . . . we saw the Arabs in their cruelty. We saw how they cut the fingers [of corpses] to steal rings and gold jewelry from the Jews. We saw how they cut throats in order to get necklaces. We saw how they cut belts to get the buckles . . . ."[14] Victor Cohen, of Tunis, told the story of his brother, who was sent to a remote rural site for his forced labor. For the first four days, he said, the Germans gave the workers no food at all. Local Arabs filled the breach by selling the workers orange peels. Then, he said, the Arabs promptly stole them back. "[The workers] were dying of hunger," he explained.[15]

Jews accused Arabs of price gouging, especially when Jews had to flee their bombed-out homes in Tunisian cities and towns and sought refuge in Arab villages in the countryside. Corinne Boukobza-Hakmoun related a family tale of her uncle, Albert Nataf, a wealthy landowner from Sousse, who handed "a massive bundle of bank notes" to an Arab in the village of Djemmal to secure refuge for his family from Allied bombing raids of their hometown.[16] Yaacov Zrivy, from a village near Sfax, Tunisia's second-largest city, recalled the huge sums Arabs charged Jews to rent houses or apartments after the Germans forced many Jews out of their homes.[17]

In Morocco, some Arab notables saw in the imposition of Vichy anti-Jewish laws an opportunity to improve both their personal finances and their political fortunes. Grand Vizier Mohamed El Mokri explained the urgency to Vichy foreign minister Paul Baudouin: Before the French established their protectorate, the Jews would take twenty years to amass a fortune, keep it for ten years until the government stole it away, and then start the cycle all over again. But twenty-eight years of French protection risked breaking this rhythm, El Mokri said, with the result that like-minded Moroccans had only two years left to work closely with Vichy to pillage the Jews if they were to keep the thirty-year cycle intact.[18] Numerous Moroccan officials were evidently willing to help make that deadline. The pasha of Marrakesh, for example, turned against the local Jewish community as a way to defend himself against the embarrassing and potentially dangerous accusation of being too pro-French. Not only did he commend the idea that local Jews should wear distinctive garb to distinguish them from Arabs, but he also went on to strike what one historian called "a major blow" against the Jews of Morocco's southern metropolis when he imposed a 100,000 franc levy on the inhabitants of the local Jewish quarter (mellah). Similarly, the pasha of Salé, Rabat's sister-city, issued an edict banning Jews from hiring Muslims.[19] And in the town of Beni-Mellal, the local Muslim governor and the French civil controller jointly decreed that any European who wanted to settle in the town had the right to choose a home occupied by Jews.[20] Indeed, Vichy officials were often eager to cultivate Arab profiteering as a way to divert the attention of a potentially restive local population. "Thanks to a prosperity to which they are not accustomed, the indigenous population is calm," wrote the provisional commander of the Tunis gendarmerie in his monthly report for August 1941. "In its large majority, they are loyal to us." To the extent such loyalty did exist—the commander almost surely exaggerated for the benefit of his superiors—it was due to the financial windfalls of the anti-Jewish campaign, not the success of pro-Axis propaganda, he noted.[21]

<hr>

As UNSEEMLY AND IGNOBLE as these acts were, if they reflected the totality of the Arab contribution to the anti-Jewish campaign in Arab lands, then these Arab indiscretions would deserve little more than passing reference in any dispassionate history of the war years in North Africa. If all the Arabs did to support the European persecution of Jews was take some pleasure and satisfaction at the comeuppance of a minority that had, in the eyes of many, disproportionate wealth and privilege—and perhaps earn some much-needed extra wartime cash along the way—then it would be unfair to charge them with responsibility in the foreigners' crimes.

But many Arabs did more than just cheer on the sidelines as Jews were marched off to forced labor. They provided the manpower—guards, foremen, train conductors, and so forth—that made the persecution possible. And, if numerous eyewitness accounts are to be believed, a sizable number often performed their tasks willfully, even eagerly. Sometimes their zealousness was characterized by gratuitous violence that bordered on the sadistic. It was against the background of the raucous cheering of thousands that these essential Arab cogs in the Nazi, Vichy, and Fascist war machinery did their jobs. The active cheerleaders and the passive onlookers created an enabling environment for the willing participants; if the first two groups had not played their part, it is uncertain whether the latter would have played theirs. For that reason, if for none other, they earn their place in the opening pages of a chapter on the Arab role in the persecution of Jews in Arab lands.

The willing participants were everywhere, performing every duty necessary to make the wheels of persecution turn. Numerous testimonies affirm that Arab soldiers, policemen, and workers all played roles—sometimes large, sometimes small—in implementing the designs of the European persecutors of North African Jewry: from the execution of anti-Jewish statutes, to the recruitment of Jewish workers, to the operation of forced labor camps. From the outskirts of Casablanca to the deserts south of Tripoli, Arabs routinely served as guards, watchmen, and overseers at those labor camps. With rare exceptions, they were feared by Jewish (and other) captives as willing and loyal servants of their Nazi, Vichy, and Fascist superiors.

Yehoshua Duweib was interned at Bizerte's notorious Philibert barracks, perhaps the harshest of Tunisia's work sites. He remembered a particularly zealous local patrolman who led a group of other Arabs in tracking down and rounding up Jews trying to escape from the hazards of nighttime bombardment. "He would gather more Arabs who threatened us and brought us back to the German army," said Duweib.[22] Tzvi Haddad, of Gabès, in Tunisia, recalled that Arab overseers—not Germans or Italians—were entrusted with marching his gang of fifty laborers to their work site in the morning and then back to town each evening.[23]

For some—perhaps even most—of these Arabs, guarding Jews and otherwise servicing the Germans, Italians, and French was a necessary if regrettable side of war. There was no joy in the job, just pay. For many, however, the Nazi, Fascist, and Vichy persecution of Jews offered an opportunity to participate in the Europeans' anti-Jewish campaign. Whether they were underlings or overseers, these Arabs became full partners in the wartime maltreatment of Jews in Arab lands.

Wherever torture occurred, Arabs played a role. Arab guards, for example, routinely flogged prisoners at "punishment camps" in the Sahara.[24] An Algerian account of brutality at Colomb-Béchar, one of the largest Vichy labor camps, tells the story of one internee who jumped through a barracks window and escaped into the desert, only to be tracked down "by Arab soldiers on horseback who dragged him back to camp tied to their horses." The captured man was then sent to a particularly hellish spot called Hadjerat M'Guil, where he was tortured and died eight days later.[25] At Djenien Bou-Rezg, another infamous Vichy concentration camp, the sadistic commandant, Lieutenant Pierre de Ricko, had at his side a team of subordinates that included a pro-fascist Alsatian, a German who moonlighted as head of a local gang of anti-Semitic hooligans, and an Arab policeman named Ali Guesni.[26] At Djelfa, in the Algerian desert, the commanding officer was another sadist, J. Caboche, who liked to strip all the clothes off prisoners and then horsewhip them. Caboche forbade his prisoners to light any fires to keep warm. On especially cold desert nights, Caboche's loyal Arab adjutant—a man known to posterity only as Ahmed[27]—reportedly took particular pleasure in making sure his charges froze.[28] An Arab served as camp overseer of the Dumergue-Fretiha farm labor camp near the northern Tunisian town of Mateur. Accounts attest to the daily regimen of gratuitous pain and torture that he meted out to the forty Jews unlucky enough to be dispatched to work under his supervision.[29]

A British officer who served on the Allied commission to investigate, and eventually liberate, Vichy labor camps, described the role of *goumiers*—local Arab soldiers—at a small punishment camp not far from the mining and railroad town of Bou Arfa, in southeastern Morocco.[30]

The camp of 'Ain al-Ourak is under the command of six former underofficers of the Foreign Legion .... It is guarded and supervised by a detachment of "goumiers" (troup of native Arabs from the southern territories) numbering about sixty. These "goumiers" ... stop attempts of escape by the men being "disciplined." They guard the camp with a bayonet on their rifles, their guns loaded, and are instructed to make use of their guns should an attempt at escape be made . . . Some of the work done by the inmates is supervised by the "goumiers" . . .

Arab guards, the officer explained, were also the camp torturers. They were the ones, he said, who supervised the *tombeau,* the punishment I described in the last chapter, and made sure the prisoners, lying in their own waste, remained still as zombies, never moving to swat a fly or evade a scorpion. "Those who dare to raise their heads expose themselves to a rain of stones thrown by the Arabs who are on guard or to be kicked, or blows from rifles," he reported.

The 1943 British Foreign Office document "Barbaric Treatment of Jews and Aliens in Morocco," which tells the story of five Polish Jews who made their way to London after being liberated from Vichy labor camps, includes harrowing details of the *tombeau* and the role that Arab guards played in implementing the torture:[31]

Typical of the offences which earned a man a stretch of *tombeau* was that of the German Jew Selgo. In January 1942, Selgo injured his leg and wrapped a bandage around the wound. The bandage kept slipping down and he stopped his road-making from time to time to pull it up. For this [Foreign Legionnaire] Gayer ordered fifteen days *tombeau.*

Like all the others, he had to lie face up night and day. He had no covering, only a tattered Legion uniform with no underclothes. He was not allowed to move or change positions in the *tombeau.* An Arab was posted over the graves to see that the victims stayed rigidly still. There were 24 *tombeau* in a row. If a man moved when the Arab was near, he got a blow with a rifle butt. If the Arab was further away and the man out of [his] reach, the guard would hurl a stone at him.

The only occasion when a man was allowed to raise his head a little was after a rainstorm when the graves filled with water. Then he was allowed a stone for a head-rest to save him from drowning. As the subsoil was clay, the water would take three days to drain away. [One of the informants] once had to lie in water for three days and nights, but he was lucky. It was during the summer and though the nights were bitterly cold, the water did not freeze.

Selgo was not so fortunate. He was sentenced in January and after a rainstorm the water in his grave froze by night. After his fifteen days he was removed from the *tombeau* with both legs frost-bitten. They took him to hospital and amputated both his feet . . . No talking among the victims was allowed, although each *tombeau* was only 40 centimeters from the next. Six Arabs mounted guard at a time and were relieved every two hours.

Gayer or one of the other guards would bring the men their meals—1 liter of water at 0800 hours, 250 grams of bread and a glass of water at 1200 hours, and another glass of water at nightfall. A man was allowed to relieve himself only during these three visits of the guard. If he could not do it then he had to do it in his clothes and lie in it. The Arab guards had no authority to allow him to leave the grave. As the majority of prisoners were suffering from severe and sanguinary dysentery, a man lying in his own filth was the rule rather than the exception.

In Chapter 3, I told the story of Harry Alexander, a Jew from Leipzig who survived two years in the desert hellhole of Djelfa, one of Vichy's harshest concentration camps in North Africa. From the moment he arrived at the Djelfa train station, Arab guards figured large in his harrowing ordeal:

Spahis are elite Arab troops. They're on horses. They're very cruel people. We were horse-whipped all the way [from the railroad station], walking two or three miles to the camp, through the sand, through the hot sun. We were beaten all the way down there. And people that fell down we had to drag them along because of the chains.

Later in his oral history, videotaped for the U.S. Holocaust Memorial Museum, Harry Alexander described the torture he suffered at the hands of the Arab guards:

For the slightest infraction of the rules, they would bury you in the sand up to your neck. And the Arabs would urinate on your head. And if you moved your head, they would take a big stone and smash your head. You weren't supposed to move. If a scorpion or a viper or ants or whatever there was would bite you, you could not move.

With no means to defend themselves, Harry and his fellow inmates resisted by not giving their torturers the satisfaction of hearing them cry out in pain.

The only way we could fight back, the only way we could protest this cruel treatment, was by not giving in to their punishment. They could beat us all they want ... and we would sit quietly and silently absorb it, without a peep. We would not even make a sound, a noise. It would hurt. It would bleed. You would be in excruciating pain. And the more we defied them in our own way, the more they would beat us ... and figure out more punishments, bigger punishments, longer punishments, more beatings, no water for the day, no food for two days, standing naked being tied to a post in the sun all day, in the hot African sun, putting a bucket of ants over your head, burying you in the sand to your neck and urinating on your head, and beating your head open—and nothing they did could make us make a sound.

Asked whether the actions of his Arab guards could be explained by the excuse that they were "just following orders," Harry gave this reply:

No, no, no! The cruelty and the barbaric manners of the guards, that came out by themselves. Nobody told them to beat us all the time. Nobody told them to chain us together. Nobody told them to beat us up with chains and whips ... Nobody told them to tie us naked to a post and beat us and to hang us by our arms and hose us down, to bury us in the sand so our heads should look up and bash our brains in and urinate on our heads. Nobody told them to do that. They told us we're supposed to be confined to work on the Transsaharien [railroad]. But nobody told them how much or how hard or how ... No, they took this into their own hands and they enjoyed what they did. You could see it on their faces; they enjoyed it.[32]

In some cases, Arab soldiers exploited their power and their weapons to terrorize Jews. After Operation Torch, Maurice Marrachi, a Moroccan Jew, detailed a litany of Arab "abuses of power" in letters to British and American diplomats. He wrote that Arab troops were unlawfully breaking into homes, extorting money, and "even passing the night in the company of the mistress of the house."[33] Arab troops were incensed at the pleasure Jews took in the speedy Anglo-American trouncing of Vichy troops in Operation Torch and retaliated by locking the gates on the Jewish quarter of Rabat for three weeks, keeping the thousands of Jews who lived in the cramped, squalid conditions of the *mellah* penned up inside. Firsthand accounts attest to the fact that—adding insult to injury—the *goumiers* also extorted food and lodging from the Jews of Rabat throughout this ordeal. Similar troubles were recorded in other cities around the sultanate, such as Meknès and Fez, often with what one historian called the "active participation" of government agents, policemen, European soldiers, and "native elements."[34]

In Tunisia, local Arab mobs—their numbers augmented by the return of Arab conscripts demobilized from the French army after its surrender to Germany—frequently turned their sights on Jews.[35] In August 1940, the towns of Kef, Ebba Ksour, Moktar, and Siliana were the scene of riots and pillaging against Jews. Triggered by rumors that Jews had kidnapped a young Muslim girl, the violence actually reflected a more general rise in anti-Semitic sentiment, with the Jews increasingly blamed for wartime shortages.[36] The French, of course, had themselves to blame for stoking anti-Jewish feeling, but now they had an even greater fear that "malcontent on the part of the Muslim masses," as Admiral Estéva, the French resident-general put it, could escalate into mass anti-French unrest.[37] Reflecting the tragic absurdity of the times, French officials blamed the Jews for their own misfortune. At one point, Vichy foreign minister Paul Baudouin urged Estéva to warn Jewish leaders in "severe and frank" language to stop agitating against Pétainism and to accept their persecution quietly. He also ordered Estéva to find quiet ways to indulge Arab sensibilities, such as freeing from prison those Arabs who had been convicted of pillage and theft for their role in anti-Jewish riots.[38] Even so, violence continued. In November 1940, there was an anti-Jewish riot in Degache. In early 1941, the same fate befell the Jewish community in Gafsa.

Then, in May 1941, the coastal city of Gabès was the scene of North Africa's worst wartime outburst of all, a three-day paroxysm of violence, pillage, and murder. What started with an attack by a gang of thirty Arabs on a synagogue, perhaps prompted by news of the demise of the short-lived pro-Nazi regime in Iraq, deteriorated into a mass frenzy of violence that left eight Jews killed and twenty injured.[39] Again, local Arab policemen were, at best, ineffective, and at worst, complicit.[40]

The rampage in Gabès was blood-curdling. Yosef Huri, a survivor, recalled what happened to his neighbor, Afila Rakach. Rakach was in her small kitchen, cooking dinner for her family, when a gang of local Arabs barged into her home. According to Huri, they grabbed a pot of boiling soup, poured it over her, tortured her in her house, stoned her, and then killed her.[41]

Another survivor, Youssef Mimoun, recalled that in one quarter of Gabès, Arab and Jewish neighbors had joined together for an evening of celebration—eating and drinking—the night before the rioting. The same people who had broken bread with the Jews one night, attacked them the next. "Although we had good relations, there were those among them who hated Jews just because we were Jews," he said.[42]

Tzvi Haddad, who lived at the end of a largely Arab street near a coffee house, remained haunted by the image of his mother, who left their home at the first sign of trouble to look for his sister. As soon as his mother got out the door, he recalled, an Arab knocked her down and then another grabbed her and tried to cut her throat. Tzvi heard his mother's screams, ran out to the street, saw blood flowing on her face and legs. Eventually, Tzvi's father arrived to rescue his wife, who, miraculously, survived. She carried a scar on her throat for the rest of her life.[43]

After the total breakdown of order in Gabès, Vichy police for the first time reacted with force and resolution. This was not born of any sympathy for Jewish victims, however. The French had more a self-interested concern: that rioting could deteriorate into anarchy and lead to further loss of French control and prestige. Indeed, colonial officials frequently noted that France's surrender to the Germans eroded the mystique of power and invulnerability the French held over the Arabs, who saw weakness and took advantage of it. As Estéva cabled his superiors at Vichy:

It is necessary to understand that German prestige has been on the rise for some time. It leads Muslims to believe themselves to be more and more on top of the Jews, since the latter keep their confidence in Britain and America . . . And in Gabès, the presence of German officers has without doubt, even without intervention on their part, let the Arabs believe they would be protected in case of riots. [I have already explained the] vexing notion among the Tunisians and even among the entourage of the Bey that Hitler is the master of the entire world and that France, in the Regency, exercises its mandate only thanks to the generosity of the Führer.[44]

To restore the perception of French dominance and control, Estéva ordered the arrest of several of the Arab perpetrators, five of whom were later executed in the Tunis kasbah. But the Gabès affair left both Jews and Arabs bruised and wary. Jews who had, for decades, put their trust in France as the protecting power felt the French were too slow to act and too solicitous of Arab sensibilities. For their part, Arabs who watched, often approvingly, as Vichy imposed stiff anti-Jewish statutes were stung that local French officials would punish them merely for stripping those measures of all legal niceties and taking them one logical step further.[45]

<hr />

ARAB GUARDS WORKING under German, French, and Italian officers at labor camps were not the only uniformed Arabs to side with the Axis powers. A small army of other Arabs volunteered for service, either directly in special German units or in paramilitary formations that fought with, or supported, Axis forces.

The Phalange Africaine—also known as the Légion des Volontaires Française de Tunisie—was first organized by Vichy officers in the aftermath of Operation Torch. The unit had 400 soldiers, about one-third Arab and the balance a motley collection of various European pro-Fascist misfits. In February 1943, the German army took full control of the Phalange. Over the next year, the unit fought against both British troops and Free French forces. Its commander, Pierre Cristofini, was convicted of treason by a French military tribunal in 1944 and executed.

A second formation—this time, all-Arab—was the Brigade Nord Africaine, a group of Algerian volunteers established under German supervision by a former French officer named Mohamed el-Maadi, a virulent anti-Semite who went by the nickname "SS Mohamed." The unit was deployed to fight the partisans of the Dordogne region of France.[46]

In addition to these paramilitary groups, the Germans tried to organize special units composed of Arab troops operating directly under their command. In January 1942, they established the German-Arab Training Battalion, which brought together Arabs who had been taken as prisoners of war after serving in the British or French armies. Volunteers hailed from Egypt, the Levant, and even as far away as Saudi Arabia, showing that it mattered little whether the hated colonialist was British or French: The Germans played on Arab dislike of both. Each soldier wore a specially manufactured cloth arm patch featuring the words "Free Arabia" written in German and Arabic. Perhaps the most famous Arab formation in the German army was the Special Formation Unit (Sonder Verbande) 287, also known as the Deutsche-Arabische Legion, which consisted of three battalions, including Arab personnel and a German officer staff. In these various subgroups, the Legion's Arab troops saw service in numerous theaters of the war, from the Caucasus to Greece to Tunisia and against Yugoslav partisans.

Generally, the Germans placed little value on the competence of these Arab volunteer units; even when they were pressed into battle, the Germans still did not view them as capable of doing more than rearguard duty or coastal defense. But there was at least one exception: An elite demolition and engineering unit was developed with nearly 100 Arabs handpicked by a certain German officer then stationed in Hammamet, Tunisia, Captain Schact of the First Parachute Brigade. Schact described them as a mix of "Moroccans, Algerians, Tunisians, Senussi, Tuaregs, Syrians, Egyptians, Iraqi and desert Arabs." The unit was flown to Berlin for training at the rigorous Wittstock Parachute School and then fought with great effectiveness behind Allied lines during the battle for Tunisia.

It is difficult to estimate the total number of Arabs who volunteered to fight alongside the Germans. One military observer suggested that up to 13,000 Arabs volunteered for service with the Axis powers during the war, about half of whom were directly in the German army and other German outfits, with the balance in the forces of Vichy France. Their direct military contribution was negligible, but, it was noted, they furnished "rolls upon rolls of propaganda film for the German war effort."[47]

There are many reasons that these men joined up with the Germans. Some were motivated by hatred of the French colonialists and admiration for any power that could defeat them. Others were keen to be on the winning side of the war, especially at a time when the Axis was in ascendance. For others, there was an economic incentive, the opportunity for work and pay when times were rough. Hatred of Jews surely played a role. As posters and flyers from the period attest, playing the "Jewish card" was a central theme of Axis propaganda and no doubt a substantial motivating factor. Although there is no specific record of Arab units participating in German-led or -inspired attacks on Jews per se, their very existence is noteworthy because they reflect a certain measure of zealous commitment by some Arabs to the larger German war effort.

<hr />

ANOTHER CATEGORY OF "VILLAIN"—a notch still higher on the ladder of collusion—included those Arabs who volunteered their services to assist directly in the persecution of Jews. No one compelled these Arabs to work alongside the German authorities, host Gestapo officers—not just regular German army men—in their homes, track down Jewish laborers, break into Jewish houses to ransack property, or inform on their Jewish compatriots.[48] These Arabs were full partners in the Nazi, Vichy, and Fascist brutality against local Jews.

Tunisia's National Archives, for example, include oral testimonies, offered by both Frenchmen and Arabs, against a man named Youssef Ben Hamida Boufheri. According to these accounts, Boufheri guided German patrols as an armed member of a German squad, pillaged homes and businesses, and even commanded a group of other Arabs pressed into labor service to work for the Germans.[49] In another file, a Vichy official recounted how "young Tunisians accompanied by [German] soldiers would present themselves at the houses of Jews and, under this threat, get themselves served something to drink and eat. The Jews consider themselves happy when [the Tunisians] don't demand their wives or daughters . . . ."[50]

Amos Shofan, whose family passed the occupation with their ill grandfather in Gabès, told of the Sabbath morning in 1943 when German troops arrived to round up Jewish laborers. With two Arab translators leading the way, the Germans entered the town's main synagogue. Amos recalled that his father asked to let the congregants finish their prayers, but the Germans refused. When the local rabbi urged everyone to go outside and accept their fate, Amos's father started a fight with the Arabs, whom he knew from the town. It was a losing battle. Together, the Arabs and the Germans beat him, dragged him on the ground, and took him and his two eldest sons to work at the local airstrip, unloading military ammunition. The Arabs, Amos said scornfully, were the worst sort of collaborators: They were "squealers."[51]

A British journalist, who entered the town of Gafsa with Allied troops just hours after it had been abandoned by the Germans, was shocked at the extent of the plunder. "All the Jews in the town have been pillaged by the Arabs acting under German encouragement," wrote Philip Jordan in his wartime memoir. "Even the doors and windows have been stolen. It is horrible."[52]

In his journal, Paul Ghez related how German soldiers and "Arab hoodlums" together launched late-night raids into Jewish neighborhoods in Tunis. At the beginning, he wrote, the forays were limited to petty larceny and harassing local passers-by. As time passed, the situation worsened. One night in mid-January, he recalled, "The Germans and their acolytes entered into private lodgings and extorted money and provisions. Two women were violated under the eyes of their husbands and children, taken under threat of revolvers." Eventually, even the German authorities grew concerned at the extent of lawlessness and mayhem produced by this German-Arab entente. German army commanders solved the problem by issuing orders prohibiting German soldiers from entering the Jewish quarter of Tunis.[53]

Jewish survivors of the German occupation frequently told stories of Arab informants. Tzvi Haddad, for example, recounted how one Saturday morning in 1943, two Arabs led two Germans to the houses of all the Jewish goldsmiths in his hometown of Gabès, extorting from each along the way.[54] According to Maurice Yaish, Arabs accompanied German soldiers throughout Tunis, picking out Jews to demand identification cards.[55] Haim Mazuz recalled how "the Arabs incited the Germans against us," pointing out Jews in the streets of the town of al-Hama; "'This is a Jew' and 'This is a Jew,'" he remembered them saying.[56] The wife of Abraham Sarfati, from La Goulette, told of Arabs who "were happy in the fact that they would make trouble for the Jews ... I would hear groups and the Arabs would lead them [the Germans] to Jewish homes, saying 'There zig-zig.' That means prostitute."[57]

Paul Ghez, who ran the Jewish recruitment service in Tunis, related the story of Arabs who were enraged by an Allied raid on the el-Aouina aerodrome in Tunis that left dozens dead. Bent on seeking vengeance, they attacked a group of Jews and denounced six of them to the Germans for having signaled to Allied bombers. Luckily for the Jews, even the Germans eventually recognized the absurdity of the charge; after all, it is patently impossible for a pilot to discern hand signals while flying at more than 15,000 feet. But, as Ghez explained, there was a long moment when the Jews feared for their lives—and with good reason.[58]

When a similar accusation was made against Victor Nataf, a young rabbinical student from Ariana, a Tunis suburb, he did pay with his life. Piecing together the story from various documents, it appears that four local Arabs from Ariana, all of whom were previously known to the Nataf family, denounced Nataf to the Germans on December 13, 1942. They accused Nataf of sending directional signals to aid Allied bombers. In fact, all Nataf had done was light Sabbath candles, which could be seen flickering through the blackout curtain that hung in every Tunis home. That same evening, a German soldier—accompanied by the four Arabs—burst into the Natafs' house, found Victor sleeping, and arrested him. Six days later, without a trial, he was pronounced guilty and shot to death. On December 21, two days after the execution, a brief announcement appeared in the *Tunis-Journal,* noting that "the Jew Victor Nataf had been condemned to death for having compromised the security of German troops."

After the Allies captured Tunisia, Victor's parents tried to convince the Free French authorities to pursue criminal charges against the four Arabs. According to the police complaint filed by Victor's mother, Ninette Nataf, one of the Arabs—a man named Said Ben Mustapha el-Ghomrasni—had harbored a grudge against the Nataf family ever since they had a financial dispute over a plan to invest in the opening of a small bakeshop. Although the Tunisian archives contain Mrs. Nataf's official deposition, the paper trail stops there. Whether the French authorities pursued the matter and arrested any of the four is not known. What is known is that the people of Ariana did not forget the injustice done to Victor and renamed the street where his family home was located in his memory. The street name, how-ever, no longer exists.[59]

A particularly vicious, though secondhand, story of extortion and murder was told by Amos Shofan, who grew up hearing from his uncle this account of what happened in the largely Arab village of Hageb al-Ayoun. During the war, local Arabs frequently shook down Jews who sought refuge near the town and threatened to tell the Germans about workers trying to avoid forced labor. In one incident, a group of Arab thieves stopped Amos's uncle and a friend on a road and demanded not only money but their clothes as well, forcing the two men to walk home naked. Later that evening, the same group of thieves broke into a different Jewish home in the village, threat-ened the family, and demanded their savings. Not satisfied with what the poor father could scrape together, one of the thieves picked up the fright-ened man's one-year-old child, took him outside, and threw him on a cactus bush. The child, said Amos, died from the thorns, a painful, agonizing death. As of 2003, when Amos gave the interview, the child's father was still alive, living in Beersheva in Israel's southern Negev region, but he has not talked about the incident in decades.[60]

Then, there was a small but influential group of Tunisian Arabs who threw their lot in with the Germans without reservation. Such was the case, for example, with the Guellaty-Okby clan, who even put their hotel on Boulevard Bab Menara at the disposition of the German authorities.[61] A number of Arabs had so thoroughly aligned themselves with the Germans that they joined in the German retreat back to Europe. These included Rachid Driss, leader of the pro-Nazi Muslim Youth (Jeunesse Musulmane), and a merchant named Hamadi Boujemaa, who reportedly earned enough money thanks to his connections with the German occupation authorities that he was able to set himself up in Switzerland. Another notable, the vil-lage shaykh of Oulad Akrim, identified so closely with the Axis that when he found himself behind British lines, he tried to escape to the German side of the front. And when the Germans left the town of Gabès, both the provincial governor and the local magistrate reportedly left with them.[62]

Following the German retreat and final collapse of Vichy rule in Tunisia, the Free French regime purged scores of officials, bureaucrats, and police-men on account of their collaboration. A significant number of these were

Arabs.[63] In many of these cases, however, the official records do not explain the real reason for the punishment: Was it because these Arabs collaborated with the Germans? Was it because they persecuted Jews? Or was it because they took advantage of the German occupation to press their nationalist, anti-colonialist, anti-French politics? In the minds of French officials—both Vichyites and Free French—agitating for Tunisian nationalism deserved much greater penalty than participating in a campaign of often violent persecution of Jews. To purge an Arab for being a secret member of a nationalist cell was understandable; to purge an Arab for collusion in anti-Jewish activities was messy and complicated. Indeed, colonial archives provide clear examples of what most likely were anti-Jewish acts cloaked in nationalist terms to make the file seem more presentable.[64] Arabs were frequently accused of "pillaging"—a crime that often meant stealing property from abandoned Jewish homes or businesses—but no reference was actually made to the Jewish connection.[65] In their fanatical repression of Tunisian nationalists, Tunisia's Free French "liberators" were no less zealous than the Vichyites. One post-liberation list of thirty-three Arabs suspected of anti-French activities during the German occupation included eight officials of Tunisia's royal court and a number of anti-French propagandists, but only one person cited for anti-Jewish activity. Another list of 106 Arabs tried and convicted for acts perpetrated during the German occupation included seven originally sentenced to death and twenty-four more who received life imprisonment at hard labor. Some had volunteered to serve with German forces; others had provided information to the Germans or helped them requisition goods; most were convicted for "pillaging" or "theft" of empty homes. Though Jews were almost surely the victims of many of these crimes, there is not a single mention of a Jewish connection in the entire file.[66] On those rare occasions when the Jewish connection is clear, the culprits did not always face justice. The one Arab cited above for "anti-Jewish activity"—Azouz Ben Mustapha Ben Hadj Ali, alias Azouz el-Gonzali—was responsible "for introducing a German soldier to a Jewish home in La Marsa to permit him to violate an Israelite woman." Despite the severity of the crime—rape—the report did not actually note whether the German's Arab accomplice was ever arrested.[67]

INDEED, IN ALL MY RESEARCH, I came across only one case of an Arab who was arrested, tried, convicted, and sentenced to prison for collaborating with foreign forces in the persecution of Jews. There may have been others, but their stories are either locked away in archives of French military tribunals, which remain closed for 100 years, or have been lost with the passage of time. The one story I did find is the gruesome saga of theft, deception, betrayal, and death that opened this book, the story of Hassen Ferjani and the three men of the Scemla family who were deported and then executed in Germany.[68]

When I met him in Paris, Frédéric Gasquet had just completed a ninety-eight-page manuscript that related just about every detail of his family's tragedy. The one part he knew nothing about was Ferjani. He had never wanted revenge and had never really thought much about him. "I never sought vengeance," he told me. "With all the horrible news I have learned about my family, I am still a very happy man who has lived a very happy life." Yet when I told him I had details of that missing chapter in his family's story, he was anxious to listen. My gift to him was, I believe, one more measure of closure. This is what I told him.

On a steamy afternoon in May 2004, I met Mustapha Ferjani in the Ben Arrous neighborhood of Tunis, a suburb that did not even exist during the war. Mustapha, then sixty-eight years old, was Hassen Ferjani's nephew, the son of Hassen's older brother Muhammad. Mustapha was a lifelong nationalist himself; he was jailed in 1954 for his political activities. After independence, he spent thirty-one years working in the Ministry of Culture, directing libraries, organizing events, and delivering lectures. I had planned to meet Mustapha in Hammamet, but he had come to Tunis to celebrate the birth of a new grandchild. Professor Habib Kazdaghli, an exacting scholar and helpful colleague of mine at the University of Tunis at Manouba, arranged the meeting. He joined me and assisted with the interview.

Mustapha met us near a small café in his daughter's neighborhood. He was nervous and wanted to make a good impression; despite the heat, he sported a neatly knotted tie and a heavy wool blazer. He was a kindly man, heavyset, with courtly manners, and a deep, gravelly voice, honed by chain smoking. One can imagine his anxiety. After all these years, a "professor"—as I was introduced by Habib—had come all the way from the United States to ask about what likely was the darkest chapter in his family's history: the arrest and imprisonment of his uncle.

As we sat down to mint tea, he started by establishing the particulars. Hassen Ferjani was born in 1907, the third son in the Ferjani family of Hammamet. Married but without children (he and his wife later adopted a daughter), Ferjani operated a small fabric shop in the seaside village of Hammamet.

We then launched into the story of Hassen and the Scemlas. Was Hassen Ferjani a German informant? At first, Mustapha temporized. There were "two versions" of the story, he explained. According to one version, it was just the Scemlas' bad luck to have been stopped by the Germans. If it had been another day, with another guard manning the checkpoint or more traffic on the street, the Scemlas would have escaped and no one would ever have heard of his uncle. According to the second version, Hassen was, in fact, an agent provocateur acting on behalf of the Germans, a cunning man who arranged the entire scheme to trap the hapless Scemlas.

So far, to his credit, Mustapha was a dispassionate storyteller, recounting what happened between his uncle and Joseph Scemla—from his own perspective, of course—without histrionics or defensiveness. Later, as he warmed to the tale, Mustapha took a different tack. Hassen, he said, believed that Scemla's son, Gilbert—the former officer in the defeated French army—was spying for the Allies. A certain pro-Vichy Frenchman in Hammamet had warned Hassen to be on the lookout: If the Scemla family was moving to Hammamet, then it was most likely connected to something sinister. Gilbert may be a spy, the Vichy sympathizer told Hassen, on a mission to provide Allied bombers with forward signals of Axis targets.

If Hassen did conspire with the Germans to trap the Scemla family (an "if" that grew weaker as our conversation went on), it was not because the Scemlas were Jewish, Mustapha said, it was because they were traitors—Tunisians who had renounced their homeland and had instead sworn loyalty to the same republican France that had brutally suppressed Tunisia's quest for independence. A half hour earlier, in the only emotional outburst of the interview, Mustapha had railed against the Tunis tribunal that had sentenced his uncle to death—"It was full of English, Jews and French," he said. Now, at the end of our conversation, he wrapped his uncle in the nationalist flag.

But even the reflected glory of nationalist pride eventually wore thin. Mustapha and other Ferjanis of his generation grew up stuck with the "affaire des Juifs," as he called it. Hassen's prison fate hung over the family like a constant shadow. "We always knew about Hassen," said Mustapha. "Every holiday we weren't allowed to be happy like everyone else, because we had to spend the holiday bringing a package to prison." Before the death sentence was commuted, he said, Hassen once believed he was so close to being executed that he even had a tearful "last visit" with his wife and mother.

But Mustapha recognized that his uncle was no common criminal. Hassen was charged with conspiracy after all, an act of perfidy that eventually led to the execution of three Jews at the hands of the Germans. (He claimed not to know the specifics of the Scemlas' execution, but he was not surprised by my description of their grisly fate.) By Mustapha's own admission, at least two of the Jews were completely blameless, and there is no evidence that the third, Gilbert, was the spy that Hassen's defenders claimed he was.

Pressed on the details of the case, Mustapha's defense of Hassen's innocence unraveled. Why didn't the Germans just arrest Gilbert, I asked, without having to go through the motions of the entire entrapment scheme? It would have been "too flagrant," Mustapha said, implying that catching a Jewish family escaping to Allied lines was somehow a more acceptable rationale for deportation than snatching an Allied spy.

But if Hassen was no common criminal, neither was he considered—at least in Ferjani family lore—a guilty man. Instead, said Mustapha, the family always viewed his uncle as "a victim." As for Hassen, Mustapha said he never heard him express remorse for what happened to the Scemlas. Then, almost as an afterthought, he mumbled something under his breath. "Maybe to himself," he said.

When I related this exchange to Frédéric Gasquet in Paris, he sighed. "What Ferjani did was really terrible. But I have difficulty thinking that someone would do what he did if he truly expected it would have been so terrible for my family. Sure, he wanted money and was willing to risk my family in the process. But it is just too horrible to imagine that he was aware that by his betrayal my father would be decapitated." I asked him what he would have hoped Mustapha had said to me. "That he asked for forgiveness," he replied. "But since he—on behalf of his family—didn't even fully recognize guilt, it would have been difficult to ask for forgiveness." Taking one more step toward the closure that he desperately sought, Frédéric concluded, "If he had asked, I would have accepted it."

———∞∞∞———

HOW MANY ARABS QUALIFY as "villains" of the Holocaust in Arab lands?

It is difficult to quantify with precision the number who played significant roles in the persecution of Jews. With more than 100 recognized sites of forced labor spread from Morocco to Libya, thousands of Arab guards kept watch over Jewish prisoners. Even more Arab policemen, clerks, and other petty government officials facilitated the operation of Nazi, Vichy, and Fascist rule. Still more lent moral, political, and sometimes practical support to the anti-Jewish campaign—the informants, the collaborators, the hooligans, the bottle throwers, and the cheerleaders—but estimating the total is especially tricky.

All in all, the number was not inconsequential. Even if 90 percent of Arabs were benignly indifferent to the fate of Jews in these countries—a high estimate, in my view, though not wholly out of bounds—that still left perhaps as many as 2 million Algerians, Moroccans, Tunisians, and Libyans as participants in, supporters of, or active sympathizers with the systematic targeting of Jews. One conclusion is clear: Without this measure of Arab support—and, certainly, without this level of Arab acquiescence—the extent of Jewish suffering in Arab lands would have been much less.

Another conclusion is clear, too: It was impossible for Arabs in countries under Vichy rule, Italian conquest, or German occupation not to know about the persecution of Jews. It was everywhere. They may have been indifferent, but they were not unknowing. Even if they tried to shut their eyes to it, Arabs could hardly avoid seeing it.

Throughout North Africa, the local version of Vichy's *statut des juifs* was promulgated through official channels and published in official gazettes with all legal niceties respected. In Morocco and Tunisia, anti-Jewish laws bore the signature of the Arab sovereign. The fact that neither monarch had a real choice in the matter did not lessen the fact that laws to which they lent their royal approval were well publicized, from the capital into the provinces. In Tunis, the Germans hung placards throughout the city that blamed "international Jewry" for the devastation of Allied bombing raids and explained that a 20-million-franc indemnity paid by the Tunis Jewish community would be distributed to local Arab charities. Jews pressed into forced labor were assembled in the heart of Tunis, at spots like the Mateur train station, just a few hundred yards from the Majestic Hotel, where the Germans were headquartered. The city's population could not have been blind to the fact that it was Jews, and only Jews, who were compelled in the first weeks of occupation to march off under armed guard, down the city's main boulevards, to forced labor camps. In the Tunisian countryside, thousands of Jews in towns and villages were forced to wear the Star of David, for all to see. In Algeria, it was Arabs and Europeans, after all, who took the slots of Jewish students expelled from schools because of the imposition of quotas. Similarly, in Morocco, Arabs and Europeans inherited jobs from Jews forced from their government posts due to anti-Jewish statutes. And so on.

Six decades ago, the Arabs of Tunis, Algiers, Casablanca, and hundreds of other places could not but have known about the "special treatment" being meted out to Jews. Admittedly, the war years in North Africa were a particularly confusing time. France was at war with itself, and it was not easy for Arabs to discern which Frenchmen—Republican or Vichyite—were less hostile to their interests and, therefore, more deserving of support. The Germans manipulated these hatreds to their full advantage, in the best tradition of divide and rule. The result was that some Arabs participated in the Nazi, Vichy, and Fascist campaigns against Jews—many willingly; others, out of necessity—while most played no role at all. None, however, could truthfully claim ignorance about what was going on around them.

Chapter 5

"The Arabs Watched Over the Jews"

A T EVERY STAGE OF THE NAZI, Vichy, and Fascist persecution of Jews in Arab lands, and in every place that it occurred, Arabs helped Jews. Some Arabs spoke out against the persecution of Jews and took public stands of unity with them. Some Arabs denied the support and assistance that would have made the wheels of the anti-Jewish campaign spin more efficiently. Some Arabs shared the fate of Jews and, through that experience, forged a unique bond of comradeship. And there were occasions when certain Arabs chose to do more than just offer moral support to Jews. They bravely saved Jewish lives, at times risking their own in the process. Those Arabs were true heroes.

———— ⌘ ————

FOR BOTH ARABS AND JEWS, war brought hardship. Wheat, sugar, oil, cloth, and other goods were scarce; disease was rampant; medicines were virtually impossible to find. For the first time in memory, black bread made its appearance on the shelves of local bakeries. Some relief came in 1941, when the United States—trying to keep Vichy from falling even more deeply in the Nazi orbit—reached agreement with Pétain's government on a controversial plan to provide France's North African possessions with some basic commodities, on condition that the goods not end up in German hands.[1] Even so, the situation remained stark. Jews suffered more than non-Jews—their rations were less than those of both Europeans and local Arabs—but survival was a struggle for all. At times of such severe privation, the old Arab adage—"Me against my brother, me and my brother against our cousin"—was the guiding principle. Families did what they could to secure the necessities of life; clans clung together against outsiders.

In such circumstances, simple acts of human kindness take on a far greater meaning than they would in normal times. Decades later, those Jews whose lives were touched by the generosity of Arabs recalled these deeds with a special fondness. To the Jews facing hardship and deprivation, it made little difference whether the Arab was a passing acquaintance or a total stranger; it only mattered that he or she was a guardian angel in a time of crisis. The Arabs who performed these noble, selfless deeds may not qualify under technical definitions of wartime "heroes," but theirs were acts of unusual sympathy and compassion at a time when they, like all other commodities, were in short supply.

Here is the story of Mirella Hassan, a Tunisian Jew who responded to an Internet posting I made soliciting stories of Arabs who helped Jews during the war:

> When I was a little girl, my parents told me often of the difficulties they had to survive in this period, and above all of the help they received from their Muslim neighbors—for food, for milk—because I had two sisters at a very young age. They [eventually] died during the war, of malnutrition. My father used to go look for goat's milk, at night during the bombardments, at the [home of local] shepherds. Mother also was nursing. A Muslim wet-nurse came to help nurse my sisters. That's all I remember; I don't recall the name, but only this help given by these Tunisian Muslims, in their own way, what they could, a gesture often made with selfless friendship, which enabled the saving of many lives. . . . That is my humble testimony.[2]

Similarly, David Guez, who passed the war in the Tunisian city of Sfax, recalled what he termed "the fair and exemplary" attitude of Arabs toward Jews. "Really, their behavior was wonderful," he said. "I won't forget the Arab who helped me and allowed me to get an extra loaf of bread every day.

Even though it was difficult to obtain bread—you had to wait in line—he [the Arab baker] would give me an extra loaf. That was a great thing."[3]

Abraham Cohen related the story of his family's flight from the Allied bombing of Tripoli. Arabs took them in and rented the family an apartment, but Cohen remembered the episode as much more than a financial transaction. "[The Arabs welcomed us] in an extraordinary way, the truth has to be told," he later said. "They received us, they gave us water and food and whoever was missing things, they brought it to us. [They were] simply partners with all of this, together; what was ours and what was theirs was the same."[4] Ezra Yosef, also from Tripoli, had a similar recollection: "Every evening there [were] bombings in the city . . . so we fled to the fields and the Arabs gave us their homes—for money, of course. [We] paid them and they went to sleep outside or made themselves tents but [there were] always good relations."[5]

Emile Tubiana, who wrote an unpublished memoir of his childhood in the Tunisian town of Béja, scene of heavy wartime fighting, gave this account of his family's flight into the countryside:

> Around noon we reached the Nezer farm which had become a commune, housing thirty families. We were warmly welcomed with hugs and kisses. The farmer set aside a stable as a dormitory for us and delivered a cart-load of hay for bedding. Everyone tried to make us feel at home, they warmed us up with a rich soup after our tiring journey. At last we felt secure and happy.[6]

Victor Cohen, from Tunis, differentiated between the hostility toward Jews displayed by Arabs in the capital city and the welcoming approach of Arabs in the hinterland. "[I]n the south, the Arabs helped the Jews. They took them to their homes in the mountains. In my family, I have uncles who got shelter at the homes of the Arabs—they gave them food, everything kosher, they had it good—but in the city they [the Arabs] gave them [the Jews] a lot of problems."[7]

Some Arabs even stepped forward to protect Jewish property from predators, be they European or other Arabs. Yaacov Zrivy, from a small town near Sfax, recalled how the Germans and their Arab collaborators instilled fear in the hearts of Jews. But still, he said, "the truth was that not everyone was like that. There were those who would hide the money of the Jews. They said: 'We will keep watch over you, that way nothing will happen to you, no Arab will do anything to you.'" And, as he said, "The Arabs watched over the Jews."[8]

And then there were Arabs who protected Jewish lives, not just safeguarded Jewish property. Tzvi Haddad, whose mother was knifed in the throat by an Arab during the Gabès pogrom, a story I told in Chapter 4, recalled an act of kindness by another Arab that occurred just seconds later:

> Who saved her? Another Arab . . . . I remember his name and the way he looks, he came with a bicycle, passing from there. When he saw me he said: "Are you the son of Rabbi Yehoshua?" I tell him "Yes." He started to yell at that Arab [who attacked my mother], he smacked his hand, and the guy fled away.[9]

During a May 2004 visit to Tunis, I was escorted around the city's Jewish landmarks by an engaging professor named André Abitbol. As we walked the streets, he told a captivating tale of one of his wife's relatives, a well-to-do man named Albert Bessis, who evidently passed much of the German occupation hiding in the cellar of an imposing townhouse at one of the city's most fashionable addresses, 19 Avenue de Paris. German officers had requisitioned the residence, one of the city's finest, and were living just upstairs. Every day, said Abitbol, an Arab chauffeur—a man remembered only as Kaddour—brought messages, packages, and mail to the Germans above and took the opportunity to deliver a parcel of food to Albert below. Thanks to Kaddour, Albert survived the German occupation.[10]

One of the fondest recollections of Arab attitudes toward Jews—moving in its simplicity—was offered by the Libyan-born Israeli Victor Kanaf, who had been known in his hometown of Benghazi as Vittorio Janch. The relationship between the two communities, he said, was "as if in a honeymoon."[11]

A number of testimonies recount stories of Arab camp guards who specifically opted out of the sadistic torture their European overseers (and many of their fellow Arabs) inflicted on Jews and other prisoners; some even secretly found ways to ease the discomfort of Jews. For example, Yehuda Chachmon was a Libyan Jew in an Italian internment camp at Giado, south of Tripoli. In this desolate spot, mistreatment was atrocious but disease even more feared. Of the approximately 2,600 Jews herded into Giado, 562 inmates died in less than a year, mostly from typhus; the death toll at Giado was the highest of all North African labor camps.[12] Still, Chachmon recalled that whereas the Italian guards treated the Jews "with brutality," the attitude of Arabs under Italian command "was excellent."

> We were in good relations with them. When they see a Jew, they don't talk to him, they don't torture him, they don't make trouble for him. The trouble only came with the Italian major in the camp . . . The attitude of the Italian police was different from the attitude of the Arab police.[13]

Even the account by five Polish Jews of barbaric treatment at Vichy labor camps in Morocco included references to humane acts by the Arab guards. In describing the setting at the discipline camp of 'Ain al-Ourak, an especially hellish place outside the southern Moroccan transit and mining town of Bou Arfa, the former internees noted that thirty Arab guards patrolled the camp, supervised by a French sergeant. According to their account, the guard troop "was changed monthly in case the Arabs began to sympathise with the prisoners." This was evidently not such an unusual occurrence, as the onetime prisoners went on to add that "there was no fear of this with the others"—that is, the French officers and Legionnaires stationed at the camp.

Indeed, in a report that recounts numerous episodes of sadistic torture meted out on hapless prisoners—Jewish and gentile alike—the flashes of humanity of the Arab guards of 'Ain al-Ourak at times peek through the story's grisly, numbing details.

> Once, when the temperature was 80 degrees centigrade [*sic*] and they had been given no water all day, the prisoners refused to work any more and went to the lieutenant in charge of the camp—Lt. Grunter (formerly an adjutant chef, a German naturalized French)—to ask for water. He refused and ordered them back to work. When they would not disperse he ordered the guards to open fire. The Arab guards purposely shot wide but two French guards wounded two men.[14]

In "shooting wide," the willful disobedience by some Arab guards almost surely saved some Jewish lives; the prisoners were aware of what the Arabs had done, were grateful to them, and reported it to the British for posterity.

Not to be forgotten are those Arabs who were persecuted, and sometimes killed, alongside Jews. In Morocco and Algeria, some Arabs were dispatched to desert concentration camps at the same time as Jews and other Vichy opponents. In Tunisia, as the Allies were on the verge of breaking through Axis lines, the Germans ultimately drafted Arabs into forced labor when the Jewish community exhausted its own manpower.

In his brutally realistic camp memoir, a Jewish internee named Jacob André Guez tells a complex story that, on the one hand, features violent Arab camp guards and Arab profiteers and, on the other hand, fellow Arab laborers and even Arabs who—on two occasions—help him and a comrade escape from Bizerte and go back to Tunis. Some Arabs are good and some are bad, but as Guez's story unfolds, Arabs come across as increasingly sympathetic and human. His story ultimately ends with Guez making his way home after an Arab wagon driver hides him among sacks of black-market coffee.[15]

Sometimes, unusual expressions of comradeship between Jewish and Arab internees at Vichy labor camps buoyed the spirits of imprisoned Jews. At Cheragas-Meridja, in the Algerian desert, Vichy banished thousands of Jews who had enlisted in the French army to fight Germans. They were designated as *pionniers Israelites,* a special status that made them prisoners in all but name. The camp also housed Arab prisoners, interned for their opposition to French colonial rule. There, a Captain Suchet, the commandant, repeatedly tried to incite tensions between Jews and Arabs. He failed, however, when the bond of their common Fascist enemy proved stronger than the mutual enmity that Suchet had counted on.[16]

It was not unusual for Arabs and Jews to face the pain and torture of Vichy labor camps side by side. At the Djenien Bou-Rezg camp, also in the Algerian desert, Lieutenant Pierre de Ricko, the sadistic White Russian who served as commandant, gave Arab, Jewish, and French anti-Fascist prisoners the same heavy workload, fed them the same inedible food, and imposed on them the same harsh discipline.[17] Similarly, at the Djelfa camp—scene of Harry Alexander's two-year ordeal described in Chapter 4—a number of

Arabs suffered alongside Jews, Spanish Republicans, and other inmates. A Czech businessman who survived eight months at the camp and later gave a riveting account of its cruelties, specifically recalled the names of several prisoners killed on the watch of its depraved commandant, J. Caboche, one of whom was an Algerian named Kaddour Belkain.[18]

If the story of Nazi, Vichy, and Fascist persecution of Jews in Arab lands is not well known, then the story of Nazi, Vichy, and Fascist persecution of Arabs in Arab lands is even less so. In the grand sweep of history, it is but a footnote. Nevertheless, these stories—and the images they conjure up—are important. Not only do they underscore the larger reality of the Holocaust's long reach into the Arab world, but they help recall a moment when at least some Arabs and some Jews shared in the suffering imposed by common persecutors.

ALGIERS WAS THE SETTING for one of the war's most remarkable episodes of Arab solidarity with Jews.

Unique among French overseas possessions, Algeria was neither a colony nor a protectorate; it was instead an integral part of France. According to French law, Algiers was as French as Nice, Marseille, or Bordeaux. But though the land was French, its inhabitants were not. In the early decades of French control, the native peoples of Algeria—Muslims and Jews, there were no native Christians—were not counted as French *citoyens*. Although they had some of the obligations of citizenship (taxation, for example), they had none of its rights. Instead, they retained their status as indigenous people and governed themselves under their own communal and religious laws.

For Jews, that situation changed in 1870, when the Crémieux decree offered French citizenship to all Algerian-born Jews who were willing, in return, to agree to submit to French personal law. To Jews who had looked to France as their life preserver against the rising storm of Arab cultural and, later, political consciousness, the Crémieux decree was a godsend. Thousands of families accepted the bargain and became French citizens.

The Crémieux decree had its enemies. It was the bête noire of France's anti-Semitic political right that—especially after the Dreyfus affair—demanded its cancellation. One constituency that lobbied strenuously against the decree was Algeria's French colonists, known as *colons*. Many of them were unreconstructed anti-Semites who argued that the Crémieux decree not only opened the doors of France to noxious Jews but also set a dangerous precedent that would one day be extended to Muslims. It was no surprise when the Pétain regime, in one of its very first acts, did precisely what the *colons* demanded and annulled the decree.

But the Pétainists went even further: They retroactively stripped citizenship from *all* Jews (and their descendants) who had ever earned it under the terms of the decree. Of the 106,986 Algerian Jews who enjoyed French citizenship on the eve of France's surrender in 1940, Vichy summarily removed citizenship from 98.5 percent. In so doing, Vichy France joined Hitler's Germany as the only two countries during the war to strip citizenship legally and systematically from their Jewish population.[19]

Satisfying the demands of French colonists was not the only reason that Vichy officials canceled the Crémieux decree. They also believed it would help bolster their flagging stature among Algeria's Arab population.[20] As noted earlier, France's swift and embarrassing defeat by Germany had hurt its prestige, a key element in keeping any restive population at bay. The Germans themselves had made further inroads among Arabs by releasing hundreds of Arab political detainees held by the French, providing special services (mosques, Arabic newspapers, and so on) to the 90,000 Arab soldiers held as French army prisoners of war in Europe, and setting up Arabic radio stations broadcasting in local dialects.[21] Vichy found itself engaged not so much in a battle *for* the hearts and minds of Arabs but rather in a struggle *against* the erosion of its power and the rise of German influence in its stead. Vichyites looked for ways to win Arab support but did not want to raise the status of Arabs to achieve it. Instead, they figured they could accomplish the same ends by lowering the status of Jews.

They were wrong. By and large, Algerian Arabs saw through the French ruse and generally refused to take part, even though some may have enjoyed short-term political benefits. "Your racism runs in all directions," nationalist leader Ferhat Abbas commented on Vichy. "Today against the Jews and always against the Arabs."[22] On the cancellation of the Crémieux decree, Messali Hadj, jailed head of the Parti Populaire Algérien, said: "[This] cannot be considered as progress for the Algerian people—lowering the rights of Jews did not increase the rights of Muslims."[23]

Surprisingly, one of the main sources of pro-Jewish sympathy among the Arab population of Algiers was the Muslim religious establishment. Here, the shining star was Abdelhamid Ben Badis, leader of Algeria's Islah (Reform) Party. Ben Badis was an intensely devout man with a modern, open, tolerant view of the world; among his many achievements was the founding of the Algerian League of Muslims and Jews. Regrettably, he died in spring 1940, before he could lend his personal strength and charisma to the Muslim response to Vichy's coming to power.

During the Vichy era, that mantle was worn by Shaykh Taieb el-Okbi. Like Ben Badis, el-Okbi was a reformist leader who cultivated close ties with the leading Jews of Algiers; the latter, in return, repaid the favor by directing Jewish donations to el-Okbi's favorite charities. El-Okbi showed his mettle in early 1942. When he heard rumors that leaders of a French pro-Fascist group, the Légion Français des Combattants, were prodding Muslim troops to launch a pogrom against the Jews of Algiers, el-Okbi did all he could to prevent it, including issuing a formal prohibition on Muslims from attacking Jews. Indeed, one historian favorably likened el-Okbi to the celebrated philo-Semitic French archbishops Saliège and Gerlier, both of whom have been recognized by Yad Vashem for rescuing Jews. This historian, however, noted one difference—that the level of "great personal risk" el-Okbi bore for campaigning on behalf of Jews exceeded those of these French Catholic prelates.[24]

From the pulpits of Algiers mosques, imams also issued instruction to local Muslims not to take advantage of Jewish suffering for financial gain. This act of self-denial, at a time when many French colonists were getting rich at the expense of Jews, was an especially noble act on the part of the local Muslim community.

Vichy law required Jewish property owners to turn over their fixed assets to conservators who would manage the business affairs in trust. In reality, this arrangement presented the conservator with a lucrative opportunity to make windfall profits; not only did the conservator receive a fee for his services, but he also had the leeway to manage the business so that it was advantageous to his own personal interests. Although a few conservators accepted the job as a way to safeguard the goods of Jewish friends, these people were—in the words of one historian—"absolutely exceptional."[25] Much more frequently, Vichy administrators used the appointment of conservators as political plums, both to reward loyal supporters and entice reluctant ones into the fold. As part of their effort to bolster popular support for Vichy, local officials repeatedly tried to enlist Arabs to serve as conservators. Everyone knew that the appointments were thinly veiled bribes.

To their great credit, not a single Arab in Algiers stepped forward to accept Vichy's offer. One Friday in 1941, religious leaders throughout the city gave sermons warning all good Muslims to refuse all French offers to serve as conservators of Jewish property. They even forbade Muslims from purchasing auctioned Jewish goods at below-market prices. Despite the economic difficulties faced by Arabs during the war, they refused to take advantage of Jewish suffering for personal gain. And, true to their imams' call, not a single Arab took the opportunity of quick financial gain either to serve as a trustee-conservator or to purchase Jewish property at Vichy-mandated fire-sale prices.[26]

In a postwar interview, José Aboulker—the brave hero of the largely Jewish resistance of Algiers—praised the city's Arab population this way:

> The Arabs do not participate [in the fight against Vichy]. It is not their war. But, as regards the Jews, they are perfect. The [Vichy] functionaries [and] the German agents try to push them into demonstrations and pogroms. In vain. When Jewish goods were put up for public auction, an instruction went around the mosques: "Our brothers are suffering misfortune. Do not take their goods." Not one Arab became an administrator [of property] either. Do you know other examples of such an admirable, collective dignity?[27]

———— ✺ ————

TAKEN TOGETHER, these stories of Arabs helping Jews offer testimony to the fact that even the harsh realities of war could not extinguish simple human generosity. At another time, in another place, many of the acts they describe would not be noteworthy. But because of when they occurred and where they occurred, these stories are truly extraordinary.

So far, most of the Arabs whose stories I have told—the camp guards, fellow prisoners, and mosque preachers cited above—have been nameless. It is only through the memory of those Jews who benefited from their kindness that we are able to recount their good deeds; these Arabs never received public recognition for opening their hearts to Jews facing persecution. Not all are anonymous, however. Thanks to testimonies, archives, memoirs, and sometimes, sheer serendipity, we are privileged to know the names of some of those Arabs who helped save Jews from pain, injury, and perhaps death.

The most famous was Sultan Muhammad V of Morocco, the third son of Sultan Moulay Yousef, scion of the Alaouite family that had ruled Morocco since 1649. Born in 1910, Muhammad was handpicked by the French to succeed his father when he was just seventeen years old. The French thought that the young prince would be a compliant client in their colonial adventure, but it was not too long before Muhammad V showed flashes of independence. Indeed, his support for the nationalist cause eventually became a nettlesome thorn in the side of the French, so much so that Muhammad V was exiled to Corsica and then Madagascar in the early 1950s. But France's strong-arm tactics succeeded only in feeding nationalist sentiments. In November 1955, the French changed tack and brought Muhammad V back to Morocco, where he was hailed a hero. In February 1956, he concluded an agreement with Paris for Morocco's full independence. The following year, he took the title of king and reigned until his death in 1961.

For Muhammad V, World War II was an especially precarious time. As the sovereign of a French protectorate, he reigned but did not rule. Apart from the small Spanish zone in the north,[28] French troops controlled the country, and the French resident-general presented recommendations to the sultan that were commands in all but name. Still, he was not entirely powerless; the symbolic influence of his office meant much to the French, and the sultan often used it to his and his country's advantage. By all accounts, Muhammad V did not share the pro-German sympathies that were common among Arab elites of the day. He was especially appalled that Vichy based its anti-Jewish laws on race (how much Jewish blood someone had) rather than religion (whether someone professed to be Jewish, Christian, or Muslim). This violated a central tenet of Islam, which welcomes converts as full members of the faith, juridically equal in status to other Muslims. Vichy's anti-Jewish laws declared people Jewish if their parents were Jewish, regardless of whether they professed to be Jewish. Not only did the new French edicts offend whatever sensibilities Muhammad V may have had regarding his concern for his consistently loyal Jewish subjects, but they also insulted the sultan's generations-old role as descendant of the Prophet and "Commander of the Faithful."

On October 31, 1940, less than a month after Pétain signed Vichy's anti-Jewish statute, the sultan affixed his royal seal to the application of the law in Morocco. But he did so only after wringing from the French two concessions: first, that Jews in Morocco would be defined by religious choice, not by race or parentage; and second, that prohibitions against Jewish professionals and quotas on Jewish students would not apply to exclusively Jewish institutions, such as religious schools and communal charities. The second concession had a very practical implication—Jewish communal life in Morocco continued without much disruption by Vichy authorities. Not only did Jewish schools escape the suffocating strictures that Vichy applied to schools in Algeria, but they continued to receive much of their budget—up to 80 percent—from the government treasury.[29] As for the first concession, its implications were more symbolic than practical. Very few Jews in Morocco avoided Vichy penalties on property and professions by proclaiming themselves Muslim. But some Moroccan Jews did take comfort from the fact that the sultan refused to allow the outsiders from Vichy to discard one of the fundamentals of Moroccan society—that his subjects were defined by faith, not by race.

In private, Muhammad V offered vital moral support to the Jews of Morocco. When French authorities ordered a census of all Jewish-owned property in the country, the Jewish leadership feared this was the precursor to a general confiscation. Secretly, the sultan arranged for a group of prominent Jews to sneak into the palace, hidden in a covered wagon so he could meet them away from the prying eyes of the French. According to one of those present, he promised the Jews that he would protect them and assured them that the census was not the first step in a plan to seize their goods and property. (After the Anglo-American invasion of Morocco, the sultan arranged for the destruction of the census documents.)[30]

As important as these private statements were, public statements the sultan made on behalf on his Jewish subjects burnished his reputation even more. At the annual Throne Day ceremony, with the elite of Moroccan and Vichy officialdom gathered at the royal palace, the sultan made a point of welcoming the leaders of the Jewish community in attendance. "I must inform you that, just as in the past, the Israelites will remain under my protection," he said in a voice loud enough for Vichy officers and at least one French journalist to get the message. "I refuse to make any distinction between my subjects."[31]

Thanks to such acts of solicitude toward his Jewish subjects, Moroccan Jewish lore celebrates Sultan Muhammad V as a savior, one of the finest, fairest, and most tolerant rulers Jews had ever known. His reputation has taken on mythic proportions, with Moroccan Jews even inventing tales of his heroism.[32] The truth is that the sultan's statements and actions on behalf of the Jews, however noble they were in sentiment, did not substantially affect the implementation of Vichy's policy of "state anti-Semitism" in its Moroccan protectorate, which the French executed either directly or through their agents in the sultan's court, such as El Mokri, the anti-Semitic grand vizier. Still, the sultan remains a beloved hero to Moroccan Jews, inside and outside the kingdom.[33]

Less famous in terms of protecting Jewish interests, but no less deserving of recognition, were Tunisia's wartime rulers, Ahmed Pasha Bey and, especially, his cousin Moncef Bey, heirs to another North African dynasty, the Husseinids. ("Bey" is an honorific title of Ottoman Turkish origin adopted by North African princes.) Like the sultan of Morocco, the beys of Tunis operated within the tight confines of a French protectorate and had little room for independent maneuver. When a Vichy emissary demanded that Ahmed Pasha sign a local version of the anti-Jewish statute, the bey had no choice but to acquiesce. And like the sultan, the Tunisian princes offered vital gestures of public support for Jews facing Vichy persecution, such as Moncef Bey's statement soon after ascending the throne expressing concern for *"all the population of the regency."*[34]

But, in some respects, the Tunisians did even more. A loophole in the Tunisian version of Vichy anti-Jewish laws gave the ruler the right to grant exemptions to native Tunisian Jews who had performed exceptional service to the state. Ahmed Bey took advantage of this oversight to exempt two leading Jewish personalities—Roger Nataf, an ophthalmologist, and Paul Ghez, the man who later served as head of the Jewish labor bureau during the German occupation. Ahmed Bey's successor, Moncef Bey, went even further. He signaled his solidarity with his persecuted Jewish subjects, as well as his independence from Vichy, by brashly awarding the highest royal distinction to about twenty prominent Jews just eight days after he ascended the throne.

Five months later, the Germans arrived. With thousands of German troops occupying his country and the prospect that the fate of the entire global conflict could be determined on its soil, Moncef Bey faced a set of circumstances that no other Arab leader had to confront. His self-interests were in conflict. A proud Tunisian, he wanted to tap the surge of nationalist spirit that accompanied France's military defeats in 1940 and 1942, but unlike so many other Tunisian patriots of the day, he knew that the Germans were themselves no friends to the idea of Arab independence.[35] A modern man, he appreciated the contributions Tunisian Jews had made to the social, economic, and cultural development of his country and wanted to do what he could to protect them from the greed and brutality of the invaders, but he did not, in the process, want to do anything that might trigger the Germans' wrath against him or his country.[36]

So, Moncef Bey played a double game. On the one hand, in November 1942, he refused President Roosevelt's direct appeal to side with the Allies and did not put up even symbolic resistance to the arrival of German forces.[37] On the other hand, he was responsible for numerous individual acts of protection toward Jews. His handpicked prime minister, Mohamed Chenik, a businessman with long-standing ties to the Tunisian Jewish community, regularly warned Jewish leaders of German plans, helped Jews avoid arrest orders, intervened to prevent deportations, and even hid individual Jews so they could evade a German dragnet. Acting in the name of the bey, cabinet ministers gave special dispensations to some young Jewish men so they could avoid forced labor and tried to intervene with German authorities on behalf of Jewish hostages. Even members of the royal court hid Jews who had escaped from German labor camps. All the while, Moncef Bey invested great effort at promoting a sense of Tunisian nationalism, across regions and religions. He not only traveled to some of the most remote parts of the country, but he also offered funds from the royal treasury to build mosques, schools, and even a mausoleum to a revered Jewish holy man. As one historian wrote, "The actions of Moncef Bey and his government prevented the

Tunisian people from letting themselves be seduced by the German sirens and above all to maintain unity."[38]

Like Sultan Muhammad V in Morocco, Moncef Bey is certainly remembered with fondness by Tunisia's Jewish community. "The Bey of Tunis did a lot to save Jews," recalled Mordechai Cohen.[39] He "actually gave the Jews equal treatment," said Shlomo Barad. "He did not allow them to be discriminated."[40] To the credit of the Bey, said Mathilde Guez of Sousse, he gathered all the senior officials of the realm at the Bardo palace and reportedly issued the following warning: "The Jews are having a hard time but they are under our patronage and we are responsible for their lives. If I find out that an Arab informer caused even one hair of a Jew to fall, this Arab will pay with his life."[41]

Although some of these memories have surely grown over time into legend, reflecting perhaps wistfulness for a bygone age, they do seem to express accurately the sentiment that many Tunisian Jews had for their country's ruling family. A sizable Jewish contingent marched in Moncef Bey's funeral procession, in 1948, despite the fact that the Free French had deposed and exiled him for allegedly collaborating with the Germans. Indeed, the gratitude of Tunisian Jews toward the princely family continued decades after the war.

When I visited Tunis in May 2004, Professor Abitbol took me to pay a call on the elderly Grand Rabbi Haim Madar, whose book-filled apartment was on the second floor of a nondescript building on Rue de Palestine. (A chief rabbi living on Rue de Palestine—such is the complexity of Jewish life in an Arab land!) His next-door neighbor, remarkably enough, was Sidi Chedli Bey, the ninety-four-year-old son of the last hereditary ruler of Tunisia. Without prior introduction, Chedli Bey warmly received us. Bedridden and shrunken with age, he nevertheless was lively, alert, and eager to talk. He told this story: When Tunisian nationalists, led by Habib Bourghuiba, declared independence in 1956, they deposed the bey and confiscated the princely family's wealth and property. Tunisia's Jews, he said, stepped forward to help. They not only paid for his apartment, but they also paid the fees for his son's education. Given the anti-royalist political environment in which it occurred, such generosity could only reflect the genuine gratitude of the bey's Jewish subjects for his support in times of crisis.

Moncef Bey was not the only Tunisian leader to trigger fond memories among Tunisia's Jewish community for helping Jews during the war. At that critical moment in the country's history, when the great powers played out their global contest on Tunisian soil, Moncef gathered around him a court and government composed of Tunisia's most worldly and enlightened men, such as the prime minister, Chenik, and the court minister, Aziz Djellouli, a liberal Muslim thinker and former mayor of Tunis. Balancing between the French authorities, the German occupiers, and the insurgent Allied forces, their task was to safeguard Tunisia's autonomy, or what was left of it, and to protect Tunisians. Helping Jews—often individually, sometimes collectively—was a constant effort. They did not always succeed. Indeed, when Claire and Lila Scemla pleaded with Djellouli to intercede to save their husbands, the story I told in the opening chapter of this book, the Arab notable wearily admitted that he was powerless.[42] But sometimes they did succeed, quietly, to secure the release of Jewish hostages, warn Jewish leaders of impending arrests, or slow down the execution of an anti-Jewish statute. For this reason, Jews in Tunisia remember Chenik, Djellouli, and their fellows as friends in times of need.[43]

One of the most remarkable examples of Arab generosity toward Jews in distress is the story of Si Ali Sakkat. At least two postwar accounts of the German occupation written by Tunisian Jews makes at least passing reference to his exploits.[44] But his selflessness is long forgotten. His is truly a lost story.

Born in the 1870s, Si Ali Sakkat hailed from a noble Muslim family, the ahl Quraysh, which traces its lineage back to the Prophet Muhammad. From an early age, Si Ali dedicated himself to a career in public service. He rose from being a humble prefect in out-of-the-way provincial towns to become the appointed mayor of Tunis. He was eventually named a minister in the princely court, where he served as *ministre de la plume et la consultation,* a position whose quaint title possessed some of the most important powers in the government, including many of the responsibilities of a modern-day minister of justice, minister of internal affairs, and chief of staff.

Si Ali was the product of the Arab liberal age of the late nineteenth and early twentieth centuries, a brief but intense burst of enlightenment and modernism that brought important European political, social, and cultural reforms to Arab societies. With its vibrant and diverse population of Italians,

French, Maltese, and other Europeans, Tunisia was especially receptive to these liberal ideals. To be sure, the moment was fleeting, and the reforms—from modern dress to written constitutions—often consisted of shallow imitations of Western style. Nevertheless, the short-lived liberal age is still cited by today's Arab reformers and democrats as proof that they are returning to their roots, not breaking wholly new ground.

Like other shining lights of the liberal age, Si Ali was known to be an enlightened, modern man, open to debate and tolerant of opposing views. Family members praise him and his wife—Lilia Baccouche, the daughter of a prominent Tunisian general—for instilling these ideals in their five children. After Si Ali's long and productive career in government, he and Lilia retired to a 740-acre farm he had purchased in the mid-1920s. There, he spent more than twenty years as a gentleman farmer, away from the nationalist maelstrom in Tunis, where men of his generation—who saw no conflict between their national consciousnesses and their loyalty to the royal court—were being squeezed, first out of politics and then out of history. Si Ali eventually died in 1954, two years before Tunisian independence replaced the ruling family with a republic.

The Sakkat family farm lies in Bir Halima, at the base of the 4,248-foot high Jebel Zaghouan, in the valley that bears the name of the mountain, a lush, broad, cereal-producing breadbasket south of Tunis. Zaghouan is celebrated for being the source of fresh water to ancient Carthage, Rome's historic competitor for dominance over the Mediterranean. Parts of a forty-mile aqueduct still tower over the road to Tunis today.

When Si Ali bought the farm, it was already a fully functioning operation. Fields of wheat took up much of the land, but there was still room for hundreds of sheep and groves of olive and almond trees. A small wadi ran through the property, feeding the well that was set up in the back of the large garden that unfolded for more than a hundred yards from beneath the window of the main house's master bedroom.

What set the Sakkat farm apart from others in the Zaghouan valley was its Spanish-style hacienda architecture. It was built in a square with a large courtyard, at the far end of which was the main house, with garages, a barn, storerooms, and other structures filling in the four sides. The most striking feature were the castles, turrets, and ramparts, and a tower that topped the hacienda walls. Inside the main house, the central hallway was graced with a ceiling that rose nearly twenty feet high, with rooms off to every side. The door to each room was decorated with inlaid tile atop the doorpost. On top of each door was an Arabic inscription beseeching Allah to grant prosperity to all who dwelled therein.

I have provided this detailed account of Si Ali's farm because that is where this story takes place. I visited the site in May 2004, escorted by Kamal Sakkat, eldest son of Hedi, the son of Si Ali to whom had fallen responsibility for the farm's upkeep. I had been looking for relatives of Si Ali for months, without success. Thanks to a stroke of good fortune, a close Tunisian colleague of mine introduced me to Kamal after realizing that he and Kamal shared the same coffee klatch in an upscale café in La Marsa, a chic suburb of Tunis. In the rundown state in which I found it, the farm looked like a ramshackle countryside ranch that Don Quixote might have stumbled upon in his wanderings through Andalusia. Seventy years ago, when Si Ali settled into the life of a gentleman farmer, it must have been paradise.

Based on the sketchy details of postwar memoirs and other sources, Si Ali Sakkat's story is as follows: At a critical point of the battle for Tunisia, fighting raged in the Zaghouan valley. With cannons firing and bombs falling all around them, a group of about sixty Jewish workers at a nearby Axis labor camp took the opportunity of the battle to escape. Seeking refuge, they found their way to the walled gate of Si Ali's farm. The former government minister turned country squire opened his home to all of them, provided them with lodging and food, and safely kept them under his care until the Allies took the Zaghouan valley on their way to Tunis and Bizerte. Thanks to him, the sixty survived what might have otherwise been a dangerous, perhaps deadly, ordeal.[45]

I went to Si Ali's farm in Bir Halima hoping to learn more. In Kamal, I had an obliging host. As he escorted me about the farm's grounds, he offered a loving sketch of his grandfather's simple kindnesses—to workers, to neighbors, to others—that provided adequate explanation of motive for Si Ali's generosity toward the Jewish laborers. Visiting the farm itself and seeing the geography also gave me a clear understanding of the opportunity Si Ali Sakkat had to lend a helping hand to Jews in need.

Kamal showed me that Si Ali's farm lies just several hundred yards from the site of a small airstrip that, he said, the Axis forces built hastily in early 1943. Indeed, it is the first property on the far side of a transit road that separated the farm from the land that housed the airstrip. Jewish laborers were evidently dispatched from Tunis to Zaghouan first to build the strip and then to clear it of debris from Allied bombs. By a contemporary account, Zaghouan was one of the worst labor sites, especially in the first days of the occupation, with Jews crowded together in hangars under the open sky, exposed to cold and rain.[46] As the Allied noose tightened around Tunis, the Zaghouan valley was on the front line. Whether the Jewish workers actually escaped or found themselves caught in the middle of the battle is uncertain; what does appear clear is that they made their way across the wheat fields and sought refuge at the imposing, fortress-like gates of Si Ali's compound.

They were lucky to come knocking at Si Ali's door. Not all landowners would have so readily offered to shelter Jews escaping from an Axis labor camp. After all, Tunisia had been the setting for pitched battles for several months, with both Axis and Allied forces winning some territory, losing it, and then winning it back again; one could never truly be sure which side would come out on top—or for how long. But the Jews who arrived at Si Ali's farm found what they were looking for—and more.

From a springtime visit to Zaghouan today, it is surprisingly easy to conjure up an image of Si Ali Sakkat, a stately Arab nobleman, opening his rambling property to a group of ragged, fugitive Jews. The Spanish-style courtyard included a warren of garages, storerooms, closets, and other potential hiding places. The main house itself contained one high-ceilinged room after another, all with the same Arabic inscription overhead. And behind the main house was an animal pen—large, broad, and deep—in which some from the group most likely found shelter. Sixty fleeing men is no small number, but Si Ali's compound could accommodate them.

Though the farm had lost some of its luster, it had lost none of its mystique. As Kamal led me through the grounds, a wife of one of his current workers came up to him and kissed his hand, just as one might imagine workers' wives kissing his grandfather's hand decades ago. Kamal asked me not to discuss the circumstances of his grandfather's act of kindness toward Jews in front of the farm laborers; they just would not understand, he said, with a hint of sadness. But back then, the bonds of loyalty and honor that defined the relationship between his grandfather and his workers were such that if Si Ali told his farmhands to open the gates, make coffee, and fetch blankets for the newcomers, they almost surely did so both in haste and in silence.

One of the most remarkable aspects of Si Ali's story—as told to me both by Kamal during our visit to the farm in Bir Halima and by his younger brother Ali, with whom I sipped beer at a Left Bank café in Paris eighteen months later—is that no one in the Sakkat family had ever before heard about their grandfather's generosity toward Jews. Even though references to Si Ali's exploits appeared in at least two books describing the wartime experience of Tunisia's Jewish community, no one had ever brought this to their attention. And according to both brothers, none of the escapees ever contacted the Sakkat family after the war to express his gratitude. Evidently, I was the first person to present the Sakkats with the story of Si Ali's heroic gesture, more than six decades after the fact.

Perhaps more amazing is the fact that Kamal and Ali had the same reaction when I described what happened in Bir Halima in 1943. Each said the story of their grandfather's generosity toward Jews rang true. That is because it sounded eerily similar to a different Sakkat family story, a tale of their grandfather's generosity toward Germans.

According to both Kamal and Ali, who each told me this story in such similar words and phrases that it seemed to have become the accepted family version, the gang of ragged men that knocked on the gate of their grandfather's farm were German soldiers who arrived after the Allied victory, not Jewish labor camp escapees who arrived before. When the Allies finally pushed the Germans out of Tunisia, forcing a crazed withdrawal of more than 200,000 German soldiers from the Cap Bon peninsula to Italy, many were left behind. A group of defeated German troops—ordinary soldiers, the younger Sakkats made clear, not SS men—found their own way to Si Ali's compound. Si Ali evidently opened his gates, gave them shelter, and put them to work on the farm, so they could evade arrest as prisoners of war. How long they stayed on the farm is not clear.

Were there really two groups of escapees who sought refuge at Si Ali's farm? Or was the story of the German troops a fictitious tale, more in tune with Tunisia's anti-French political sensibilities, concocted to cover up Si Ali's generosity toward the Jews? It really does not matter. The two Jewish historians who wrote about wartime Tunisia more than a half century ago had no reason to fabricate a story of Si Ali's courageous rescue of Jews, so we have no reason to doubt it happened.[47] The fact that Si Ali never spoke of this, that it never became part of the proud Sakkat family legacy, and that its place in family lore was taken by an alternative, more politically correct, tale of wartime hospitality does not detract from that. And even if the two tales are true, the fact that Si Ali's farm was a place of refuge for young, scared, defeated German conscripts a continent away from their homes does not lessen the importance of what Si Ali did for the Jews. It only confirms his basic humanity.

Chapter 6

Anny's Story

F ROM THE DAY I BEGAN THIS RESEARCH, I was convinced that there must be stories of Arabs who saved Jews that had never emerged. Soon after I began to search in earnest, I realized that it would not be simple to find sixty-year-old needles in a haystack made more complex by the overlay of contemporary Middle East politics. At least I had the Internet to improve the odds.

In November 2002, I posted an e-mail message at harissa.com, the web-based meeting place for discussion on all aspects of Tunisian Jewry. Harissa is the "hot sauce" that lends spice to so much Arabic cuisine and a fitting name for a cyber-gateway into the richness of Tunisian Jewish life. Two days before Thanksgiving, I received a response from a seventy-one-year-old woman in Los Angeles named Anny Boukris.

In that first message she sent me, Anny wrote: "The Arabs saved many Jews, hurt also other Jews. I don't know very well these stories. I remember very well only our story." She then related the broad outline of a remarkable tale from her childhood in the small seaside town of Mahdia. She wrote that during the war, an Arab man scooped up her family in the middle of the night and hid them on his farm, safely away from the sexual predations of a depraved German officer who had his sights on Anny's attractive mother. Her account was captivating. It was precisely the sort of story I was convinced existed but had yet to find.

I wanted it to be true, but was it? Anny's telling raised as many questions as it did answers: What was the relationship between the Arab "hero" and the German officers? What was the frequency of German rape of Jewish women during the occupation? When exactly did the Boukris family flee to safety? Anny was only eleven years old when all this happened; her account had a number of suspect gaps and inconsistencies. I showed the e-mail, shorn of any personal reference to Anny or her family, to two respected Tunisian Jewish historians—one in Paris, the other in Jerusalem. Both of them dismissed it, without hesitation. It was a concocted story, they both said, totally without foundation. One of them flatly told me that rape of Jewish girls by German soldiers did not occur. The other simply noted that the story sounded too far-fetched, too fantastic, to be true.

These professional assessments fed my doubts, but the tenacity and passion that had made Anny hold on to her family saga over half a century were too powerful to set aside. Anny's story grabbed me. I wanted to meet her face to face and probe more deeply, but I was living in Morocco at the time and could not get to California. So, I moved on to other aspects of my research. In the meantime, Anny moved, from LA into a retirement complex in Palm Desert, two hours outside the city. Every few weeks I would receive an e-mail message from her, and the riveting story of her family's Arab guardian angel would gnaw at me once again.

Finally, I decided to hire an interviewer to visit Anny in my stead and tape her story. With luck, I found Zepporah Glass, a consummate professional with extensive experience taking oral histories from Holocaust survivors. On October 8, 2003, Zepporah drove to Palm Desert and spent the day interviewing Anny. It was just in time. Eight weeks later, after having told her story for the first time in rich detail to someone who had come just to listen to her, Anny died.

Zepporah's interview produced an eighty-three-page transcript. It provided a far more detailed account of Anny's childhood, hometown, and family life than anything Anny had previously e-mailed me. It also contained a much more nuanced, exacting recounting of the tale of the righteous Arab who, she claimed, saved her family from the Germans. This is her story.

Anny was born on September 17, 1931, in Mahdia, a town along Tunisia's eastern shore. She was the second of three children of Jacob Boukris and

Odette Boccara. Before the war, her father was the local representative of Vistanda, a producer of gas stoves, and Anny's house at 58 Rue Ali Bey was always full of the latest household appliances. She fondly recalled a comfortable, well-appointed home and a large, close-knit family. Anny described lively Sabbath dinners together—conversations flying in rapid-fire French and Italian, and with their Arab maid, in Arabic. Anny's was an altogether happy, unremarkable early childhood, filled with tutors, scouts, fun at the beach, and friendships with Jewish and Arab kids alike. Through her child's eyes, Anny's reminiscences of the early years of the war—the nightly blackouts, the air raids, two bombings in Mahdia harbor, and so on—are more playful than scary. Even a bout of what she called scoliosis—the discovery of a substantial lump on her back—that took her and her worried parents to doctors in Sousse and eventually Tunis did not blacken her spirits for long. "I have only nice memories of my childhood up to, you know, '42," she said.

Her story begins with the arrival of the Germans in Mahdia. Right away, the Germans set out requisitioning Jewish properties to board their troops. A soldier came to the Boukris's house, with a local Frenchman as interpreter, and told the family they had one hour to leave. Anny, who was home at the time, remembered the scene. It was a Thursday. The knock at the door came without warning. The family had suspected something might happen and had prepared for this eventuality. They had stocked up on provisions, packed all their expensive heirlooms in a small room, and placed a large bookcase in front of the door. It was a useless exercise. The German soldier inspected the house and quickly found the hiding place. He carted all its contents away, in boxes constructed from the very bookcase that had failed to guard the door. What the eleven-year-old Anny cried over most was the loss of her stamp collection.

That day, the Germans expelled Anny and her family from their home and transformed 58 Rue Ali Bey into a barracks for newly arriving troops. In the frenzy, Anny's father kept his wits about him and arranged for his family to seek refuge in an olive oil factory a mile and a half from the center of town. Aunts, uncles, and cousins joined them there, as well as the families of the Uzzan brothers, who were neighbors and friends. The living space was cramped, the dozen or so children rarely allowed to leave, and every day the men had to perform day labor for the Germans.[1] Nevertheless, the small community managed to set up an alternative life there. The market was still open, kosher food remained available, and, Anny recalled, Friday evenings were still set aside for Sabbath dinners.

Late one night, several weeks into the Boukris's stay at the oil factory, there came another knock at the door. This time, said Anny, the caller was an Arab named Khaled Abdelwahhab, the son of a wealthy landowner and former minister to the court of the bey, Hassan Husni Abdelwahhab. Hassan Husni was one of Tunisia's most celebrated public servants, an erudite man known for his scholarship and belles lettres. His name is memorialized on Tunis street signs and even a room at the national library.[2] In Anny's telling, Hassan Husni and her father had been close friends. The handsome man at the oil factory door was Hassan Husni's only son.

Khaled told them they were at great risk; they had to hurry and he would take them to safety. Everyone should come, he said, the extended Boukris family as well as the neighbors who shared the oil factory lodgings with them. They packed their belongings, though this time—their possessions much reduced—there was no choice about what to take, they took it all. By shuttling back and forth through the night, Khaled eventually managed to get everyone settled at his family's farm in the small village of Tlelsa, about twenty miles west of Mahdia. By dawn, the oil factory was empty.

Anny recalled a huge farm, filled with groves of almond, olive, and apple trees, and a large swimming pool "modeled after an American one." The families slept in tight quarters, beds squeezed together and lined up right next to each other. But it was comfortable and safe; she recalled no sense of imminent danger. Every day, a local woman would come to bake fresh pita bread, which was a special treat.

Near the farm was a German Red Cross encampment that tended to injured soldiers. Many of its workers knew about the Jews being hidden at the farm but kept quiet about it. Some even brought food or bandages when someone at the farm was hurt. Anny recalled one kindly German who came almost every day. Her uncle Neldo later explained that the German told him his mother was Jewish.

Anny, her family, and her neighbors—about two dozen people in all—passed the rest of the German occupation of Mahdia at the Abdelwahhab farm. She left the property only once a week, when much of the Mahdia Jewish community gathered at a Jewish-owned farm four miles away. There, the local rabbi presided over the kosher ritual slaughter of chickens for the next day's Sabbath dinner. Khaled came to see them just about every day. Though she felt safe on the farm, Anny still remembered this as a time filled with fear.

They had stayed on the farm for about four months when, in April 1943, British troops arrived in Mahdia, and it was deemed safe to go home. When the Boukris family arrived at their house, they found a sty. Their German "guests" had littered the house with animal bones and garbage. Overwhelmed by the stench, the family moved to an uncle's house for Passover. They then began their lives anew.

Later, when she was older, Anny's parents explained to her why Khaled Abdelwahhab had spirited them away in the middle of the night.

As one of the leading citizens of Mahdia, Khaled was in frequent contact with foreign troops, German and British, who occupied the town. He evidently made a special effort to socialize with the German officers, as a way to ingratiate himself with them and thereby learn more about their plans for the town. It was, said Anny, "a kind of spying."

At one point, Khaled learned that the Germans had set up a house where they could regularly take their pleasure with girls and young women. "They used to visit them and do whatever they wanted," she said. With her halting English and old-world demeanor, Anny never used the words "rape" or "sex," but that is what she meant. At least some of the girls at the German bordello were Jews. Anny recalled that two Jewish girls, traumatized by the experience, eventually committed suicide.[3] She also said she later heard stories of the bordello herself from a Jewish midwife married to a Muslim man, whose job was to clean the house for the Germans.

Apparently, Khaled did what he could to protect the young girls. He regularly sent his cook, Amor, to the bordello with trays of Tunisian delicacies and bottles of fine wine. Khaled himself would often arrive to oversee these repasts, personally pouring glass after glass. Sometimes he succeeded in getting the Germans to drink so much they would bypass the girls and head straight for bed.

Before long, as a welcome visitor to the bordello, Khaled became a confidant of one of the German officers. One night, the German told Khaled that he had his sights on an especially beautiful Jewish woman—"he wanted her and was going to bring her the day after for his own pleasure." From the German's description of the woman—referring, most likely, to where she lived and who her family was—Khaled realized that the German was talking about the attractive, blond, blue-eyed wife of the gas appliance salesman, Anny's mother, Odette.

That night, Khaled was particularly liberal with the wine, trying to pour enough—in Anny's colloquialism—to "make [the German] drink to death." When the officer finally went to sleep, Khaled drove directly to the oil factory, where he knew the Boukris family had found shelter. There, he told Anny's parents what he had learned and then began to whisk everyone there off to his farm. "We left like that," said Anny.

Jacob and Odette Boukris were forever grateful to Khaled Abdelwahhab for the selfless kindness extended to them and their family. Exactly how much of a risk he took to protect Anny's mother from being raped by a German officer is not clear. In the eyes of the Boukris family, Khaled feared for Odette's life and for the safety of her entire family. Jacob and Odette also believed that Khaled himself could have been killed if the German found out that Khaled had tricked him to save a Jewish woman.

For years thereafter, Anny recalled Khaled as a frequent, honored guest at Sabbath dinners, one who took a special delight in the family's tasty chicken couscous. Years later, even after she married and moved inland, to the central Tunisian town of Sbeitla, Khaled made a point of stopping by and saying hello to Anny when he passed through. Anny never heard her parents talk with Khaled about his wartime generosity, but it was the unspoken bond that linked all of them together.[4]

Anny's story was unlike any other I had heard in the course of my research. Yad Vashem's standard to consider a candidate for its honorable designation "Righteous Among the Nations" is "when the data on hand clearly demonstrates that a non-Jewish person risked his (or her) life, freedom, and safety in order to rescue one or several Jews from the threat of death or deportation to death camps without exacting in advance monetary compensation."[5] By Anny's telling, Khaled Abdelwahhab meets the test; he would merit recognition as a "righteous Arab." But was it true? How much was fact? And how much was the vivid imagination of an eleven-year-old girl, images of a reality she believed to be true, locked into her consciousness six decades ago?

A seventy-one-year-old's memory of a sixty-year-old event does not stack up well against the authority of eminent historians. But then I began to receive a series of e-mails from a wonderful colleague, Shira (Chantal) Simhony, who at the time was a university lecturer in Tel Aviv. Shira is a native of Ariana, once a bustling Arab-Jewish town that has since been absorbed as a suburb of metropolitan Tunis. Her father, Georges Sarfati, served as Ariana's vice mayor and was the wartime representative of the town's Jewish community to the French and German authorities. Shira responded to one of my earliest Internet postings and has provided invaluable support to this project ever since. She knew Anny personally and, like me, had a powerful connection to her story. An indefatigable researcher, Shira took up my charge to find evidence to support Anny's testimony. She did just that, bit by bit.

Speaking to Tunisian Jewish women in ways that were simply impossible for me, Shira learned that many were terrified of the sexual predations of German soldiers. Shira e-mailed me about her conversation with a woman from Sousse, named Giselle, whose family moved to the town of Moknin during the war. Giselle said that it was common knowledge that German troops sought out Jewish girls to "have fun" with them. "If the Germans found a young woman," Shira quoted Giselle as saying, "they would have taken her to their camp and the woman was not seen again." Though Giselle was just fourteen years old when the Germans arrived, her family's fear for her safety was so strong that they set up an elaborate plan to hide her in a well whenever a German unit passed through Moknin.

In another e-mail, Shira detailed a conversation with an eighty-seven-year-old Tunisian Jewish widow living in Paris, named Gabrielle Bokobza, whose husband had come from Mahdia. She vividly recalled that many of the town's Jewish families split up during the German occupation, with women and children fleeing to the safety of the countryside while the men stayed behind to perform forced labor. Of special relevance to Anny's story, Mrs. Bokobza said she remembered that the Germans had set up a bordello in Mahdia and had put an older Jewish woman from Eastern Europe in charge of the enterprise. Perhaps this was the "Jewish midwife married to a Muslim man" of whom Anny had spoken.

Then, several months later, Shira sent me a message that at least seemed to provide direct confirmation that Germans did rape Jewish girls. In it, she relayed a story she had been told by the niece of a Jewish woman, originally from Tunis, who had been raped by three German soldiers. According to the niece, her aunt eventually married and had four children, but she never fully recovered from the trauma. This woman (no useful purpose is served by divulging her name) had nothing to gain by concocting a tale of such personal anguish, which she had evidently carried in silence all these years. Given the details provided to Shira by the woman's niece, there is no reason to doubt it. If that story was true, I thought, then it lent credence to Anny's. After all, if some Jewish women had been raped by German soldiers, then the idea that German officers wanted to rape Anny's mother or bring her to a house of "kept women" could not be dismissed so easily.

In May 2004, I flew from Rabat to Tunis, with the express purpose of trying to prove—or, as the case may be, disprove—Anny's story. Through friends in Tunisia, I had tried for months to find more news about Khaled Abdelwahhab and his family, hoping to learn his side of the story, but I had had no luck. So, I looked instead for ways to confirm what Anny had told Zepporah. By several strokes of good fortune, I found precisely what I was looking for.

In her interview, Anny had described in detail her daily life growing up in Mahdia. She also mentioned in passing the names of her childhood friends. Two whom she recalled with special fondness were Arab girls, the Chlaifa sisters, Suha and Salha. The three had gone to school together, shared meals, and played in each other's homes. On arriving in Tunis, I consulted one of the researcher's handiest tools—the telephone book—and found two Mahdia phone numbers under the name Chlaifa. To my great delight, one of the numbers was answered by the warm, welcoming voice of Najla Chlaifa, the wife of Suha and Salha's nephew, Hussein. I made arrangements to drive from Tunis to Mahdia the following day in order to visit Najla and Hussein.

Mahdia is located on the southern part of the Gulf of Hammamet, down the coast from the important port city of Sousse. In the tenth century, Mahdia served as the capital of the Fatimid dynasty, and it still boasts a walled medina, called Bou Jerras, which, as my *Lonely Planet* guidebook noted, has "a maze of vine-shaded squares and narrow cobbled streets."[6] The main entry into the medina is through an impressive arched gate, the Skifa al-Kahla, on the far side of which used to be Rue Ali Bey. I wanted to find Anny's house, but the street has since been renamed—and renumbered—and there is no trace of number 58. Much of the old town spreads westward along a small peninsula, at the eastern end of which is the lighthouse of Cap d'Afrique. Just at the tip of the cape is one of the world's most scenic cemeteries, where waves lap back and forth over white gravestones dug deep into the rocks. Najla noted wistfully that people buried in that cemetery were fortunate to have both their bodies and souls spend eternity in paradise.

In their small yet comfortable apartment, overlooking the sea on the north side of town, Najla and Hussein told me some exciting news: Both Suha and Salha were still alive and, equally important, reasonably alert. The people of Mahdia were proud of the fact that Arabs and Jews had lived and worked together for centuries, they said, and though they did not recall the Boukris family clearly, they were sure their aunts would have ample memory of the war years. But they said circumstances were such that they could not take me to meet the sisters. A family feud had been raging for years, a story of rivalry and jealousy that ultimately found its way into local courts. I lost track of the precise nuances of who allegedly stole what from whom, but I understood clearly when Najla explained that neither Suha nor Salha was likely to speak with me if I came with an introduction from her or her husband. It would be better to just knock on their door. When Najla then telephoned one of the aunt's daughters to confirm they were at home, she learned that a distant cousin had died earlier that day. Suha and Salha were sure to be on their way to the deceased's home, she warned, so I had better move quickly.

About twenty minutes later, I knocked on a large, blue-painted wooden door across from Mahdia's small commercial port. When a maid opened the door, I asked to speak with Madame Hamza, Salha's married name. I was in luck. Salha was just leaving the main house, at the far side of a courtyard, dressed for mourning. She was on the way to meet her sister down the street and then they would walk together to the home of the deceased cousin. I introduced myself briefly, and before she had a chance to think twice, I asked if she recalled a young Jewish girl she played with six decades ago named Anny Boukris.

Imagine the scene from Salha's point of view. In this small fishing village, very little upsets the slow, predictable pace of everyday life. Then, out of the blue, comes a strange man, an American "professor"; he shows up at her door, without invitation or even warning, to ask about a childhood friendship more than a half century old. To say Salha was caught off guard is an understatement.

But there was a solidity to Salha that quickly showed through. (I don't doubt that she was a central protagonist in the Chlaifa family feud!) It took her only a moment to find her bearings. And when she did, she walked right on by me, through the gate and into the street. Truth be told, I think it was only because she was impressed by the sleek, black, chauffeur-driven Mercedes sedan she saw parked in front of her home—the car and driver having been loaned to me for the week by a generous Tunisian friend—that she turned around and spoke to me. I could either come back tomorrow, she said, or I was welcome to walk with her now. Taking no chances that she would change her mind, I walked with her eastward along the main road, the maid trailing discreetly behind. About 150 yards on, an even more diminutive elderly woman stood waiting by another large, painted door. It was Salha's older sister, Suha.

As we walked, Salha began to warm up to me. When we reached Suha's door, she suggested we go inside, where we could talk beyond the sound of passing cars. She then told Suha that I had asked about Anny Boukris. Hussein, their nephew, had warned me that, of his two aunts, Suha's memory was less sure, but to my amazement, she began to rattle off Anny's family tree as though she had studied for a quiz. "Anny Boukris?" she asked. "Her sister's name was Eva? (Yes.) Her parents were Jacob and Odette? (Yes.) Didn't Jacob work at the gas station after the war? (He did.) Odette was a Boccara, no? (Yes.)" After a few minutes like this, both she and Salha said they not only remembered Anny and her family, but they recalled that the Boukris and Chlaifa families had a history together that went back years earlier, when Anny's grandfather had worked as secretary to their own grandfather.

I then turned to the real subject of my visit and asked them about Anny's wartime story. I did not want to lead them on, but I couldn't be sure they would volunteer personal information to someone who was still a total stranger. I told them that I had interviewed Anny several months previously, before she died, and that she had told a striking tale about her family's experience during the German occupation. Did either of them know what I was referring to? Again, it was Suha, the older of the two, who answered first.

"The farm," she said. Anny and her family spent some months at a farm in Tlelsa. It was too much to assume she could recall the name of the landowner, so when I mentioned "the Abdelwahhab family," Suha said, "Yes, it was Khaled Abdelwahhab who took them away." I pressed on, hoping to get confirmation of the reason for the rescue—Khaled's fear that Odette would be raped by the German officer—but they did not know that part of the story. (Indeed, Anny said her family never talked about it.) When I specifically asked whether they recalled any stories of German soldiers having sexual relations with Mahdia Jewish girls, I seemed to hit up against a wall of culture and memory. The Chlaifa sisters said neither yes nor no; both, almost simultaneously, raised their shoulders, as if to ask me not to ask.

Within minutes, the interview was over. Suha and Salha had told me, without prompting, what I had hoped to hear: Anny's story, at least in its broad strokes, was true. According to them, the Boukris family did indeed pass the German occupation of Mahdia at the Abdelwahhab farm. Before driving back to Tunis, I had one more stop to make. If successful, I could add another layer of confirmation to Anny's account. The next destination was Tlelsa.

If you had no reason to stop in Tlelsa, you wouldn't. With a handful of ramshackle shops, a clinic, and a primary school along the main road, it isn't really much of a town. When we passed a sign indicating the town limits, I asked the driver to pull into a small mechanic's shop. A group of men were chatting in the back. I asked the manager if anyone could point me toward the farm of Khaled Abdelwahhab. Seeing the sedan in which I arrived and perhaps fearful of a big city tax inspector, they remained quiet. When I kept talking in my hodgepodge of Arabic and French and explained that I was an American professor who had traveled a long way because something important had happened on the farm during World War II, their demeanor eased.

After all, no Tunis bureaucrat could concoct a story (or an accent) like that. One of the men then volunteered to take me to the farm, the entrance to which was only a few hundred yards away.

The farm was just as Anny had described it. It was a huge property, stretching out for hundreds of acres south of the main road. It was filled with almond, apple, and olive trees, just as she said. To the left of the front door of the single-story main house was a large, low-hanging barn. And on the far side of the house, partially obscured behind high grass, was a pool, with dozens of old, rusted fountain spouts rising from the center of its base. Evidently, this is what Anny meant when she referred to the pool being "modeled after an American one."

The farmhouse itself was boarded up; it had clearly been vacant for quite some time. My guide explained that Khaled had died a few years earlier, childless, and no one had taken responsibility for the farm. (My surmise about the locals' fear of a tax man was evidently well founded.) Some of the farm's former laborers made an effort to keep it from falling completely into disrepair, but, he said, the farm had not actually been worked in years.

There I stood, in the place where an Arab man rescued a Jewish woman and her family from the threat of the Germans. The Chlaifa sisters had corroborated Anny's story, and the visit to the Tlelsa farm had confirmed it. Driving back to Tunis that evening, I was elated. I wish I could have told Anny.

FIFTEEN MONTHS LATER, I received further confirmation of Anny's story. At a cocktail party in New York City, I met a Tunisian Jew named Lionel Uzzan. As we played Tunisian Jewish geography, I learned that Lionel's family came from Mahdia and that his ninety-two-year-old grandmother, Lyvia Boukhobza Uzzan, was still living in Paris. At the time, I was focused on finding proof of the suicide of a Jewish girl in Mahdia as the key to substantiate Anny's story, and I asked Lionel to ask his grandmother if she could remember any such story. Only later did I realize that Lionel's family name—Uzzan—was the same as the name of the relatives who took up lodging in the olive oil factory with the Boukris family. When I called Lionel soon thereafter, he said he was sorry, but his grandmother had no recollection of a suicide. By this time, though, I was ready with a barrage of questions about the Uzzans themselves.

A week later, I got my reply. Lionel's relatives confirmed everything. Of course they knew the Boukris family, including Anny's parents and her siblings. At least six members of the Uzzan family had been living with the Boukrises at the olive oil factory when the Arab gentleman came in the middle of the night to protect them. They didn't recall Khaled's name, but they remembered the farm where they and Anny's family passed the rest of the German occupation. According to Lyvia, the Arab was an acquaintance of her husband, Moshe Uzzan, who owned a sardine factory in town. Lyvia also said Lionel's aunts, Edmée and Elda, had fond memories of the Chlaifa sisters, who were their childhood schoolmates.

Lionel was stunned. He had never before heard this story of his family's rescue.

----- ❈ -----

STILL, THE STORY WAS NOT FINISHED. Thanks to the exquisite detail of Anny's interview, she and her family were three-dimensional figures. They were real people who lived and loved and carried with them the memories of the war years—including the relief of evading what might have been—for the rest of their lives. Anny, I believe, bore the burden of truth for all of them. She ultimately found peace only after she had told her story to someone who truly wanted to listen. But the hero of the story, Khaled Abdelwahhab, was just a blur. I knew nothing about him except the most important part, his selfless act of rescue. I wanted to know more. I was convinced there was more to know.

Two years of looking for the Abdelwahhab family and I had had no luck. Friends in the academic community knew nothing. I visited the head of the Tunisian National Library, Dr. Hsouna Mzabi, and even though the library itself boasted a room named after Hassan Husni Abdelwahhab, he had no idea what had happened to the family of the patriarch. When I enlisted the help of well-connected officials in the Tunisian government and the U.S. embassy, I received some leads to members of Khaled's extended family but nothing close enough to help me learn more about Khaled himself. The Abdelwahhabs—heirs of a celebrated Tunisian nationalist, one of the most illustrious writers in the history of Tunisian literature—seemed to have disappeared. (And this time, the telephone book was no help.)

Then, once again, serendipity struck. In September 2005, I received an e-mail from a remarkable woman named Hayet Laouani, one of my dearest friends in Tunisia. Hayet is a onetime schoolteacher who was working as a bookkeeper in her husband's shipping company when he died prematurely. Instead of retiring to a life of upper-class leisure, Hayet took over the firm. She put in sixteen-hour days, working the docks, getting to know the longshoremen, learning everything about shipping that she would never learn in business school. Through years of hard work and the haze of countless cigarettes, she earned the confidence of her workers, her suppliers, and her clients and built the company into a shipping powerhouse, responsible for about one-fifth of all Tunisia's international shipping. If that weren't enough success for one Arab woman in a world of Arab men, Hayet then was asked to run the Tunisian National Federation of Transport. Among other responsibilities, that job put her in charge of Tunis's taxi system. One has to throw all conventional notions of Arab culture out the window just to imagine this long-haired, rosy-cheeked, cherub-faced woman of a certain age giving orders to hundreds of grizzled, big-city Arab cabbies.

Hayet had been a great source of help and support throughout my research. She opened doors, put cars at my disposal, and eased my way at times when I wanted to be free from the strings attached to favors from others. Then, in September 2005, she sent me a "eureka" e-mail. The workers at Khaled's Tlelsa farm were wrong: Khaled may have had no sons to work the farm but he was not childless. Hayet had found Khaled's daughter.

Six weeks later, a friend of Hayet's picked me up at a downtown Tunis hotel. He was Ahmed Smaoui, the man who led Hayet to Khaled's family. Short, stocky, armed with a quick wit and forever tending a pipe, Ahmed led a life that paralleled the history of modern Tunisia. As a young student, in the early days of the republic, he had been arrested and sent for a year to a desert jail camp for his outspokenness against the Tunisian regime, but he eventually won over the men who run this small, almost claustrophobic country with his competence. At different times, he ran the national railroad, the national airline, and the Ministries of Social Welfare and Transportation. When Ahmed was in government, Hayet told me, he repeatedly clashed with her, but they later became good friends. Ahmed's connection to this story was the fact that he served for more than a decade as a senior official in the Ministry of Tourism. All those years he sat in the same office with Khaled Abdelwahhab.

Ahmed drove me and Hayet to meet Khaled's daughter in the chic neighborhood of modern-day Carthage. Her name, he told me, was Fafou, diminutive of Safia. Along the way, he told me that Fafou wasn't Khaled's only child. There was another girl, he said, the daughter of a Venezuelan opera singer Khaled had married in Spain. My hero, I was beginning to realize, had led quite a life.

It was nearly 9:00 PM by the time we walked up the long stone stairway to the discreetly elegant, whitewashed home in Carthage where Fafou lived with her husband. The house was filled with archaeological treasures, relics from Carthage's past, most of which, I came to learn, were collected by Khaled. Indeed, the house had been built by Khaled, who gave it to his daughter.

Fafou greeted us warmly, though tentatively. Given that a strange American had come with two Tunisians she had never before met to talk with her about her father, her reticence was no surprise. As we sat down to tea and Ramadan sweets, she told me the outline of her father's life. When she paused, Ahmed filled in with details. Here is what I learned.

Khaled Abdelwahhab was born in 1911, the only son among the five children of Hassan Husni, the famed author. From an early age, Khaled was a cosmopolitan, unbound by the confines of his small-town roots. He studied art, architecture, and archaeology, and was a lover of great music, fine wine, and good food. As a young man, he traveled widely, not only to France, where most young Tunisian men of means went to seek their fortunes, but even to America, where he spent two or three years in the early 1930s learning art and architecture in New York. He was, in Ahmed's words, an elegant, refined, cultured man, both an aesthete and a gourmand. His zest for good food and conversation was infectious; to have dinner with him, said Ahmed, was more than a meal, it was an experience. To top it off, Khaled was dashing, debonair, and strikingly handsome. Family photos that Fafou dug out for me to see told the story better than words: Her father was blessed with movie-star looks, a Tunisian Paul Newman.

Khaled was the type of person whose occupation was not the central focus of his life. It was only well into our conversation that the question of "what he did" even figured in a discussion of "who he was." Fafou could only recall two jobs her father ever held. For many years, he was "an adviser" in the Ministry of Tourism. It was not clear what he actually did in this job, but Khaled seems to have concerned himself with the care and preservation of Tunisia's rich archaeological legacy. Fafou also recalled that her father spent some time in the Ministry of Agriculture, as chief of staff to the minister. Khaled was a man of the world, she said, but he loved nothing more than the fruit, nuts, and flowers of his farm in Tlelsa.

Fafou herself had inherited her father's good looks. She was a beautiful woman, also of a certain age, though she had a hint of sadness in her eyes. When I told her the details of Anny's story, that her father spirited away the Jewish families in the middle of the night to hide them on the Tlelsa estate, she was nonplussed. Like Si Ali Sakkat's two grandsons, she had never before heard the story of her father's righteous deed. The only wartime tale in the Abdelwahhab family repertoire was related to me by her husband, who recalled Khaled regaling them with the story of a German officer burning his tongue when Khaled introduced him to harissa, the spicy Tunisian hot sauce. But Fafou said she was not surprised by her father's help to the Jews. In her case, I think she had long ago gotten used to surprises from her father.

What I learned that evening only confirmed key aspects of Anny's story. Khaled would have been thirty-two years old at the time of the German occupation, the right age with the right ruggedly handsome looks that Anny described. He was precisely the sort of person who would have prepared lavish repasts of food and drink for German officers, if only as a way to wean information and learn their intentions. (Indeed, the harissa story confirmed that Khaled served meals to German officers.) A bon vivant with an eye for the ladies, he was also the type to whom a German officer, after a few drinks, might confide his sexual desires. From his time abroad, in Paris and New York, Khaled almost surely came into contact with Jews in a richer and more varied way than even the most open-minded of his countrymen back home. He loved his farm and would naturally think of Tlelsa as a place where he could safeguard people the way he tended for flowers and trees. He was his own man, an impulsive iconoclast who would not think twice about knocking on the door of an olive oil factory in the middle of the night to spirit the inhabitants to safety if he thought that was the right thing to do. On top of all this, he was an experienced keeper of secrets. Putting all this together, Anny's story rang truer than ever.

Khaled Abdelwahhab died in 1997, at age eighty-six. He had no sons; there are no more Abdelwahhabs to carry the family name. His legacy, however, lives on in Anny's story. I asked Fafou what her reaction would be if the world knew about her father's selfless wartime deed. She said she would not mind. Perhaps his will be the first Arab name honored by Yad Vashem as a "Righteous Among the Nations."

Chapter 7

In the Heart of Europe

A S WE HAVE SEEN in the last two chapters, just across the Mediterranean from the carnage of Europe, some Arabs saved Jews during the Holocaust. The distances are not that great. At its narrowest point, across the Straits of Gibraltar, Morocco is only eight miles from Spain. Tunisia, the northernmost point of Africa, is just ninety miles from the Italian island of Lampedusa. Algiers, the de facto capital of Arab North Africa, is an overnight steamer ride from Marseille. Nevertheless, the sea has served as a gulf to keep these stories virtually unknown to this day.

But what about within Europe itself? Stories of Arabs who collaborated with the Nazis in Europe—like Haj Amin al-Husseini, mufti of Jerusalem— are well known. Were there also Arabs who saved Jews in Europe?

There was certainly opportunity. Europe was home to a sizable Arab community even before the start of the war, composed primarily of veterans among the half-million Muslims who served in the French army in World War I and their families. As World War II approached, the French hastily recruited another large group of Arabs—nearly 350,000—to serve in its army. When France fell, huge numbers were taken captive by the Germans. Most were placed in special prisoner-of-war camps, in which the Germans separated Arab soldiers from Europeans and sought to win them over to the Axis cause by offering halal food, providing Arabic news and entertainment, and even building mosques inside POW camps. Before long, the Germans

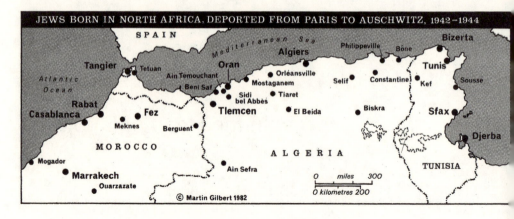

MAP 7.1 "Jews Born in North Africa, Deported from Paris to Auschwitz, 1942–1944," reprinted from Martin Gilbert, *The Routledge Atlas of the Holocaust,* 3rd edition (London: Routledge, 2002), p. 127.

decided the best investment they could make to gain the loyalty of their Arab prisoners was to release them. Most returned to North Africa, then under Vichy rule, but thousands remained in France, swelling the local Arab population.[1]

At the time, France's Jewish population also included thousands of Jews from Arab lands. The year 1940 marked the seventieth anniversary of the Crémieux decree, which extended French citizenship to the Jews of Algeria; two generations of Algerian Jews had had the opportunity to move freely across the Mediterranean and throughout metropolitan France. Over the years, thousands more had traveled from Morocco and Tunisia to study, work, and live in France. In addition, when war broke out, about 2,000 Jews from Arab lands, not French citizens, were themselves caught in Europe. Rootless and friendless, with few resources and little protection, these refugees faced especially difficult times. Twelve hundred of them eventually perished in gas chambers and concentration camps.[2]

In this environment, it is only natural that expatriates from the Arab lands of North Africa—Arabs and Jews—had some contact with each other. For a recent Jewish emigrant from Constantine living in Lyons or a stranded Jewish traveler from Marrakesh stuck in a refugee camp outside Nice, Arabs hailing from their hometowns were probably more accessible than local

Frenchmen. And for many Arabs in those same locales, the culture of Sephardic Jewish life—its sights, sounds, and smells—were, most likely, more familiar than the local French way. Given the depths of French anti-Semitism under Vichy, on both the official and popular levels, it would not be surprising if some Arabs had helped some Jews. If that were true on the southern coast of the Mediterranean, then it stands to reason that it would also be true on the northern coast of the Mediterranean. The real surprise would have been if none of the Arabs in France helped any of the Jews in France facing the evil of Vichy.

Until now, however, no Arab has been recognized for his role in helping to save Jews inside Europe itself. If that changes, a prime candidate is one of the most influential and well-known Arabs of his day, the head of what could be considered the most important Arab institution in Europe. The institution is the Great Mosque of Paris. The man was named Si Kaddour Benghabrit.

The Great Mosque occupies an entire city block on Paris's famed Left Bank, not far from the bookstores of the Sorbonne and just a half mile or so from the seat of French Christendom, the Cathedral of Notre Dame. The mosque is an imposing structure, enclosed within tall, thick fortress-like walls and cornered with minarets that taper into the sky. Built in the 1920s, it was a gift from the French government to recognize the 100,000 or so Muslim soldiers who died in World War I, about one-fifth of all Muslim soldiers fighting in the service of France. But its creators conceived of the mosque as more than just a symbol of French gratitude; in their mind, the mosque served a practical function, too. Through it, France sought to create a special connection between Paris and its Arab immigrants and, through the latter, to the influential religious authorities (and powerful religious sentiments) of the countries from which they came. It was, from the start, as much a political institution as a center of prayer.

Si Kaddour Benghabrit (the abbreviated Algerian form of Sidi Abdelqadr Ben Ghabrit) was a religious leader, spiritual guide, and deft, well-connected political actor all at the same time. According to his official biography, he was born in 1868 in the Algerian town of Sidi Bel Abbès, was schooled in the study of Muslim law, and was on track to follow a traditional path moving upward through the Muslim religious hierarchy. But in his mid-twenties, he made a detour that would change his life: He took a position as an inter-preter with the French legation in the international port city of Tangiers. For the next two decades, as France deepened its protectorate over Morocco, Benghabrit was a Zelig-like character who found a way to serve both French officialdom and the court of the Moroccan sultan—managing the French consulate in Fez in 1903, convincing the new sultan to accept a French mili-tary mission there in 1908, helping to negotiate a French-Moroccan border agreement in Paris in 1910, working with the sultan on a French-German accord in 1911, and so on. For a time, he even served as chief of protocol to the sultan himself.[3]

Over the years, Benghabrit proved himself intensely loyal to France, and as French officials often attested, he provided invaluable service to French interests.[4] But if he was deeply enmeshed in the world of French diplomacy, Benghabrit always kept at least one foot in the world of Muslim religious in-stitutions. World War I was a turning point. In early 1917, he became presi-dent of a prestigious international foundation that supervised and protected Muslim religious endowments and holy places, headquartered in Algiers. Then, later that year, in a new role as French honorary consul-general, he undertook missions in North Africa and in Europe to minister to Muslim troops serving in the French army. He spent the last two years of the decade in the service of the French foreign ministry, monitoring postwar diplomacy over the fate of Syria, and then, in 1920, he began a project that would con-sume the rest of his life. That year, the French parliament turned to him to establish a mosque in Paris. When the magnificent, green-roofed structure formally opened six years later, Benghabrit was installed at its head as rector. Both the sultan of Morocco and the president of the French republic were in attendance. At the ceremony, Benghabrit said the latter's presence conse-crated the "eternal union" of France and Islam.

While he continued to undertake official missions on behalf of the French government, Benghabrit served as the head of the mosque until his death in 1954. He was buried inside the mosque's walls. In a way, he chose the right time to die. Though he was eulogized as "the most Parisian of Muslims," the "eternal union" he praised three decades earlier was coming apart. The year of his death coincided with the start of the long, bloody struggle for Algerian independence from France; within two years, France's two other Arab protectorates—Morocco and Tunisia—were fully independent. Benghabrit had been ahead of his time in knitting a life that blended his traditional roots and his allegiance to a cosmopolitan France. By the time of his passing, that sort of life of fusion and compromise had become old-fashioned. In that sense, Benghabrit was not unlike Si Ali Sakkat, Mohamed Chenik, and other Arabs of the liberal age. Time eventually passed them all by.

Why does Benghabrit deserve to be included among Arab rescuers of Jews? Stories of the mosque's role in aiding Jews during the war have circulated for years. The principal source was a North African Jew named Albert Assouline, a captive in a German prison camp. According to Assouline, he and an Algerian named Yassa Rabah escaped together from the camp and stealthily traversed the countryside across the French-German border, heading for Paris. Once in Paris, they made their way to the mosque, where, evidently thanks to Rabah's connections in the Algerian community, the two found refuge. Eventually, Assouline continued his journey and joined up with Free French forces to continue the fight against the German occupation.

Like many escape stories from World War II, Assouline's story was full of terror, adventure, and good luck. But the most fantastic part of the story was his claim that the mosque provided sanctuary and sustenance to Jews hiding from Vichy and German troops as well as to other fighters in the anti-Fascist resistance. "No fewer than 1,732 resistance fighters found refuge in its [underground] caverns," he wrote in a 1983 article for *Almanach du Combattant,* a French veterans' magazine. "[These included] Muslim escapees but also Christians and Jews. The latter were by far the most numerous."[5] According to him, the senior imam of the mosque, a man named Si Mohammed Benzouaou, took "considerable risk" by hiding the Jews and providing many (including many children) with certificates of Muslim identity, with which they could avoid deportation and certain death. Assouline's account was rich in graphic detail. He recalled, for example, one "hot alert" when German soldiers smelled the odor of cigarettes and, convinced that Muslims were forbidden to smoke, searched the mosque looking for hidden Jews. According to Assouline, the Jews were able to escape via sewer tunnels that connected the mosque to nearby buildings.

Assouline's stunning story described the mosque as a virtual Grand Central Station for the Underground Railroad of Jews in France. If France's most influential Arab, leader of its most important Muslim institution, was actually responsible for saving Jewish lives, it would turn on its head conventional thinking about the role Arabs played during the war and would catapult Benghabrit and his mosque colleagues into the pantheon of those recognized as "righteous." But was it true?

From the outset, there was one great hole in Assouline's story: Not one person has ever come forward to corroborate it. In the sixty years since the war, not a single person—Jewish or non-Jewish—has testified that he or she had found refuge in the mosque. Not one person has mentioned the mosque as a place of hiding in his or her wartime memoirs; not one person has mentioned the mosque's hospitality in an oral history; not one has replied to the many requests made via Internet bulletin boards and chat rooms, including those I posted myself, searching for alumni of the mosque's sanctuary to Jews. The specificity of Assouline's claim—not "around 1,000" or "more than 1,500" but exactly "no fewer than 1,732" people were hidden in the mosque, he said—lent it compelling credibility. (He said he came up with this number by reviewing a file of ration cards he saw in the mosque.) But no less compelling was the absence of a single independent testimony to support his claim.

At the same time, the fact that none of the 1,732 has ever come forward to provide corroborating testimony from his or her own wartime experience is not itself sufficient reason to reject Assouline's claim; the absence of other firsthand accounts does not prove that the mosque did *not* play a role in defense of Jews. Indeed, threads of evidence from various other sources suggest that the core of Assouline's story—that the mosque and its leaders provided aid and succor to Jews during the war—may in fact be true.

Derri Berkani certainly believed Assouline. A French documentary filmmaker, of Algerian Berber origin, Berkani was so moved by the untold story of the mosque that he made the 1991 film *Une Résistance Oubliée: La Mosquée de Paris* (*The Forgotten Resistance: The Mosque of Paris*). This half-hour movie, which aired on French television, follows the story of a young Frenchwoman whose Algerian grandfather, a fighter in the French resistance, was killed on a street near the mosque. She, in turns, looks inside the mosque for an explanation of a death she never understood. What she finds is a story of a community that protected the unprotected, from North

African escapees from German POW camps to American and British paratroopers who found medical care and refuge in the French-Muslim hospital nearby. Most of all, the story focuses on Jews, especially Jewish children.[6]

Assouline, a thin man with dark, sunken eyes and a long, pointed black-and-white beard, appears on film to tell the tale of his flight decades earlier from a German prison camp and his relief in finding refuge inside the mosque. The film takes viewers inside the tunnels beneath the mosque, where Assouline says hundreds found safety. He adds intriguing details: that Benghabrit had a special button installed that he would push to trigger a warning alarm in the event of a police raid and that, in emergencies, Jews would huddle in the mosque's main sanctuary, which was known to be off-limits to non-Muslims, including German soldiers with their prying eyes. In addition, Berkani provides the testimony of a physician in the municipal department of public hygiene, a man named Ahmed Somia, who tells the story of a young Jewish orphan, seven or eight years old, whom Benghabrit hid in the safety of his home. "Si Kaddour felt that we had to do something for this child," he said. The solution was to provide the boy with a false birth certificate from the mosque that certified him as a Muslim and allowed him to live openly.

Berkani's film is understated yet powerful, moving in its simplicity. It is anti-Hollywood, the antithesis of a slick, sugary attempt to pull at the viewer's heartstrings in order to build sympathy for Benghabrit and the role of the mosque he led. But it has one flaw: Other than Assouline's account, there are no direct testimonies from rescued Jews. There are no archival documents. There is no real proof.

Assouline's story received a boost in June 2005, when Salim (Simon) Halali, a world-renowned singer, died in Cannes. Born in 1920 to a poor Jewish family in Annaba (formerly, Bône), near the Algerian-Tunisian border, Halali hailed from a local Jewish-Berber tribe. When he was just fourteen, he made his way to France, where he was eventually discovered singing in a cabaret. It was not long before Halali became France's most celebrated "oriental" singer. For the next forty years, he was a fixture of Andalusian music, predecessor of today's *rai* trend, beloved by millions. His music blended the rhythms of his Jewish, Berber, and Arab roots. When Halali died, critics eulogized him as "the most beautiful Arab male voice of the post-war years."[7]

Halali, it seems, owed his success—and his life—to the mosque of Paris. Virtually every obituary of Halali, on both sides of the Mediterranean, told the same story: Halali escaped certain deportation and death thanks to the generosity and ingenuity of Benghabrit. French writer Nidam Abdi explained in the prestigious Paris newspaper *Libération* that the twenty-year-old Halali found himself all alone in 1940, after his closest friend joined Radio Berlin, the Nazis' premier propaganda organ. When Vichy started its pursuit of Jews, Halali turned to the mosque for help. Benghabrit, a cultured man who had been a fan of Halali's, did not fail him. To protect Halali from the grip of Vichy's anti-Jewish laws, Benghabrit evidently provided him with a certificate of Muslim identity. But because Halali was such a public figure, Benghabrit had to go one step further. To lend credibility to Halali's claim of Muslim roots, Benghabrit arranged to have the name of Halali's grandfather engraved on an abandoned tomb in the Muslim cemetery in Bobigny. This unconventional ploy provided incontrovertible proof of Halali's Muslim origins and enabled him to survive the war years in safety.

Berkani's film does mention Halali's story in passing; it was evidently common knowledge. But the repetition of Benghabrit's exploits on Halali's behalf that appeared in countless obituaries, including in mainstream newspapers like *Libération*, lends it special credence. Still, repetition is not proof.

From France's wartime archives, it is clear that the men who ran the mosque had ample opportunity to help Jews. This was especially the case when the occupation authorities turned to the mosque to determine whether people who claimed to be Muslim really were.

For a certain number of Jews living in France—it is impossible to know how many—passing as Muslim was a clever ruse to avoid confiscation, arrest, or deportation. This was a particularly useful ploy for Jewish men, since Muslims, like Jews, are circumcised, often the defining test of Jewishness for Vichy and Nazi Jew-hunters. The fact that Jews and Arabs in North Africa shared so many surnames made it possible for some Jews to pass as Muslims. But German and Vichy inquisitors were zealous in tracking the bloodlines of accused Jews at least two generations back. Cases of people who claimed to be Muslims but who were suspected of being Jewish were complicated; birth records and marriage registers—if they existed at all—were somewhere on the far side of the Mediterranean, perhaps in a remote town or village, maybe tucked away in a local mosque or the haphazard files of a village headman. So, instead of dispatching its own agents to search for documentary proof, the Germans turned to the mosque of Paris, whose word on the matter was accepted as final. Sometimes, the mosque certified claimants as Muslims; sometimes, it rejected claims and the accused were considered, under the law, as Jews. The mosque, then, certainly had the opportunity to determine the fate of these people. Whether it deliberately chose to help Jews, protecting the real identity of the claimants regardless of the evidence, is the key issue.

Therefore, in October 2005, I went to Paris to ask the current head of the mosque, Dalil Boubakeur. Since no survivors had come forward to testify to the role of the mosque, I thought, perhaps the mosque itself would attest to its role. Given the tense, suspicious, and often hostile relationship between Jews and Muslims in France, I doubted it. Throughout much of Europe, Jews and Muslims are like the Hatfields and McCoys, groups that revile each other with a mutual venom that runs deep. And France is ground zero. It is home to both the largest community of Muslims in Europe (not including Turkey) and the Continent's largest community of Jews. But in absolute terms, France's 6 million Muslims—10 percent of the French population— are ten times the number of French Jews. Anti-Semitism is a plague among some quarters of France's Arab community, with attacks on Jews, Jewish institutions, and Jewish property a frequent occurrence. Because of the sheer demographic weight of Muslims, French authorities deal gingerly with the problem. "There is no anti-semitism in France," President Jacques Chirac once famously said.[8] This in a country that only a half century earlier celebrated anti-Semitism as an official policy of the state, a country whose Jews are today leaving for Israel in such numbers that—as British chief rabbi Jonathan Sacks has noted—they are fueling a boom in Jerusalem's real estate market.[9] Chirac's willful blindness on the depth of French anti-Semitism was reflective of the general French reluctance to address the whole spectrum of political, social, economic, and cultural problems of the republic's Arab and Muslim underclass—problems that exploded in October 2005, with a rampage of violence that France had not seen since 1968.

Given the raw, tense relationship between Arabs and Jews in France, I had low expectations that any Muslim leader would embrace a legacy of

Muslim rescue of Jews during the Holocaust. The usual refrain—"We had no part in the Holocaust"—was safe ground, and I did not expect Muslim leaders to tread far from that position, even if the role in question concerned saving Jews. The fact that my interlocutor was Boubakeur further steeled me for disappointment. Boubakeur is not only rector of the Paris mosque, he is also president of the governing body of all French Muslims, the Conseil Français du Culte Musulman (CFCM). This is an especially sensitive post, whose de facto responsibilities include both representing Muslim interests before the French government and transmitting French government interests to the Muslim community. Even in the best of times, this job requires acute political skills and deft social and cultural balancing. My interview with Boubakeur took place just a day before the eruption of the October 2005 riots. For French Muslims, it was clearly not the best of times.

Like all previous mosque rectors, Boubakeur is Algerian by birth. As the son of a previous rector, he was born into the thin crust of French-Muslim elite. He is a physician by training, with a French medical degree in addition to his diploma in religious studies from Egypt's venerable al-Azhar University, seat of orthodox Sunni Islam. He is a thoroughly accomplished man, able to move easily between the worlds of politics, science, philosophy, and religion. Boubakeur's biography is full of awards received, titles earned, books published. He is not shy about his accomplishments. In fact, Boubakeur's business card includes eleven lines of description, eight in English and three in Arabic.

Before the interview, I had been warned to expect nothing but platitudes. One Sorbonne scholar I met explained to me that Boubakeur had no interest in lifting the veil on the role one of his predecessors, Benghabrit, may have played in protecting Jews during the war. Current-day attitudes toward Jews are so troubled that the Arab and Muslim communities in France would erupt in outrage if the mosque welcomed proof that it had provided sanctuary to Jews; the mosque certainly would not provide it willingly, I was told.

Generational politics added another layer of complexity. Benghabrit, I was reminded, lived and died loyal to France and was opposed to the rise of nationalism in his native Algeria in the 1930s, 1940s, and 1950s. When that politics fell out of fashion, Benghabrit's star dimmed; he is, as a result, no longer an iconic figure in the Muslim community. Boubakeur represents a

1. Gilbert Scemla, who with his father and brother, was deported from Tunisia to Germany where they were all executed: "They were condemned only because they were Jews." *(Courtesy of Frédéric Gasquet)*

2. Marshal Henri-Philippe Pétain meets Algerian religious leaders during their visit to Vichy, 1942. *(USHMM, courtesy of Serge Klarsfeld; Beate Klarsfeld Foundation)*

3. *(Below)* José Aboulker, hero of the Algiers Jewish underground. *(Courtesy, Collection of the Musée de l'Ordre de la Libération, Paris)*

4. *(Above)* Morice Tondowski, Polish-born French Legionnaire, was interned at Berguent, Vichy France's only all-Jewish labor camp in North Africa. *(Courtesy, family of Morice Tondowski)*

5. One of the few structures still standing at the desolate site of the Tendrara labor camp, along the track of the Trans-Sahara railway, eastern Morocco. *(Courtesy of Jennie Litvack)*

6.   SS Col. Walter Rauff, designer of mobile gas vans, led Nazi efforts to terrorize the Jews of Tunisia. *(Courtesy, Ullstein Bild/The Granger Collection)*

7.   *(Center)* Jewish workers marching through the streets of Tunis, en route to a forced labor site, December 1942. *(Courtesy, Bundesarchiv)*

8.   *(Left)* A Tunisian Jew, wearing a five-pointed yellow star, cleans the street as a German soldier looks on. *(Courtesy, Bundesarchiv)*

9. *(Above)* Site of Philibert Barracks, Bizerte, the worst German labor camp in Tunisia: "Lice and parasites became their most loyal companions." *(Author's photo)*

10. *(Right)* This modest monument to Tunisian Jews killed during Nazi occupation, including Jewish laborers and Jews deported to death camps in Europe, stands in a corner of Tunis's main Jewish cemetery. *(Author's photo)*

11. *(Left)* Jewish survivors from the Bergen-Belsen concentration camp returning home to Libya, 1945. *(USHMM, courtesy of Yad Vashem Photo Archives)*

12. Sultan Muhammad V, pictured in 1945 with Charles de Gaulle in Paris, lent vital moral support to Morocco's Jewish community. *(AP Photo)*

13. Moncef Bey, wartime leader of the only Arab country to suffer a full-fledged German occupation, is remembered with affection by Tunisian Jews. *(Courtesy, Government of Tunisia)*

14. (*Above Left*) Mohamed Chenik, philo-semitic prime minister of Tunisia, "very likely saved Jewish lives, perhaps at risk to his own." (*Courtesy, Government of Tunisia*)

15. (*Above Right*) Si Ali Sakkat, former mayor of Tunis, gave shelter to sixty Jewish workers who fled a labor camp during the height of battle. (*Photo, courtesy of Ali Sakkat*)

16. Adorned with turrets and towers, Si Ali Sakkat's Spanish-style hacienda was visible from a great distance. Si Ali's grandson, Kamal Sakkat, stands in the foreground. (*Author's photo*)

17. *(Right)* Anny's parents, Odette Boccara and Jacob Boukris, pictured in their wedding photo. *(Courtesy, the late Anny Boukris)*

18. *(Left)* Khaled Abdelwahhab, Arab guardian angel who protected Anny's mother from the sexual predations of a German officer. *(Courtesy, family of Khaled Abdelwahhab)*

19. Si Kaddour Benghabrit, pictured welcoming German officers to the Great Mosque of Paris in March 1941, was responsible for helping up to 100 Jews evade persecution. *(Courtesy, Centre de Documentation Juive Contemporain)*

20. Dalil Boubakeur hosts President Jacques Chirac in April 2002, the first visit by a French head of state to the Great Mosque of Paris in 76 years. (*AP photo*)

21. Father Emil Shofani, right, leads a group of Jewish and Arab Israelis on an unprecedented visit to Auschwitz in May 2003. (*AP photo*)

different generation with different politics; indeed, the French media frequently links him to the generals who run the Algerian government, heirs of the revolution against French colonialism. But the story is even more complicated: now, the politics of Boubakeur's generation finds itself criticized by more radical Islamists, including sympathizers to the extremists who fought a terrorist war against Algeria for much of the past fifteen years. In this ideological sandstorm, any story that burnished the image of Benghabrit could only tarnish Boubakeur's and, at the same time, further inflame the more radical elements among French Muslims. I assumed Boubakeur was sure to do all in his power to avoid this combustible mix.

With this as background, I arrived at the mosque at the appointed time. When I got out of my taxi, I was astonished to find that the driver had dropped me off at the front door of a bustling café. I was totally disoriented. This was Ramadan. Could the mosque really run a fully operating Parisian café, serving espresso and croissants, in the middle of the holy month of daytime fasting and prayer? Wasn't that sort of like visiting the Western Wall on Yom Kippur, the Day of Atonement, only to find Hasidic Jews manning a cheeseburger stand? A harried waiter confirmed that this was indeed the Great Mosque of Paris. When I pressed, he mumbled that the entry to the sanctuary and the mosque's administrative offices was on the other side of the building, on a quiet side street. I hurried around the block and found Pierre Thénard, a helpful French diplomat I knew from his Washington days. He had arranged the Boubakeur interview for me. Pierre explained that the café made a tidy profit that supports the mosque's operation. The mosque even cleared a few euros from charging customers for access to its hammam, he said. The capital of French Islam, I was beginning to learn, was not as I had expected it to be.

We entered the mosque and found ourselves a world away from Paris. With its intricately tiled mosaics, cool gardens, and carved wooden latticework, it was more like being back in North Africa. After a short wait, a female secretary ushered us into the rector's surprisingly cramped office.

Boubakeur is a short, stocky man in his mid-sixties, with a broad and fleshy face, wire-rimmed eyeglasses, and a few long strands of hair washed flat back across his scalp. He greeted us warmly, almost effusively. A cane was nearby, and he needed it to stand when we shook hands. When Pierre and I left an hour and a half later, Boubakeur nearly fell over when he rose to show us the door. His infirmity, however, did not diminish his presence. He had all the qualities of an effective communicator: He never let go of eye contact, he gestured expressively when he talked, he spoke beautifully and with empathy. He knew how to connect with his audience.

After a few words of greeting in Arabic, we spoke French, and Boubakeur launched into a monologue on the historic links between Jews and Muslims. "In the past there existed special elements of common human-ity, of our common life, a symbiosis between us that regrettably has been in-terrupted by the politics of the second half of the twentieth century," he said. In the corridor, Pierre had told me he had arranged the interview by writing Boubakeur's office a note describing me as an influential leader of the "American Jewish lobby"—this is not true; I direct a nonpartisan research institute, not a lobby group—so Boubakeur, it seems, was trying to establish what he thought would be his bona fides with me. I feared that this lecture was the start of a fifteen-minute courtesy interview in which Boubakeur would spin platitudes but say nothing of substance. Without being rude, I quickly asked him the questions I had come to ask: What was the mosque's role in the war? What did he know of stories that the mosque had served as a refuge for Jews? Did the mosque, in fact, save Jews during the war? With-out a flicker of hesitation, he said he knew the stories. He also said they were, to a large extent, true.

"The mosque represented the sensibilities of the Muslims of North Africa toward their Jewish brothers," he explained.

> It was a natural phenomenon. But from the view of fifty years later, given the experience of the massive crime that befell the Jewish people, the ex-tent of which we now know, and the establishment of the state of Israel and the blockage of political relations between Jews and Arabs, it regret-tably looks differently . . . The new sociology of the world is different than it was in the 1940s and certainly different from what it was in Andalusia. What happened then [in the 1940s] was very symbolic but exemplary.

I was surprised. Boubakeur did not sidestep the issue of the mosque's role on behalf of Jews, indeed he was proud to talk about it and to claim it on behalf of French Muslims. At the same time, he was careful to place it in a wider historical context that afforded him the safety of distance and detachment and enabled him to separate his pride at past heroics from the complicated realities of current events. As significant as his admission was, I wanted specifics. I asked him: What actually happened inside the mosque during the war? Here again, Boubakeur was careful to make fine and important distinctions.

He confirmed the fundamentals of Assouline's account. "The main testimony of evidence about the events in the mosque," said Boubakeur, "was given by a man named Assouline, a French aviator who was a prisoner of war who escaped in 1940 with a Muslim Arab from Algeria named Rachid. Rachid brought Assouline to the mosque. Underneath the mosque there are caverns and an underground river, which makes it an excellent place to hide. They hid here." (In Assouline's account, his Algerian friend had a different name.)

Boubakeur said that Assouline's account of his personal saga was true. But he then summarily dismissed Assouline's provocative claim that the mosque provided sanctuary for a large group of desperate Jews. "Assouline later said that up to 1,700 Jews were hidden here. That is a legend." The mosque's underground tunnels were an officially designated air-raid shelter, Boubakeur countered, open to all. Although some Jews took refuge there, he said, they came as Parisians looking for cover, not as Jews seeking protection. Boubakeur added that he personally had walked down into the tunnels years earlier, shortly after his installation as rector, and saw a sign that read *"Abri"* (French for "shelter") that he assumed was left over from the war. But even as he rejected Assouline's story, Boubakeur did leave a small crack open: "And if some others were hidden here, it was certainly not on the scale that Assouline talked about." Still, the mosque's official view, enunciated by Boubakeur, was that Assouline's tale was a myth.

So far, Boubakeur had defended the mosque's humanity toward Jews in general without admitting to any specific acts on their behalf, other than hosting Assouline for a few days in 1940. This was a virtuoso performance; it would pass a test of political correctness from both his Muslim constituents and non-Muslims, including Jews, looking for signs of his stance on questions of tolerance and civic responsibility. But as far as the mosque's wartime role, I was beginning to get a sinking feeling that Boubakeur was keen to project the image of helping Jews without actually confirming any specifics of that help.

I moved on. Did the mosque provide certificates of Muslim identity to Jews, enabling them to evade Vichy laws? When Boubakeur said yes, immediately and without hesitation, I was astonished.

"It is true that the mosque provided certificates of Muslim identity to some Jews," he said. "This was possible because, especially for North African Jews, the names are very close." Boubakeur went on to explain that the mosque had both motive and opportunity to implement the certificate scheme. The motive was selfless—to enable Jews to avoid persecution by providing an acceptable rationale for their circumcision. The opportunity took advantage of a "double game" that, he said, characterized the complex relationship between the German occupation authorities and the Muslim community of Paris.

"The Germans were always pressing the mosque, trying to impose themselves on the mosque to use it for propaganda among Muslims," he said.

> They always wanted to have visitors here; at one point, we feared that Hitler himself would make a visit. We tried to resist but it wasn't always possible. Some German senior officials did come; pictures were taken, etc. In 1943 [after the Allied invasion of North Africa], the Germans changed tack and imposed more restrictions on the mosque's activities. Earlier on, everyone was playing a "double game." Sometimes, the Germans may have closed their eyes to what was going on among Muslims here; sometimes, people here may have closed their eyes to doing things with the Germans.

Even if Muslims and Germans were engaged in an intricate "double game," I asked, shouldn't one consider the mosque's actions on behalf of Jews as courageous? After all, I asked, isn't it one thing to have personal, human contact with persecuted Jews, and another thing for the mosque itself to risk its status by helping those Jews? "Yes, yes, yes," he nodded. "Absolutely, it was courageous. It was very courageous. Courageous and natural at the same time."

I was dumbstruck. Boubakeur, titular head of the Muslims of France, had confirmed a central thread of the story of the mosque's role in defense of Jews. I pressed on for details. He reminded me that recipients of the certificates were primarily Jews from North Africa, that while some Ashkenazim (European Jews) may have benefited, it was essentially an effort to assist Jews from Arab lands. All told, he said, a maximum of 100 certificates of Muslim identity were issued.

Once again, Boubakeur was careful to place the story of Muslim certificates in a specific historical and political context. "It definitely happened," he went on. "But it wasn't an organized process. It was individual by individual. And it was clandestine." Boubakeur explained that he did not believe that there was a concerted effort by the mosque hierarchy, representing the institution, to safeguard Jews with the provision of false identity papers. Instead, this was done on a case-by-case basis, he said, with individual Muslims bringing individual Jews to seek help from mosque leaders. And, he said, Benghabrit was probably not the key player. That role belonged to the chief imam of the mosque, Si Mohamed Benzouaou.[10] "Benghabrit was there, overlooking the mosque, but he focused on external affairs, politics, relations with the state," said Boubakeur. "He surely knew what was going on and closed his eyes to it, but it was the imams inside the mosque who actually helped the Jews."

Benghabrit was clearly a sensitive issue, as the Sorbonne scholar had warned me. I pressed Boubakeur on the role his predecessor actually played in protecting Jews. As head of the mosque, wasn't he responsible for everything that went on inside these walls? Could mosque authorities issue 100 identity certificates without his personal stamp of approval? Isn't it appropriate, therefore, that Benghabrit receive official recognition as a rescuer of Jews? Boubakeur temporized. Many Muslims saved Jews, he said. Muslims were in the resistance. Muslims fought for the Allies. Muslim doctors did remarkable things for Jews. But there are few documents for these acts. "We have an oral tradition, not a written one," he explained.

Boubakeur then told me a fascinating tale. Apparently, I was not the first to come to ask about the mosque's wartime role. Representatives of Yad Vashem, Israel's official Holocaust memorial, had come, too, he said. As the institution that determines whether stories of rescuing Jews are true and whether the do-gooder merits formal recognition as a "Righteous Among the Nations," he said that Yad Vashem was interested in learning the truth of claims about Benghabrit.

"We showed them what we have," Boubakeur said. "I am proud of what this mosque did. I urged them to recognize the mosque, not any particular individual. But Yad Vashem said it only recognizes people, not institutions." As a second-best option, Boubakeur said, he proposed that Yad Vashem authorize the installation of a plaque that he would hang near the entry to the mosque. "It would say, 'In this mosque, Jews were saved during the war.' But Yad Vashem said no." (After returning from Paris, I immediately wrote an e-mail to Mordechai Paldiel, longtime head of the Yad Vashem department responsible for vetting the candidacies for the "Righteous Among the Nations" designation, and asked for his view of Boubakeur's account. After several exchanges, Paldiel told me that Yad Vashem's representative in Paris did meet with Boubakeur and explained to him the criteria for recognition as one of the "righteous." He also confirmed that Yad Vashem would not have lent its imprimatur to the idea of a plaque on the mosque. The origin of the meeting—whether Boubakeur approached Yad Vashem or vice versa— is still unclear.)[11]

Still, Boubakeur did not want to address the core issue. If indeed Yad Vashem recognizes only people, not institutions, didn't Benghabrit's overall responsibility for the mosque mean that he deserved to be recognized for saving up to 100 Jews during the war?

That was a line Boubakeur did not want to cross. "Benghabrit was a complex man," he said. "To some, he was a collaborator; doing things at the same time as being a rescuer. You need to know—those were complex and difficult times. To survive, you had to do certain things. And above all, he wanted to protect the mosque."

Boubakeur's anxiety was palpable. Scrutiny of his predecessor's personal role in defense of Jews would invariably underscore the gray, murky world in which Benghabrit operated during the war—a world memorialized by German propaganda photos that show Benghabrit accompanying German officers on visits to injured troops and hosting German officers in the courtyard of the mosque itself. My own view is that the grayness of Benghabrit's wartime past did not seem to be different than that of other rescuers. Oskar Schindler, for example, saved Jews by finding ingenious ways to keep them on his list of workers, but he did not mind using their labor to keep his company running. Still, at a moment when relations between the French Muslim population and wider French society were already on the edge of explosion, Boubakeur could not have welcomed the prospect of the mosque being in the eye of a tornado of questions—"Was Benghabrit on the side of the angels? Did Benghabrit make a deal with the devil?"—concerning its founder's role in World War II. Boubakeur's response was to steer the spotlight away from the personal exploits of a former mosque rector whose pragmatism might be misunderstood either by today's generation of French Muslims or by wider French society—or both.

"So, about saving Jews, there is no doubt about the role of the mosque," Boubakeur said conclusively. "But about Benghabrit, I am prudent. Benghabrit closed his eyes to what was going on [on behalf of the Jews] and let it happen. I can't say more. He is buried here. I respect him and his memory. Of course, we keep the legend [about Assouline's claim of 1,700 Jews hidden beneath the mosque]. Reality is a bit different. But even so, even if it was one Jew saved, that by itself is an important fact."

Then, when I thought our conversation had run its course, Boubakeur surprised me once again. He picked up a thin folder that sat on the table in front of him and pulled out a single sheet of paper. It was a copy of a document from the French Archives. Dated September 24, 1940, the document was a note to the French minister of foreign affairs from the deputy director of the ministry's Political Department. In it the writer—a bureaucrat identified by the initials "P. H."—informed his superior about a certain peculiar action taken by the German authorities in Paris. The brief, typewritten note read as follows:

> The occupation authorities suspect the personnel of the Mosque of Paris of fraudulently delivering to individuals of the Jewish race certificates attesting that the interested persons are of the Muslim confession. The imam was summoned, in a threatening manner, to put an end to all such practices. It seems, in effect, that a number of Jews resorted to all sorts of maneuvers of this kind to conceal their identity.

> Vichy, le 24 septembre 1940.
>
> Le directeur politique adjoint.
>
> NOTE POUR LE MINISTRE.
>
> Les autorités d'occupation soupçonnent le personnel
> de la mosquée de Paris de délivrer frauduleusement à des
> individus de race juive des certificats attestant que les
> intéressés sont de confession musulmane. L'imam a été sommé
> de façon comminatoire, d'avoir à rompre avec toute pratique
> de ce genre. Il semble, en effet, que nombre d'israélites
> recourent à des manoeuvres de toute espèce pour dissimuler
> leur identité ./.

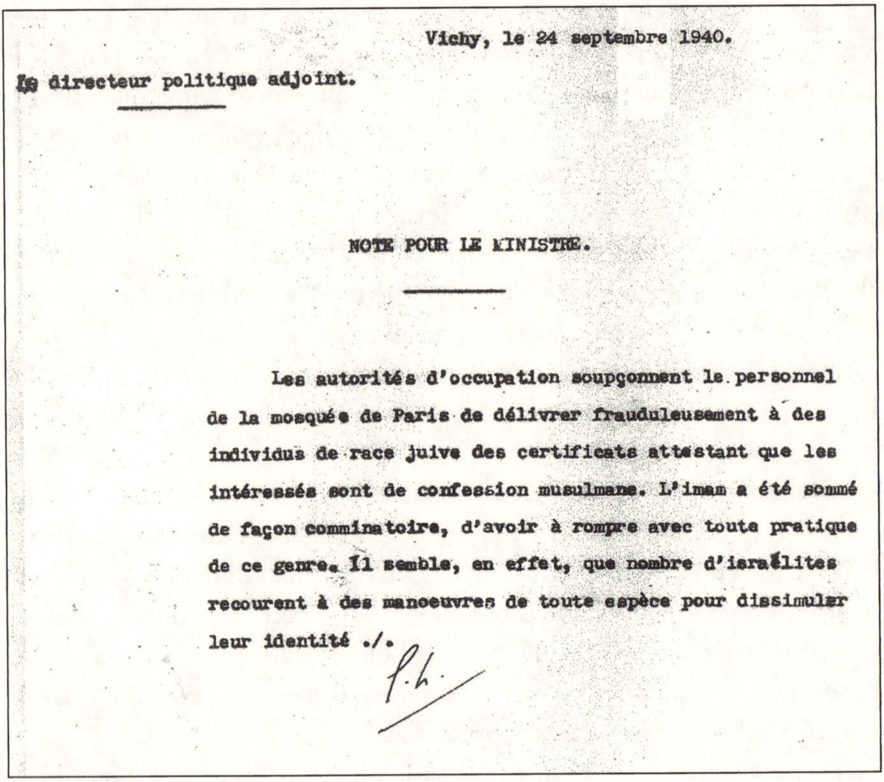

FIGURE 7.1   Dalil Boubakeur handed me this French archival document during our meeting at the Great Mosque of Paris. It attests to the fact that German officers ordered Si Kaddour Benghabrit to stop helping Jews.

There, in black and white, was the smoking gun, documentary evidence that the Germans suspected mosque officials of providing certificates of Muslim identity to Jews. If the problem had caught the attention of the Germans just two months after they took control of France—and only days before the Germans issued their first anti-Jewish ordinance in the occupied zone—then it had to be serious.[12]

My conversation with Boubakeur ended almost exactly where it began, with my host lamenting the fact that a bygone era of brotherly relations between Arabs and Jews had fallen victim to the conflict between Israelis and Palestinians. Boubakeur even summoned a Jewish historian, who arrived so quickly that he seemed to be on retainer, to read out a syrupy letter praising Boubakeur's selfless commitment to religious understanding, communal tolerance, and philo-Semitism. It seemed like a well-rehearsed command performance. The tableau reminded me of one of the more farcical images of Middle Eastern politics: Yasser Arafat hosting his "minister for Jewish affairs," an anti-Zionist rabbi from the ultra-ultra-orthodox Neturei Karta sect. If this was all staged for me, as it certainly seemed to be, then Boubakeur was truly pulling out all the stops. After all, he had clearly prepared for this meeting; before I arrived, he had the file with the French archival document discreetly placed on his desk, ready to be played like a trump card. Here, the head of French Islam was burnishing his pro-Jewish bona fides to me, an American Jewish historian, when the only bona fides I was really interested in occurred six decades ago.

For a further twist on this story, one need look no further than Benghabrit's official biography found on the mosque's Web site.[13] There, the mosque webmaster seems to look more generously on Benghabrit's wartime role than does the current mosque rector. The Web site not only includes praise for the "active role" the mosque played during the war "in saving Jews and resistance fighters," but there is even reference to "the late friend of the mosque, Abraham [*sic*] Assouline, [who] advanced the figure of 1,700 persons." On close inspection, however, it is clear that Assouline's claim is left hanging even there; it is neither endorsed nor rejected. Even in cyberspace, it seems, Boubakeur—like Benghabrit before him—made sure his institution treads carefully between two worlds.

In the end, what matters is the fact that Boubakeur confirmed, with powerful supporting evidence, the fact that at least some Arab officials of the Great Mosque helped some Jews survive the German occupation, most likely at great personal risk. Boubakeur's position, like his life more generally, represents an elegant compromise. According to him, the mosque did hide Assouline and provide up to 100 Jews with certificates of Muslim identity they used to conceal their identities; he left open the possibility that a small number of other Jews found refuge in the mosque; he rejected Assouline's claim that 1,732 Jews and other resistance fighters hid in the tunnels beneath the mosque. "True enough," Yad Vashem's Paldiel wrote me. "The Imam was warned by the authorities. At the same time, it is important to know more [about] what exactly took place in the Mosque and who exactly were involved in giving out false documents to Jews."[14] True enough, the details matter. I asked Boubakeur if he would authorize a more complete search of the mosque's records for further clues about the distribution of certificates of Muslim identity. He said yes. The next day, riots broke out in the Paris suburbs and Boubakeur was at the center of the storm. I never heard from him again.[15]

In my view, the fundamentals of the story matter most. Whether Benghabrit the person or the mosque as an institution deserves recognition for helping to save Jews is less important than the fact that acts of rescue took place. In the heart of Europe, some Arabs saved some Jews during the Holocaust.

Chapter 8

A Crack in the Wall

Y AD VASHEM, Israel's national memorial to the Holocaust, an impressive, awe-inspiring complex of museums and archives in Jerusalem, is hallowed ground, both for the Jewish state and the Jewish people. It is the place that connects the story of a small country on the eastern shore of the Mediterranean to the most heinous crime of history.

The "Righteous Among the Nations" are central to that narrative. These are, by last count, the 21,310 brave, selfless non-Jews who risked their "life, freedom, and safety in order to rescue one or several Jews from the threat of death or deportation to death camps without exacting in advance monetary compensation."[1] They include some of the most famous heroes of World War II, such people as the Swedish diplomat Raoul Wallenberg and the German industrialist Oskar Schindler. Honorees range across nationalities and religions. Every country in Europe is represented, as is just about every Christian denomination. Muslims from Turkey, Bosnia, and Albania are among the righteous, too. Even faraway countries little touched by the Holocaust have their "righteous," like Brazil (Luis Martins de Souza Dantas), Japan (Chiune-Sempo Sugihara), and China (Feng-Shan Ho and Pan-Jun-Shun).[2]

But nowhere on that roll of honor is an Arab recognized for his efforts to save a Jew. When I began searching for righteous Arabs, I had a modest goal—to tell the story of a single Arab who saved a single Jew during the

Holocaust. If I could do this, I thought, then perhaps at least one Arab could take his or her place among the exalted group of the righteous. It did not make sense to me that Arabs were so exceptional, so uniquely inured to recognize human suffering, that not one of them had stood up to protect a Jew facing Nazi, Vichy, or Fascist persecution.

Where Arabs lived, such persecution certainly existed. It did not descend to the level of extermination or even mass killings, but—as in Tunisia—that was more for lack of time than lack of will. Even in that small country, hardly central to German imperial designs, where the Nazis never controlled more than one-third of the country and where Allied bombs fell day and night, the invaders still found the wherewithal to dispatch the SS to set up the scaffolding of the "final solution." This included officially sanctioned torture, confiscation, deportation, and murder. If the tides of war had turned in different directions, this almost surely would have evolved into full-fledged genocide.

Not only did such persecution exist where Arabs lived, but Arabs played a role at every level. Some went door-to-door with the Germans, pointing out Jews for arrest. Others led Jewish workers on forced marches or served as overseers at labor camps. They manned the railroads that took bewildered European Jews deep into the Sahara, prepared the gruel that passed for food at torture sites, patrolled the streets of Bizerte, Tunis, and Sousse, armed with guns and clubs, looking for Jewish escapees. Some took these jobs because they needed the money to feed their families; others volunteered because they were zealous about their work. Every person's story was different, but the common thread that connected them all was their shared undeniability. There can be little doubt that a great many Arabs had the opportunity to protect Jews from what the Germans and their partners were doing to them.

Did not a single Arab rise to the occasion? Were Arabs so different from, say, Ukrainians? Latvians? Albanians? I don't think so. In fact, I believe that Arab behavior during the years when the Germans and their allies controlled their countries was not so different from the behavior of Europeans when Germans and their allies controlled *their* countries. Specifically, most were indifferent; some played a supporting role in the persecution; and a smaller group did what they could to protect Jews, defend them, or just ease their suffering.

With the benefit of time and distance, none of this should really be surprising. But ignorance on this topic, especially among people who should know better, is nearly universal. Wherever I went, whoever I talked with, whenever I broached the subject, I provoked reactions that ranged from skepticism and doubt to disbelief and avoidance.

Perhaps the most unexpected response I encountered in the early stages of research was the level of utter consternation among Arabs who had never before heard of the persecution of Jews in their countries during World War II. Indeed, I have had numerous conversations with moderate, worldly, well-educated Arabs who were astonished to hear the stories I told them. Setting aside whatever role Arabs themselves may have played in this persecution, these contemporary Arabs could not themselves believe that any systematic targeting of the local Jewish community took place in their homeland. These, I should add, are sophisticated, knowledgeable, sympathetic people, without any hint of Holocaust denial in their bones. And I have no doubt they are telling the truth, as they know it. They are merely echoing history as it has been passed down to them, both in its official version and informally, through family recounting.

Typical in this regard is a certain Arab friend of mine, a highly successful senior bureaucrat in a major international organization. When I first broached the topic of my research in conversation, he looked at me with a polite bemusement that, before long, transmogrified into a mix of disbelief and incredulity, with a dash of horror added for good measure. It was bad enough that I, a foreigner, was delving into domestic matters within his country. It was worse still that I was proposing to examine a chapter of his nation's history that he didn't even believe existed. I think he was insulted that I would suggest that what might possibly be a few, isolated incidents of anti-Semitism—they happen everywhere, don't they?—could be stitched together into a well-knit campaign of persecution, especially one to which a significant number of his countrymen contributed. At the same time, I think he was at least slightly concerned for my sanity, or at least my professional reputation.

My friend's hurt response exposed a mild form of the Arab consensus view about the Holocaust in general. In the minds of many Arabs, the murder of 6 million Jews is somehow history's perverse revenge upon the Arabs. The script for this Arab passion play is simple: Jews may have been crucified by warped Christians, but the Christians then sought expiation for their guilt in the creation of Israel. The real suffering, however, was endured by the Arabs, whose land was stolen to make possible Christian atonement for wartime guilt. After all, whatever suffering Jews endured was far away and for a limited time; Arabs suffer in their homeland, for generation after generation.

One by-product of this narrative is what can be called crude Holocaust "celebration." Propagandists of this ilk idolize Hitler and regret only the absence of a "new Hitler" who could complete the unfinished work of the original. That is the view, for example, of a former Moroccan army officer, Ahmed Rami, who founded Radio Islam in Stockholm a quarter-century ago.[3] There are times when this raw delight in the murder of Jews finds its way into mainstream Arab discourse. A favorite outlet for this sort of Hitler worship has been a state-owned newspaper in Egypt called *al-Akhbar.* "Thanks to Hitler, of blessed memory, who on behalf of the Palestinians, revenged in advance, against the most vile criminals on the face of the earth," ran one of many similar editorials. "Although we do have a complaint against him for his revenge on them was not enough."[4] Such Holocaust celebration, however, is not the chief by-product of the Arab Holocaust narrative. There is no legacy of mass murder of Jews in Arab lands, and many Arabs, to their credit, are simply repulsed by the idea; it is just too crude, too coarse, too vulgar to contemplate. As a result, Hitler worship has remained a fringe phenomenon.

The much more common by-product of the Arab Holocaust narrative is Holocaust denial. This phenomenon takes two main forms. Extremists, both Islamic fundamentalists and radical secular nationalists, deny the Holocaust altogether. For them, the death camps, the cattle cars, the macabre scientific experiments, and the chimneys burning with the smell of human flesh are all part of a great ruse designed to win sympathy for the Jews and enable them to steal Palestine from the Arabs. The Holocaust itself becomes the big lie, the greatest conspiracy of all time. The methodical murder of millions of Jews simply did not happen. As a columnist in a state-run Egyptian newspaper wrote in 2002,

> [Jews] are a catastrophe for the human race. They are the virus of the generation, doomed to a life of humiliation and wretchedness until Judge-

ment Day . . . They are accursed, fundamentally, because they are the plague of the generation and the bacterium of all time. Their history always was and always will be stained with treachery, falseness, and lying. Historical documents prove it . . . With regard to the fraud of the Holocaust . . . Many French studies have proven that this is no more than a fabrication, a lie, and a fraud!! That is, it is a "scenario" the plot of which was carefully tailored, using several faked photos completely unconnected to the truth. Yes, it is a film, no more and no less. Hitler himself, whom they accuse of Nazism, is in my eyes no more than a modest "pupil" in the world of murder and bloodshed. He is completely innocent of the charge of frying them in the hell of his false Holocaust!![5]

But in polite Arab company, it is out of bounds to praise Hitler, Auschwitz, or *Mein Kampf*, a best-seller in many quarters of Arab society. Even an uncompromising, absolutist Holocaust denial is frowned upon. It is too shocking, too brazen, too bound up with the conspiratorial mindset from which many moderate, modern-educated Arabs are themselves trying to escape. So, instead of denying the fact of the Holocaust, the more acceptable view is to deny its enormity. The result is that across the Arab world, it is conventional wisdom to discount the numbers of dead and to dispute the magnitude of the horror.

"Holocaust minimization" is so widespread in Arab media and Arab scholarship that to cite a list of examples can have the effect of diminishing the venality of each one. Iran's president Mahmoud Ahmadinejad—who is Persian, of course, not Arab—drew international condemnation in 2005 with his dismissal of the Holocaust as a "myth." But he was not the first Middle Eastern head of state to advance this view. Forty years ago, Arab nationalist hero Gamal Abdul Nasser, president of Egypt, told a German newspaper that "no person, not even the most simple one, takes seriously the lie of the six million Jews that were murdered."[6]

In Western eyes, these men are (or were) radical leaders of outlaw states, and condemnations of their comments were often tinged with a certain bemusement at their crude, boorish ways. It is not so easy to be dismissive of similar views advocated by an Arab leader universally praised for his condemnation of terrorism and his moderate approach to peacemaking—

Yasser Arafat's successor as Palestinian president, Mahmoud Abbas. In 1982, Abbas earned his doctorate from a Soviet academic institution on the basis of a dissertation titled "The Other Side: The Secret Relations Between Nazism and the Leadership of the Zionist Movement." A central thesis of this work is Abbas's accusation that postwar Zionists grossly inflated the number of Jewish victims of the Holocaust for their own political interests. As Abbas argued:

> During World War II, forty million people of different nations of the world were killed. The German people sacrificed ten million; the Soviet people twenty million; and the rest [of those killed] were from Yugoslavia, Poland, and the other peoples. But after the war it was announced that six million Jews were among the victims, and that the war of annihilation had been aimed first of all against the Jews, and only then against the rest of the peoples of Europe. The truth of the matter is that no one can verify this number, or completely deny it.[7]

Here, the death of a young Jewish girl has the same moral standing as the death of her Nazi killer, "sacrificed" by the German people. Since they all have claims on our conscience, German claims—numerically speaking, that is—may be even greater than Jewish claims.

The purpose of Abbas's dissertation, like many others produced by Arab "scholars" of the last half-century, was to inject relativism into the discussion of the Holocaust. Yes, Jews suffered, this argument goes, but in a century that produced genocides in Cambodia, Bosnia, and Rwanda, the mass killings of Jews during World War II were hardly unique. Shrinking the Holocaust down to size lays the foundation for the political objective of Arab Holocaust denial, which is to undermine the Jewish people's claim to a national home in Palestine. If the Holocaust were something unique, in which the world's most advanced society nearly succeeded in wiping out one of the world's oldest peoples, then it stands to reason that the victims deserve special remedy. After all, human history does not reach its nadir every day. Providing special protection for these victims by helping them realize their goal of creating a state of their own, where the eternally homeless would never again live at the whim of the local despot, is a reasonable solution. And

Palestine, site of their ancient homeland, is a reasonable place to do this. But if Jewish suffering were just another in a long list of unfortunate events in which the weak suffered at the hands of the strong, then it loses its specialness. After all, the world cannot indulge every people that has a claim on its conscience.

Less than two years after it was submitted in Russia, Abbas's dissertation was translated into Arabic and published in Jordan, with a new introduction by its author. It is now a standard work, widely cited by Arab students, politicians, and propagandists. In recent years, Abbas has rejected the idea that he ever denied the Holocaust, but he has not publicly repudiated his early work. "I wrote in detail about the Holocaust and said I did not want to discuss numbers," he told an Israeli interviewer when he first became Palestinian prime minister in 2003.

> I quoted an argument between historians in which various numbers of casualties were mentioned. One wrote there were 12 million victims and another wrote there were 800,000. I have no desire to argue with the figures. The Holocaust was a terrible, unforgivable crime against the Jewish nation, a crime against humanity that cannot be accepted by humankind. The Holocaust was a terrible thing and nobody can claim I denied it.[8]

His protestations aside, what Abbas did not publicly admit was the inherently political context of his work. Abbas's dissertation was part of the Palestinian ideological struggle against Israel, a high-stakes battle in which facts and memories are weapons and legitimacy is the prize. Even so, it is important to note that his dissertation was not the product of some youthful indiscretion. Abbas, born in 1935, was forty-seven years old when he received his doctoral degree.

In some quarters, Holocaust denial has morphed into a perverse identification of Jews with Nazis. Ironically, the only time many Arabs recognize the magnitude of the Holocaust is when they ascribe to Jews the role of Nazi persecutors of Palestinians. Take, for example, an article by Abd al-Aziz al-Rantisi, leader of the radical Palestinian terrorist movement Hamas, penned before he was killed in an Israeli counterterror operation. Titled "Which Is Worse: Zionism or Nazism?" Rantisi wrote, "When we compare the Zionists to the Nazis, we insult the Nazis—despite the abhorrent terror they carried out, which we cannot but condemn. The crimes perpetrated by the Nazis against humanity, with all their atrocities, are no more than a tiny particle compared to the Zionists' terror against the Palestinian people."[9] These views are not limited to Islamic radicals; they can be found among Arab mouthpieces of the radical left, too. In August 2005, for example, the pan-Arab satellite channel al-Jazeera aired an interview with a Palestinian-Jordanian author named Dr. Ibrahim 'Alloush. In his broadside against America and Israel, 'Alloush said, "Nazism crossed [Germany's] borders and invaded the territories of others under various pretexts. Nazism oppressed others and exploited the media. Nazism is what the Zionist movement is doing . . . and what the U.S. government is doing. I am not defending Nazism, but Nazism is a thing of the past. The new Nazism of today wears the robes of new liberalism. The new Nazism is imperialistic and Zionist policy, witnessed on a universal and globalized level today." 'Alloush, by the way, lived in the United States for thirteen years and earned degrees from Ohio University and Oklahoma State University.[10]

Such bizarre views aren't just the province of fringe propagandists. On the contrary, they have become mainstream. Egypt's state-owned *al-Ahram* newspaper is the largest in the Arab world. Its editor, appointed by the president of Egypt himself, is often viewed as the mouthpiece of the regime; when he speaks, millions of Egyptians listen. For many years, the editor was Ibrahim Nafie. In August 2002, he was charged by a French court with incitement to anti-Semitism and racist violence for having permitted the publication of an article titled "Jewish Matza Is Made from Arab Blood." That was just one of a long series of anti-Semitic articles that appeared in Nafie's newspaper, including many examples of the most vulgar form of equating Nazism and Zionism. A colleague of mine, David Makovsky, wrote Nafie directly to ask if he would repudiate this horrible accusation. In his reply, Nafie would not budge: "The comparison between Israeli colonial system and Nazism is, in my view, valid. An occupation regime which conducts targeted killing, destruction of agricultural fields, house demolition, arbitrary shooting, administrative arrests of a huge number of Palestinians and the execution of prisoners of war is indeed comparable to Nazi practices against Jewish and non-Jewish communities."[11] In other words, the methodical effort to exterminate an entire people and the terrible, regrettable by-products of a century-long war between Arabs and Jews in Palestine are "comparable."

Compared with much that passes for free media in the Arab world, Nafie's view is rather generous. In popular Arab culture, Zionism is actually considered to be a far more heinous crime than Nazism. On Israeli Independence Day in 2001, 12,374 people participated in a pseudo-scientific "Internet poll" on al-Jazeera satellite television. The question of the day was "What Is Worse: Zionism or Nazism?" The response: 84.6 percent said that Zionism is worse than Nazism; 11.1 percent said that Zionism is equal to Nazism; just 2.7 percent said that Nazism is worse than Zionism. "All that is left for me to do is to congratulate the Zionists for this painful result," intoned Faisal al-Qasim, the most popular anchorman of the channel's most popular talk show. "Indeed, they have excelled in exceeding the Nazis."[12]

The idea that Nazism's brutality, aggression, violence, and cruelty are somehow essential elements of Zionism, that they are as much part of Zionism's DNA as anti-Semitism is part of Nazism's, was brought home to me one day by a good Moroccan friend of mine. This person is a wonderfully open-minded Arab liberal, a battle-hardened campaigner in the fight against the fascism of Islamic fundamentalists and in support of real democracy for her homeland. When we lived in Rabat, the capital of Morocco, she shared Hanukkah latkes at my family's dining-room table; when she visited us back home in Washington, she watched as my kids marched in a Purim parade at our local synagogue. Not a drop of anti-Semitism runs in her blood. One day, talking about Middle East politics, she proudly told me she believes Israel certainly has a right to exist. "It is not Israelis I hate," she said. "It's Zionists." I was perplexed. Zionism, after all, is Jewish nationalism, the movement to create a sovereign state for the Jewish people. How can a thoughtful, caring, highly intelligent person support Israel's right to exist and at the same time denounce Zionism?

The answer, I learned, is in the meaning of the word "Zionism." To her, the definition of the word has almost nothing to do with the quest for Jewish statehood. Zionism means something else. As she matter-of-factly explained, the essence of Zionism is the "purposeful infliction of pain and suffering on Arabs and Muslims." By this definition, to be a Zionist is to harm Arabs and

Muslims; one cannot be a true Zionist without causing continual misery and ongoing torment to the people whose land was stolen to make possible the Jewish state. In this mindset, the failure to achieve peace between Arabs and Israelis is not the fault of missed opportunities, poor leadership, or even the success of the assassins who killed statesmen like Yitzhak Rabin and Anwar el-Sadat. Rather, peace is elusive because Zionists want it so. By this thinking, Zionists can *only* triumph through the intentional killing of Arabs and Muslims.

Though my friend would never draw this conclusion, her definition of Zionism actually gives rise to a neat, though monstrous, equation: Zionism is to Arabs as Nazism is to Jews. There is also a corollary to this: Just as not all Germans were Nazis, so too not all Israelis are Zionists. Regrettably, so this thinking goes, Israel is controlled by Jewish Fascists, the way the Third Reich was run by German Fascists. That distinction makes it possible to endorse Israel's right to exist but to reject the ideology that animates Israel's existence. Everyone thinks of Zionism this way, my friend told me. It is what kids are taught in school, what parents pass on to their children, what believers hear in the mosque.

For me, this was a stunning revelation. If Arabs and Israelis do not even share a common definition of the words they use, then the gulf between them is wider than I feared. If this is how some of the most enlightened Arab liberals think, I realized, then one can only shudder about the rest of Arab society. And if this discourse of denial, this unconscious morphing of Jews and Nazis, reflects a deep-seated Arab view of the world, then imagine how heretical it would be for Arabs to talk about any role—good or evil—they themselves played in the Holocaust.

In Tunisia, where Nazism touched Arabs the most, I learned this lesson well. Several years ago, when I first embarked on research for this book, I had an idea—in retrospect, an absurdly naive idea—to commemorate the sixtieth anniversary of the Allied liberation of Tunisia from German occupation. In my dreams, I could see a solemn ceremony in which Tunisian government officials, Tunisian scholars, Tunisian journalists, Tunisian Jews, and members of the far-flung Tunisian Jewish expatriate community would come together to recall liberation and pay their respects to the memory of those Tunisians—Jews and Muslims—who suffered at the hands of the

Nazis. It did not take long after I arrived in Tunis on my first trip there for reality to intrude. My first interviewee was a renowned historian at a major Tunisian university, an internationally recognized expert on Tunisia's Jewish minority. When I asked him to describe popular reaction in his country the day Allied troops finally "liberated" it from Nazi occupation, a quizzical look appeared on his face. After a moment's hesitation, he replied, "Liberation? What are you talking about? The departure of the Germans meant the return of the French, who were infinitely worse!" To a Tunisian—a Muslim Tunisian—that was undoubtedly true.

Another bracing moment came when I was welcomed into the home of the family of Mohamed Chenik, overlooking the Mediterranean coast in the fashionable seaside village of Sidi Bou Said. Chenik, Tunisia's prime minister during the German occupation, should be a candidate for recognition as a "righteous Arab." A prominent businessman and onetime head of Tunis's Chamber of Commerce, Chenik counted many Jews among his friends and acquaintances; even his personal lawyer was Jewish. According to stories from various historians, he walked a fine and dangerous line between safeguarding Tunisian state interests vis-à-vis the Germans and using his position to warn Jewish leaders of impending arrests by the Germans and securing dispensations from forced labor for the sons of Jewish friends. He very likely saved Jewish lives, perhaps at risk to his own. These were truly noble deeds, regardless of whether they were performed to help a friend, to salve a conscience, or just to pay off an old business debt.[13]

Few Tunisians remember people like Chenik anymore. A pragmatic, worldly man of the Arab liberal age, he was thrown out of office after the Free French replaced Vichy, only to return to the prime ministry to lead negotiations for autonomy from France in the early 1950s. But ever since 1956, when Tunisia received its ultimate independence, the country's nationalist catechism has been to lionize Habib Bourghuiba, father of a free Tunisia, and in the process discard the memory of pre-independence leaders like Chenik. Since I was offering this forgotten statesman a political resurrection of sorts, one that would bring honor to his name, I had fully expected his family to embrace revelations of Chenik's wartime role in defense of Jews. Part of me had even expected his efforts to help Jews to have become part of Chenik family lore, passed on from generation to generation. I even had a delusion that an elderly member of the family might unearth from some dusty closet a diary, some photos, or, most fantastically, a letter of thanks from a saved Jew or some other piece of evidence of Chenik's righteousness. At the very least, I expected the family to thank me for my efforts and enthusiastically support my further search for proof of their patriarch's good deeds.

I was wrong on all counts. The dozen or so members of his family who gathered to listen to my tale were warm, polite, generous, and welcoming. They plied me with tray after tray of delicious sweets and several rounds of coffee and tea. Through the smiles and the handshakes, though, it was clear they wanted nothing to do with my recitation of Chenik's exploits. We never heard stories like this before, they said, and if what I told them were true, he still did nothing special. I was offering them the possibility to have their father (or uncle, or grandfather, as the case may be) remembered by people all over the world as one of the righteous of his generation and they wanted nothing of it. They urged me to return if I had irrefutable proof of their father's acts of kindness, but they had nothing to help me—not a scrap of paper, not a name of a special Jewish colleague, not a single memory. As they showed me the door, figuratively and literally, I was sure they were hoping never to hear from me again.

The Chenik family was not unique. As I pursued my research in one Arab country after another, I witnessed numerous examples of Arabs not wanting to be associated with anything that could suggest that the tentacles of the Holocaust stretched into their own backyard.

In Morocco, for example, I spent hundreds of hours poring over maps, archival documents, and specialty magazines to learn the most minute details of the construction of the Trans-Sahara Railway. This was the never-to-be-completed train whose tracks were laid by European Jews and political prisoners deported by Vichy France to labor camps and torture sites deep in the Sahara Desert. I was convinced that a treasure trove of information lay in the dusty files of the Moroccan National Railroad, which took over the bulk of the defunct Trans-Sahara line decades ago. If I had had access to those files, I believe I would have found lists of "workers"—slave laborers in everything but name—who were technically on the railroad's payroll, as well as invoices from the French and third-country companies that supplied the tractors, earthmovers, and other heavy equipment that made the railroad's construction possible. (As I was later to confirm through other sources, most of the heavy equipment was, unfortunately, American—made by Caterpillar and delivered to French control just months before the fall of France and Vichy's coming to power.) But Moroccan railroad officials were hypersensitive to any connection linking the persecution of Jews and the operation of their railway. Once they found out I was interested in the story of Jews who worked the railroad during the war, they would have nothing to do with me. It didn't matter whether I was trying to wring maintenance documents from a provincial depot chief in faraway Oujda or trying to gain access to official company archives in the capital city of Rabat. The Moroccans were unfailingly polite, as Moroccans are, but unshakable nonetheless. I was later told by a knowledgeable Moroccan friend that the railway people feared I was doing research for a legal claim to be filed by Holocaust victims, like one that had been lodged against the French national railway. If true, it was an irrational fear, given that Morocco—a French protectorate at the time—would bear no legal responsibility for the operation of the Trans-Sahara. But just by raising questions about the operation of the railway during wartime, I had opened a Pandora's box so powerful that it appeared to spook them into a posture of denial.

I confronted this sort of response even when I was looking for confirmation of the most positive Arab connections to the Holocaust, stories of Arabs saving Jews. In Egypt, for example, I labored fruitlessly in search of a phantom Holocaust hero I early on labeled the "Arab Wallenberg."

This story has its origins in the very first interview I undertook for this project, a conversation with an elderly Jewish woman named Dora Wortsman. A friend of a friend had pointed me toward Dora, a warm, affable woman who kept a small, tidy home in Queens, New York. Sitting at her dining-room table in June 2002, Dora told me the fascinating story of her older sister, Risa.

In 1936, when she was just fifteen, Risa went to a dance in her native Vienna and met an Egyptian chemistry student who called himself Harry. (His real name was Hussein.) From that moment, the dashing Harry and the beautiful Risa began what Dora called an "on-off relationship." Two years later, in March 1938, Hitler's armies marched into Austria. The writing was on the wall for Vienna's Jewish community, so Risa and Harry decided to marry. But in order to register their marriage appropriately, the couple had to travel to the Egyptian embassy in Berlin—no easy feat for a Jewish girl and an Arab man, even then. Nevertheless, two months later, the couple succeeded. Though Egypt had its own king and government at the time, it was a British protectorate, similar to Morocco's relationship with France. With an Egyptian marriage certificate in hand, Harry and Risa were eligible for Egyptian travel documents, enabling them to leave Vienna for London. Once there, Harry secured visitor visas for Dora and other members of the family. Most were saved before the Nazis dispatched Vienna's Jews to death camps. "We could not have done this if not for my Arab brother-in-law," Dora said.

For me, the most intriguing character in the story was not Harry, whose righteousness was a product of love for his wife and her family. I was interested in the Egyptian diplomat in Berlin. If this consular officer provided Harry and Risa with an *authorized* marriage certificate that enabled them to escape Nazi-occupied Austria, was it possible that he—or other Arab diplomats—provided Jews with *unauthorized* documents that enabled them to escape, too? After all, a cosmopolitan Egyptian diplomat would surely have come into contact with Jews, both in the multicultural environment of prewar Cairo or Alexandria and in the country where he was posted. Opportunity was virtually certain, and potential motives were numerous. From my perspective, it matters little whether this Arab diplomat helped Jews out of personal friendship, for sheer humanitarianism, or for financial gain. It only matters that he helped Jews.

From that point on, I did everything I could to prove his existence. If true, this "Arab Wallenberg" would have been a pale version of the real Wallenberg, but any act of rescue, in my view, deserves its recognition. So, I began my search in earnest. I contacted associations of Jews from Egypt in search of any wartime stories of Jews receiving travel documents from Arab diplomats. Nothing. I tracked down relatives and colleagues of Arabs who served in European diplomatic posts during the war. Nothing. Finally, I focused my efforts on gaining access to the consular records of Egypt's European diplomatic missions in the years just before the outbreak of full-scale war, in 1939. Those marriage and birth registers, I believed, might list the names of Jews who escaped Europe through the intercession of an Arab diplomat.

I started contacting every Egyptian official I knew. I wrote the foreign minister, a jovial, approachable man whom I knew well from his many years as ambassador to Washington. I never received a reply. I then went to see the national security adviser, a longtime political survivor who had kept an iron grip on the "American file" in Egyptian foreign policy for many years. Though he looked me in the eye and promised to help, I never heard another word from him. I wrote diplomats and journalists, scholars and politicians, and the response was always the same—silence. Though one would think Egyptian officialdom would be eager to unearth proof of a great humanitarian act by an Egyptian diplomat, one that would burnish Egypt's less-than-stellar image in the United States, none of my requests to Cairo ever even received a reply.

In October 2003, I read the Internet transcript of a debate on Middle East politics held before a packed crowd of students at the American University of Cairo and thought I had found a champion who would secure the necessary access for me.[14] The speakers were C. David Welch, the American ambassador, and Ahmad Kamal Aboulmagd, a prominent Egyptian thinker. Aboulmagd is what can be called a "crossover intellectual." On the one hand, he is someone thoroughly at ease in the Western world, a professor of law and former head of the World Bank Administrative Tribunal, a man who served in the early 1970s as Egypt's minister of sport. On the other hand, he is one of Egypt's most respected Muslim theologians, a member of the Supreme Council of Research at Cairo's al-Azhar University, the seat of Sunni Muslim scholarship, and the author of such works as *A Contemporary Islamic Point of View*.

At one point in their sometimes heated exchange, Aboulmagd turned to Welch and said:

You cannot continue to blackmail the world with something so horrible [as the Holocaust]. We all condemn the policies of Hitler and the Holocaust, but enough is enough. There is a moment of saturation and, let me be very blunt on this, world Jewry is in danger, because of the very irresponsible policies of the Government of Israel, supported by some unaware leaders of the Jewish community in the United States. I hate to see a day where there is an unleashing of dormant general anti-Semitism, in

Europe, particularly, and maybe in the United States. But we Arabs are not part of it. We are not part of the Holocaust. We never persecuted Jews.

There was my opening, I thought. Aboulmagd himself had broached the issue of the Arab role in the Holocaust. Such an enlightened man, I believed, would appreciate learning the details of the Holocaust's long reach into Arab lands and might be able to open the right doors in Cairo for me. So, I twice wrote him letters, sent through his son, a diplomat at the Egyptian embassy in Washington, providing details of the Nazi, Vichy, and Fascist persecution of Jews in Arab lands. I asked him to use his good offices to help me gain access to Egyptian consular records of the late 1930s. Noting the absence of an Arab among Yad Vashem's list of "righteous" non-Jews, despite the existence of more than 100 sites of German, French, and Italian labor and punishment camps on Arab soil, I begged for his intercession: "Didn't *some* Arabs help or rescue *some* Jews? And if indeed some Arabs did rescue some Jews, then isn't that a positive, constructive answer to Arab Holocaust denial?" I didn't receive an answer. Then, in 2004, when Aboulmagd came to Washington, I met him and asked him directly for his assistance in gaining access to the files. Yes, he said, he promised to help. As is the case with every entreaty I ever made to an Egyptian, I am still waiting.

***

ARABS, HOWEVER, do not have a monopoly on refusing to come to grips with the Holocaust's long reach across the Mediterranean. One of the strangest phenomena I came across in my research was the extent to which many Jews are unwilling to embrace the fact that Jews of Arab lands suffered persecution, too. Of course, the fate of those Jews never even approached the horror of the Jews of Europe. But that alone does not diminish what Jews in Arab lands had to confront. Built on law and implemented with the full power of the state, their Holocaust-era persecution was far more pervasive than the episodic spasms of violence and retribution those Jews had experienced in previous centuries. Oddly enough, though, Jews living in Arab lands today are themselves among the least likely to press for recognition of their communities' suffering six decades ago.

Just two generations ago, North Africa was home to thriving, robust Jewish communities. Jewish communities from Marrakesh to Tripoli were heirs to a legacy of excellence and achievement in medicine, law, science, philosophy, and commerce that dates hundreds of years before the Enlightenment opened a crack in the door for European Jews. Today, Jews are an endangered species in Arab lands. In Morocco, where 250,000 Jews once lived, there are, at most, 5,000 year-round Jewish residents left, the vast majority concentrated in the country's commercial capital, Casablanca. In Tunisia, once home to nearly 150,000 Jews, there are just about 1,500 remaining, clustered mostly in the cloistered communities on the island of Djerba. In Algeria and Libya, the situation is even worse. An official of the American embassy in Algiers told me in 2005 that there were no Jews living in Algeria; the "head of the Jewish community," he wrote me in an e-mail, lives in Paris. In May 2004, the *Jerusalem Report*, an Israeli magazine, ran a brief but poignant story on the death of Rina Debash, the eighty-something-year-old described as "the last Jew of Libya."[15]

As for the Jews that are left in Morocco and Tunisia, it would be a mistake to view them simply as representative microcosms of the communities they once were. In successive waves of emigration over the last fifty years, propelled by rising anti-Semitism and spillover from the Arab-Israeli conflict, more than ninety-eight out of every 100 Jews in Morocco and Tunisia left their native land. Most settled either in Israel, the French-speaking countries of Europe, or in Canada. The few who stayed remained for various reasons. Some were too rich to leave, tied to the land of their birth by immovable assets and the desire to maintain a certain standard of living. Some were too poor to leave, choosing a known poverty at home rather than risk an unknown poverty abroad. Others, primarily women, were married to Muslim men and opted for a different identity. The few who remained behind constituted just a remnant of these once-grand communities, not a representative sample.

Whatever the reason, when everyone else either chose to relocate to the Jewish state or the liberal democracies, these Jews chose to go from a substantial religious subgroup to a tiny minority in a vast sea of Arabs and Muslims. In comparison to contemporary America, it is as though the size of the Jewish population shrank from Methodists to Taoists in a single generation.

That decision had consequences. The normal pattern of Jewish minorities around the world is to compensate for a natural sense of insecurity through loyalty and patriotism to their host country. Whether in Britain, France, or America, Jews answered the call to fight Nazi Germany by enlisting in huge numbers. In Muslim lands, Jews were already *dhimmis*—subordinate, tolerated, "protected people" who paid special taxes in order to secure the protection of the ruler to defend their lives and property. Generation after generation of *dhimmi* status bred among many Jews a sense that unswerving loyalty to the ruler provided the only safety shield against the capriciousness of the Muslim masses. When the vast majority of Jews left these countries, the tiny group that stayed behind compensated for their lack of numbers by clinging to the local rulers more tightly than ever. The fewer the Jews, the greater the fear, and the more loyal they became.

These are not irrational fears. For centuries, Jews in Arab lands have known that "the golden age of Andalusia" was always less golden in reality than it has become in memory. Yes, they were usually spared the slaughter of York, the star chamber of Spain, or the pogroms of Poland, Russia, and Ukraine, but that relative standard did not lessen the oppressive taxes, daily humiliations, and periodic outbursts of violence that defined daily life for the Jews of Arab lands. In recent years, the rise of radical Islamic extremism has added a modern-day wrinkle to these Jews' age-old search for survival. In 2002, a terrorist group linked to al-Qaeda bombed the Ghriba synagogue in Djerba, killing twenty-one persons. In May 2003, another al-Qaeda affiliate launched five suicide attacks on one night in Casablanca, in which thirty-two bystanders were killed. At least three of the sites—a Jewish cultural center, a Jewish cemetery, and a hotel frequented by Israeli and Jewish tour groups—were Jewish targets. These events highlighted the urgency of the Islamist threat as well as the reality of Jewish vulnerability. Remarkably, not a single Jew was among the dozens killed in these suicide attacks. But the warning was clear.

A few months before the Casablanca bombings, my family was invited to that same Jewish cultural center for a Hanukkah party. I had expected a small affair, with a few dozen people in a stuffy room eating greasy potato pancakes. What I found was a lush, sprawling campus of pools and tennis courts, teeming with more than 300 people. Kids were everywhere. Magicians performed. Food and drink were fresh, hot, and plentiful. And there wasn't a security guard in sight. When I asked one of our hosts, a successful entrepreneur with young kids of his own, why no one even checked our bags or looked in the trunks of our cars, he explained to me the local formula for Jewish survival. "The king protects us," he said in a loud voice. Then, in more hushed tones, he added, "And everyone here has a packed suitcase under the bed."

Today, Jews in Arab lands are fiercely devoted to those countries' rulers. Though the political systems are different—in Morocco, the ruler is a progressive if near-absolute monarch; in Tunisia, he is a tough-minded secular autocrat—the pattern of behavior is the same. Jews are the ruler's staunchest defenders, since anything that tarnishes the ruler's image lessens his ability to protect them. When Western human-rights advocates criticize the regime for rigging some election, arresting some opposition leader, or closing down some newspaper, leaders of the local Jewish community usually rise to its defense. Wary of any change that could dilute the power of local rulers, many Jews quietly but firmly warn visiting journalists and traveling diplomats that it would be dangerous to press rulers to import fashionable cultural trends from the West, like democracy, too quickly. More power to the people means less to the rulers, they argue, and weak rulers would be unable to protect the Jews from the people.

Most of all, these Jews do not complain. Not about taxes, not about petty discrimination, not about glass ceilings that usually keep Jews from ever rising too high, and not about the regime-permitted assaults on Jews as useful scapegoats when they do. As a Jew from America, where Jews complain about everything, and as a frequent traveler to Israel, where complaining is a national pastime, living among the dwindling community of Jews in an Arab land was a jarring personal experience. In public, at least, these Jews just never complained about anything.

To my surprise, this phenomenon even extended to Jewish memories about World War II. When I asked Moroccan and Tunisian Jews in their sixties, seventies, and eighties about the persecution of the war years, a common reply was, "What persecution?" Not a single Moroccan I spoke with even knew (or admitted to knowing) about the presence of labor camps or torture sites for Jews and other political prisoners on Moroccan soil. In

Tunisia, I even met a Jew who had nice memories of the Nazis. Now one of the leaders of the local Jewish community, this man worked as a fifteen-year-old laborer under the glare of German rifles at a construction site during the war. "I honestly have nothing bad to say about the way I was treated," he explained to me. "They [the Nazis] were always fair and courteous." He was not alone. In other conversations, local Jews often protested the notion that their parents or grandparents suffered from rioting, pogroms, vandalism, or other violent acts at the hands of Arabs prior to or during the war. This is a chapter of their history that most Jews in North Africa simply choose to ignore. The Jewish Museum in Casablanca, the only such institution in an Arab country, is a cultural gem tucked away in a leafy suburb. When I asked the curator about spasms of violence launched against the Jewish quarters in Morocco's large cities during the war, he became almost apoplectic; he vehemently denied that any such thing could have occurred. And, as if reading from a script, virtually every Jew I met in Morocco and Tunisia offered a vigorous defense of the role played by local Muslim princes—especially the sultan of Morocco and the bey of Tunis—in protecting "their Jews" (some of which was true, of course). One prominent Jew in Tunis, twice decorated by the Tunisian government for his civic contributions, even tried to convince me that the family of the country's *current* president deserves praise and respect for having hidden Jews during the war. (I didn't hear that claim from anyone else.) To be sure, there were notable exceptions to this trend. In La Goulette, a seaside suburb of Tunis, a wonderful friend and irrepressible historian, Danielle Hentati, took me to visit the new Jewish nursing home, where gendarmes have been posted since the Ghriba synagogue attack in 2002. Inside, a bronze plaque recognizes the generosity of Jewish philanthropists from Baltimore. There, we listened to two octogenarians relive painful memories of surviving the hellish German labor camp in Bizerte. But generally, when I asked Jews in Morocco and Tunisia about their own and their families' experience during the war, the usual refrain was, "It wasn't so bad."

Only after several of these conversations did it occur to me that this sort of denial among Jews of Arab lands is part of their overall strategy for survival. As the last remnant of a people who had mastered the art of living as a tolerated community—sometimes protected, often abused, always second-class—over 1,400 years of Muslim rule, these Jews long ago made peace with their lot. Their silence about the persecution they suffered at the hands of the Nazis and their Vichy or Fascist allies is just the latest in a string of silences. This is the same reflex that prompted Jews in these countries to rush to the microphone after the Djerba and Casablanca bombings to assure the world that "everything's fine." It isn't, of course. Life for Jews in these countries hasn't been fine for a long time, and it is getting worse. Young Jews are voting with their feet. On a walking tour of Tunis in 2004, Professor André Abitbol took me through the halls of the Lycée Carnot, the elite high school that produced generations of the country's doctors, lawyers, and other professionals. At one time, Abitbol said, Jews filled half the student body; he himself served as vice president of the alumni society. But in 2004, he said, only three Jews—all girls—graduated from high school *in the entire country.* At such a pace, the community (outside Djerba, at least) is doomed. The ones that are left have made their choice. To survive requires them to dissimulate, to submerge who they are and what they feel, because honesty would be too painful, too embarrassing, and surely too dangerous.

Jews who did leave these Arab lands have a different approach. Much depends, of course, on when they left—whether it was immediately upon the establishment of the state of Israel in 1948; with independence of their Arab homelands in the 1950s and early 1960s; with the nationalization of property and the Arabization of education that followed soon thereafter; with the spasm of anti-Jewish riots triggered by Israel's lightning victory in 1967; or in the wake of the last major Arab-Israel war in 1973. And much depends on where they went—to Israel, Europe, or North America. But the one thread that ties together these disparate waves of emigration is a sense of grievance. After all, these were the ones who left. Something compelled them to leave, and rarely was the allure of the return to Zion alone powerful enough to do that. Like many emigrant groups, these Jews are nostalgic for their roots. They work hard at retaining old-world customs, holiday recipes, communal ties, and time-honored traditions. Thousands fill the seaside resorts of Tunisia and Morocco each summer or return for annual pilgrimages at the shrines of local Jewish saints. But nostalgia can only smooth over the hard edges of memory. These Jews left for a reason.

Some of them, especially in the earliest waves to leave, arrived in their new homes with memories of persecution at the hands of Germans and their allies that were still fresh and vivid. But part of the rude awakening many of them found in their new homes was the fact that their suffering did not seem to count. Whether in Israel, Europe, or North America, the Holocaust was commonly viewed as "the destruction of the European Jews," as Raul Hilberg had titled his landmark 1961 work. That left no room for Jews of Arab lands. Indeed, like hundreds of thousands of others who suffered during the Holocaust, many of these Jews applied for compensation for their forced labor and restitution for stolen property. They were almost always rejected. For decades, no one recognized them as legitimate claimants. Not France, whose wartime regime was the driving force behind the establishment of labor camps and torture sites in Morocco and Algeria. Not Germany, which sent the SS to persecute Jews in Tunisia. And not Italy, responsible for interning thousands of Jews in Libya.

Saddest of all is the fact that recognizing the status of Holocaust survivors from Arab lands is even a matter of dispute among Jews. In April 2004, two leading experts on Jewish demography prepared reports for the International Commission on Holocaust Era Insurance Claims. As reported by the Israeli newspaper *Ha'aretz,* the scholars were asked a very simple question: How many Holocaust survivors are alive today? Using essentially the same definition of "survivor"—"any Jew who lived for any period of time in a country that was ruled by the Nazis or their allies is called a Holocaust 'survivor' or 'victim'"—they came up with wildly different conclusions. Jacob Ukeles, an American, estimated the number of living survivors at 687,900; Sergio DellaPergola, a professor at Hebrew University, offered the much larger figure of 1,092,000. The main difference was that DellaPergola included Jews from Arab lands; Ukeles did not.[16] These dueling statistics have more than just academic significance. They help to determine the allocation of huge sums in still-to-be-disbursed Holocaust-era compensation funds. With the boost of North African Jews, DellaPergola's statistics showed nearly half of all survivors living in Israel, compared with only 38.5 percent in Ukeles's accounting. Given that tens of millions of dollars are at stake, this is no small difference.[17]

Even to this day, even among Jews, the question of whether Jews in Arab lands suffered pain, loss, and even death at the hands of the Nazis and their allies is not settled. In April 2006, Yad Vashem unveiled its first full-scale curriculum to teach junior high school students about the experience of North African Jews during the war. "More than once when I've led groups [through the museum], I've heard children say the Holocaust only affected the Ashkenazim," Yael Richler-Friedman, head of Yad Vashem's Curriculum Development Department, told an Israeli newspaper. "It's 'common knowledge' at Yad Vashem that it's a problematic issue, and there was a feeling that we couldn't ignore it." Filled with photos and testimonies, the 114-page teaching tool is sure to trigger a great leap forward toward including North African Jews within the Holocaust narrative. But still, there is reluctance. On the key question of whether North African Jews should be viewed as victims of the Holocaust, the curriculum's authors punted; they presented both sides of the issue and avoided coming down on either. In some quarters, the question of the Holocaust's long reach to Arab lands still divides Jews rather than unites them.[18]

But there is hope for change, thanks in large part to two breakthrough, if overdue, accords between the German government and the Conference on Jewish Material Claims Against Germany, which was founded in 1951 to represent the interests of Jewish victims of the Holocaust. In May 2005—sixty-two years after the expulsion of German troops from North Africa—German authorities reached agreement with the Claims Conference, as the advocacy organization is commonly known, to pay compensation to survivors of nearly 100 labor camps in Morocco, Algeria, and Tunisia.[19] Then, after another round of negotiations in June 2006, Germany agreed to include Jewish labor camp survivors as claimants in pension programs provided by the German government. "It is the first time that the suffering of women and children in Tunisia has been recognized, and it is very significant historically," said Gideon Taylor, the Claims Conference's executive vice president.[20]

One of the greatest sources of pride I derive from years of research for this book is the fact that I was able to provide the Claims Conference with supporting evidence that helped convince the German government to right this historic wrong. In August 2003, when I was living in Morocco, I received an e-mail from Dr. Wesley A. Fisher, head of research for the Conference, who had heard about my research through the grapevine of Holocaust historians and asked whether I had specialized information on labor camps in North Africa. Over the next several months, I collected testimonies, photos, and rare registries of camp internees found in obscure archives. "It made my day," the head of the Slave Labor Research Team wrote me when he received documentation I sent him.[21]

When I heard news of the June 2006 agreement, I thought back to my visit with Bizerte veterans at the nursing home in Tunis. At the time, their stories seemed so forgotten amid the global campaign to remember the Holocaust. Today, awareness is growing, thanks to the affirming power of history. To me, there is great irony, and great satisfaction, in the fact that research that began as an effort to find an Arab who saved a Jew played a modest role in making room for forgotten Jews in the collective memory of the Holocaust.

AMONG ARABS, there is also some good news, as the walls of denial, ever so slowly, begin to crumble. In recent years, a growing number of Arabs have begun to chip away at the popular consensus of Holocaust denial. Of course, much of the Arab educated elite always knew this consensus to be false, but many continued to feed it because it was politically useful. To many in the Arab world, denying the Holocaust—or its ideological first cousin, equating Zionism with Nazism—has been an easy and convenient way to sustain popular hatred of Jews and the Jewish state, a useful tool to divert popular attention from such domestic problems as corruption and despotism. Arabs fighting against Holocaust denial do it for precisely the opposite reason, to remove a major psychological impediment to Arab-Israeli reconciliation.[22]

A powerful example of this occurred in September 2000, when Jordan's Prince Hassan bin Talal, brother of the late King Hussein and a descendant of the Prophet Muhammad himself, was among the special guests invited to a ceremony marking the rededication of the lone remaining synagogue in the Polish town of Oswiecem. At one time, Oswiecem had been a majority Jewish town that boasted more than two dozen synagogues and a thriving Jewish community. All that changed when the Germans chose it to become the industrial core of the "final solution," and Oswiecem came to be known by the German name of the death camp built nearby, Auschwitz. A visionary New York philanthropist named Fred Schwartz came across the old synagogue, which had been used as a rug warehouse throughout Poland's Communist rule, and led a campaign to make it the anchor of a bold renewal of Jewish life in the place most widely identified, by Jews and non-Jews alike, as hell on earth. I have known Fred for twenty years, and when I suggested he invite Hassan to the ceremony, he came up with the idea to give this Muslim prince the special honor of nailing the mezuzah into the synagogue's front door. Hassan's very presence gave the event a unique and poignant currency. "After survival comes revival," he said in his deep baritone at the dedication ceremony. "For all of us this is a message that death is not the end of life."[23]

Though Hassan's visit was all about politics—how could such a deep expression of Muslim solidarity with the most horrific of Jewish experiences not be viewed through the lens of politics?—it was not overtly political. Keeping politics out of these sorts of initiatives is no easy feat. Take, for example, the high-profile May 2003 visit to Auschwitz by a joint delegation of 120 Israeli Arabs and 130 Israeli Jews. The brainchild of a tireless campaigner for Arab-Jewish understanding named Emil Shofani, an Israeli Arab who is a Greek Orthodox priest and educator, the purpose of this trip was to sensitize Arabs to the searing experience of Jews during the Holocaust. For months prior to the trip, Shofani organized seminars among Arabs and between Arabs and Jews, both to prepare the travelers for what they would see and to reach a common understanding among them as to why they were going. The latter was summed up in a communiqué issued by the Arab participants two months before they departed for Poland.

> We the undersigned, a group of Arab citizens in Israel, fear the deterioration of relations between Arabs and Jews in our land ... Out of human responsibility, and in the belief that it is possible to change the atmosphere of Jewish-Arab relations in Israel, we are initiating this human initiative. We seek to feel the pain of the other side. The two peoples cannot abandon the path of bloodshed unless each understands and internalizes the pain of the other, and the fears of the other that pushed them to the line of fire, conflict, and war. Understanding this principle, we have decided to delve deeply into history and swim in the Jewish past ....

Even before they left Israel, the delegation—the largest group of Arabs ever to visit Auschwitz—was pilloried by some in the Arab press for being stooges of the Jews. One Greek Orthodox official in Jerusalem vowed to organize a counterpilgrimage of Jews and Arabs to the refugee camps of Sabra and Shatilla in Lebanon, site of a 1983 massacre of Palestinians by Christian militiamen under the protection of Israeli troops.[24] Still, the Shofani group was not deterred. "It's such a powerful experience to be here that I cannot speak," said Nujeidat Shafi, a forty-six-year-old Arab from Israel's Galilee region, after visiting Auschwitz's Death Wall, where thousands of Jewish prisoners were shot to death.[25] The organizers worked hard to keep politics from intruding in the trip, though they knew that politics was, in fact, its whole rationale. As one participant, a woman named Saida Nusseibah, later wrote in an on-line journal, "The pain was too great. You could hear the walls crying, having to absorb the sorrow of what happened to the Jewish Nation. The pain was too vast for words. Yet what of my people's pain?"[26]

For Shofani, politics was the context, but he understood that for the Holocaust to be an essential part of the Arabs' learning experience, participants had to park their personal political views at the door. For Khalid Mahameed, politics is welcome right into the living room.

In April 2005, after spending about $5,000 of his own money, Mahameed officially opened the Arab Institute for Holocaust Research and Education. Housed in his law offices in Nazareth, Israel's largest Arab town and the scene of violent tensions between Muslims and Christians, the museum is, in Mahameed's words, "the first Arab museum of the Holocaust." Its purpose, he said, is for Arabs to understand the intense Jewish need for a safe haven. "Israel was established on the ashes of the Holocaust. This is how Jews around the world see Israel," he told a press conference at the museum's opening. "Understanding the fact that personal security is perhaps the major concern of Jews in Israel and elsewhere, as a direct outcome of the Holocaust and the feelings of persecution, is extremely important." Mahameed is not shy about admitting that for him, the underlying political objective of the museum is that Arabs need to learn about the Holocaust in order to come to grips with their own statelessness. "The Palestinian people paid the price for the Jewish Holocaust in that they became the refugees and remained without a country," he said. "The fact that Jews were murdered in Germany led to Palestinians not having a state." Among Arabs, Mahameed's museum is controversial; neighbors have cursed him in public and his family ostracizes him, he says.[27] Among Jews, the response has been profound ambivalence, which is not surprising for a Holocaust museum founded on the idea that Palestinians bear the burden of Jewish suffering. In a press release, the Anti-Defamation League praised the museum as a potentially "worthy pursuit" but warned it against "propagat[ing] the classic anti-Israel use of the Holocaust and promot[ing] anti-Semitism."[28]

As the intimate strangers to the saga of Israel, there is something appropriate about Israeli Arabs groping for ways to come to grips with the Holocaust. One does not have to accept Mahameed's political conclusions to recognize that Israeli Arabs have had a firsthand experience with Holocaust memory unlike that of any other community of Arabs. Although some of the most grotesque forms of Holocaust denial and identification of Jews with Nazis proliferate in mosques and newspapers just across the Green Line, in the Palestinian towns and villages of the West Bank and Gaza, Israeli Arabs like Shofani and Mahameed—each in his own way—are breaking new ground. Immersed in politics, they do not seek truth for truth's sake alone. But in the scarred, chastened world that Israeli Arabs inhabit—a world that is neither fully Israeli nor fully Arab—that would be too much to ask.

Outside the narrow confines of the Arab-Israeli arena, there are also some positive signs of a countermovement against the coarse Holocaust denial that passes for political debate throughout polite Arab society. In March 2001, for example, the government of Lebanon refused to allow Holocaust "revisionists," including the notorious Institute for Historical Review, to convene an international conference in Beirut. The late prime minister Rafik Hariri banned the event after a group of fourteen prominent Arab intellectuals, hailing from Morocco to Syria, signed a letter calling for "this anti-Semitic undertaking" to be canceled.[29] Eventually, peripatetic Arab Holocaust deniers found a venue in Amman, Jordan, where the Jordanian Writers Association, a rabidly anti-Israel group, played host to the conference in May 2001. It is not news that the revisionists eventually found a home in some Arab capital, though the fact that they ended up in one of just two Arab countries to have a peace treaty with

Israel says much about the depth of that peace. What is newsworthy is that a coalition of Arab intellectuals and Arab politicians was brave enough to force them to search for one.

In capsule form, the debate among Arab intellectuals on the appropriate response to Holocaust denial can be found on the Web site of a fascinating on-line initiative called the Legacy Project, which describes itself as "a global exchange on the enduring consequences of the many historical tragedies of the 20th century." In 2001, the project posted a "virtual symposium" on the theme of "the Holocaust, seen from the Arab world."[30] Three Arab intellectuals contributed essays. Rami G. Khouri, a Jordanian Christian who spent his formative years in the United States, offers the realist view that Arabs need to come to grips with the Holocaust not because of some moral imperative but because failure to do so would put them at a global disadvantage. "The reality is that, in the mass media and most corridors of political power, we in the Arab World continue to be judged heavily on the basis of our attitudes and policies towards Israel and the modern Jewish experience," he writes. "This is irritating and even offensive to most people in the Arab World, but it remains an inescapable fact that we are better advised to address than simply to curse." In contrast, Abdou Filaly-Ansari, a liberal Muslim theologian from Morocco, presents the enlightened view that Arabs need to remedy the fact that "the Holocaust has a 'disturbed' presence in contemporary Arab opinion . . . It is a kind of non-event, and is sunk within a larger historical context, as one of many episodes of comparable size and meaning." But the most stunning of all is an essay by Anwar Chemseddine, the pseudonym of a professor of English at a university in North Africa. Titled "The Arabs' View of the Holocaust Is Indeed Troubled," it is no wonder that Chemseddine decided to write under a false name.

His thunderous essay rails against Khouri's view that the entire debate about the Holocaust and Holocaust denial is a fringe issue, important only to small groups on the political margins. On the contrary, Chemseddine argues that if Arabs are finally to escape centuries of closed-mindedness and truly engage the modern world, it is essential that they first recognize the universality of the Holocaust. "The genocide's principal significance today is that it stands out as the archetype of the crime against humanity," he writes. "It is this crucial relationship between the Holocaust and modernity that Arab opinion fails to understand . . . The Holocaust is not Europeans killing off 'their Jews' (a calamity restricted to Europe, as is often heard), but a horrific event that must engage all humanity precisely because it is a crime against humanity." At the conclusion of his essay, Chemseddine makes a startling statement that I have never seen another Arab make, before or since. Arabs not only *should* engage the Holocaust out of a commitment to universal values, he argues, but they *must* engage it if efforts at reform within Arab societies stand any chance of success. "There are many admirable, high-minded intellectuals in the Arab world fighting and risking their lives for issues like human rights, liberty, democracy, justice, and so on, but it is amazing that no one has thought of why and how these issues are pertinent to the Holocaust, nor of why and how reflection on the Holocaust is essential to them," he writes.

He is the first Arab I had ever come across who asserts that Arabs have an interest in discovering the true meaning of the Holocaust not so they can understand Jewish suffering or even so they can connect with the last century's most heinous crime but because the Holocaust experience was, as Chemseddine puts it, "essential to them." Through the good offices of the Legacy Project, I was able to track him down. We not only met each other and became friends, but he proved invaluable in helping me trace the family tree of an Arab rescuer I discussed in an earlier chapter. Still, "Chemseddine" prefers to keep his real name out of this book. He knows that mainstream Arab political culture is just not ready to deal with the likes of him yet. And he is not ready to face mainstream Arab political culture, either.

So far, all these efforts to tear down the wall of Arab Holocaust denial have been based on opening Arab eyes to the facts of twentieth-century European history. No Arab has ever tried to tap into Arab history itself, by telling the story of the Arab encounter with the Holocaust, the details of the Holocaust's long reach into Arab lands, or the human sagas of Arabs who helped Jews facing wartime persecution. For an Arab to explore the Holocaust as Arab history would require great courage. It is no easy task. But it is one that would be made easier if Jews challenged Arabs to face their own history of engagement with the Holocaust. Instead, one of those cultural oddities that Jews and Arabs share is a reluctance to address their common historical memory of the Holocaust's Arab chapter.

This brings me full circle, to the fact that there is not a single Arab among the 21,310 people recognized by Yad Vashem as "Righteous Among the Nations" or, as far as I know, among any of the other memorials established by Jewish institutions to honor non-Jews who risked their lives to save Jews during the Holocaust. Indeed, only recently has the Holocaust experience in Arab lands emerged as a topic of interest and discussion within the Jewish mainstream. It was not until 1997 that Yad Vashem published its first scholarly volume on the wartime persecution of Jews in Libya and Tunisia; three documentaries on the travails of North African Jews finally aired on Israeli television in 2005; schoolteachers only received their first specially designed curriculum on the topic in 2006.[31] If, in some quarters, controversy still swirls around the question of whether Jews who outlasted the Nazi, Vichy, and Fascist persecution in Arab lands merit recognition as "Holocaust survivors," it is no surprise that institutions devoted to Holocaust remembrance, such as Yad Vashem, have not yet begun to grapple with stories of Arabs who may have saved Jews during the war. I understand that Yad Vashem is not a detective agency; it scrutinizes the bona fides of would-be "righteous" but does not hunt for heroes the way Simon Wiesenthal once hunted down villains. Still, that does not obscure the fact that the letter that I twice sent to Ahmed Kamal Aboulmagd, the liberal Egyptian theologian, asking for his help in gaining access to archives that may prove the existence of my still imaginary "Arab Wallenberg" could just as easily have been written to the head of Yad Vashem: "Didn't *some* Arabs rescue *some* Jews? And if indeed some Arabs did rescue some Jews, then isn't that a positive, constructive answer to Arab Holocaust denial?" In my view, the answer to both questions is yes. In the course of research for this book, I came to the sad conclusion that there are two main reasons that no Arabs have been included among the list of the "righteous": first, many Arabs (or their heirs) didn't want to be found, and second, Jews didn't look too hard.

I believe the research for this book only scratched the surface of what can be uncovered about the history of the Arab encounter with the Holocaust, in general, and the role of Arab heroes, in particular. When I started this project, I set out to find one Arab who saved one Jew facing wartime persecution. After many false starts and dead ends, I eventually met that goal and more; these pages tell the stories of several Arabs I believe merit recognition under rigorous definitions of "righteous." Then, in the final days of my last research trip to Tunisia, in October 2005, something curious happened—new leads to stories of Arab rescuers began to fall in my lap so fast that I did not have time to pursue them. When I sat with Khaled Abdelwahhab's daughter in Carthage, for example, my two Tunisian helpers—Hayet Laouani and Ahmed Smaoui—both told me their families hid Jews during the German occupation, but they only knew the murkiest of details. Later that night, as we took a festive Ramadan stroll through the old city of Tunis, I purchased a copy of an obscure biography of a long-forgotten Tunisian physician from the town of Nabeul, a man named Mohamed Tlatli. Among his claims to fame, his biographer noted, was that Tlatli protected Jews during the German occupation by hiding several on his family farm and providing others with medical certificates excusing them from forced labor.[32] Then, the very next day, I spent an hour with award-winning Tunisian filmmaker Abdel Latif Ben Ammar, who told me that he himself had nearly made a movie about Arab shepherds from Tebarka, in western Tunisia, who hid Jews fleeing from German persecution during the war. "It happened all the time," he told me. "Arabs would share what they had with the Jews—their small huts, their meager food, their tattered clothes. And when the Germans would come looking for Jews, the Arabs would say they are their cousins." The film never got made, he said, because nervous post-9/11 investors were just not interested in a story that showed Arabs actually saving Jews. "In France, they told me I was crazy for trying to do a film that showed a poor, illiterate Arab as the good guy and the Germans as the bad guy. After all, they said to me, we French and we Germans are building a partnership in the new Europe."

If I stumbled on all these stories in just my last seventy-two hours in Tunis, then there is still a treasure chest of history waiting to be discovered. But time is short. Witnesses, like Anny Boukris, are dying, and their stories are dying with them. On my last trip to Tunis, I learned that both Grand Rabbi Haim Madar and his neighbor Sidi Chedli Bey, the son of the last hereditary ruler of Tunisia, had died. Typing the words to this chapter, I received an e-mail from London with the sad news that Morice Tondowski, the Polish Jew whose sheer will to survive carried him through the torture of Berguent and Foum Deflah, had died, too. It is commonplace these days to say that there is a race against time to chronicle the memories of Holocaust survivors before they are lost for eternity. As tragic as that would be, those lost memories could never erase the thousands of oral histories, videotapes, and testimonies that have been taken of Holocaust survivors from Europe. But for the dwindling number of survivors from Arab lands, the race isn't even on.[33]

Just as I am convinced that there remains much more to unearth about the Arab encounter with the Holocaust, I am also convinced that growing numbers of Arabs may be ready to listen. In January 2005, I visited Amman, the capital of Jordan, as a guest of the U.S. State Department. My hosts wanted me to talk about U.S. foreign policy, but I had a second agenda: I wanted to talk to Arabs about their role in the Holocaust. Every time I suggested to my handlers that they arrange an occasion for me to deliver a speech on this topic, they politely changed the subject. So, I took matters into my own hands and contacted an old acquaintance, a professor at the University of Jordan, and asked whether he would be willing to host a seminar for me to talk about "the search for Arab heroes of the Holocaust." My acquaintance, himself no stranger to academic controversy, agreed and generously arranged for a roundtable discussion with what he called a "small quality audience." Beyond the tree-lined promenades, the playing fields, and the stone-faced classroom buildings, it is important to note that the University of Jordan is not a typical university, at least by American standards. A sizable number of its 34,000 students are adherents to a radical Islamic fundamentalism and the campus itself is a place where the most innocent event—a female student tutoring a male student; a male instructor offering research advice to a female undergraduate—can be misread and transformed into a frenzy of protest and violence. Therefore, it was with no small measure of trepidation that I went there on a chilly winter afternoon to deliver what may have been the first-ever speech to an Arab audience, in an Arab country, about the Arab role in the Holocaust.

Then, the remarkable happened—nothing. Twenty or so people sat around the seminar table and listened respectfully as I described the deportation of Jews from Europe to Morocco and Algeria, the setting up of labor camps for thousands of Jews in Tunisia, and the typhus-induced deaths of hundreds of Jews at Italian camps in Libya. Many took notes when I told the stories of Arabs whose role was essential to the operation of Nazi, Vichy, or Fascist programs to persecute Jews. They courteously and attentively heard my recitation of the exploits of Arab heroes, such people as Si Ali Sakkat and Khaled Abdelwahhab. And when it came time for me to stop talking and for them to respond, not a single person questioned the facts that I had presented.

To be sure, not everyone agreed with my findings. A number of people disagreed vigorously with the idea that Arabs bore any responsibility for their actions during the war and dismissed any acts of "righteousness" as ordinary human kindness, without any deeper meaning. So, for about an hour, we had a lively debate about the Holocaust's long reach into Arab lands. Imagine that! I had a lively debate with a group of Arab students and scholars, at a major Arab university, in an Arab capital city, on the meaning of the Arab encounter with the Holocaust. It almost seemed like a normal college seminar, but it wasn't, by any means. Together, we all crept through a crack in the wall of denial and took a small step into a new, more hopeful world. It was only a beginning, but it was something. And for me, it was thrilling.

EPILOGUE: A POEM

Catherine Tihanyi was the translator of Michel Abitbol's book, *The Jews of North Africa During the Second World War,* from French into English. Her poem, first published in 1988, is the only one I found that describes the experience of Europeans deported to French labor camps in Morocco and Algeria.

Once upon a time, on the sparkling
shores of the Mediterranean . . .

HEIMATLOV: a stateless person
(Merriam-Webster)

Look upon me
I am Heimatlov
cry the red sands of the desert
to the translator rooted
at the window pane of time
But how can the translator translate
this silence?

———

The snow falls
on the broken circle
of Heimatlov's thatched village
His soft brown eyes
look back in flight
as he zigzags through Europe

His journey's a jagged line on the map
all the way to the port
of voices and suns and ships
where the sea flows so bright
through his thankful fingers
On the other side
the soldiers took him to make a railroad
in a desert camp
Saida, Djelfa, Mangoub,
In-Fout, Bidon, Berguent,
Foum-el-Flam, Fort Cafarelli?
Heimatlov is somewhere
in the small places of the map
of French North Africa
"where the usual mode of punishment
was a hole in the ground
in which the victim had to lie down
5 feet and ¼ long 2 feet and ½ wide"
The translator clutches the calculator
in vain
against the cry
of the red sands
of Fort Cafarelli
where Heimatlov is in the hole
for days
of fire and ice
And the soldiers throw stones:

>   This one's for the pain in my guts
>   This one's for the fear in my heart
>   And this one's for the war
>   which you caused
>   This one's for Roosevelt
>   This one's for Churchill
>   This one's for Hitler
>   And this one's for Stalin
>   This one's for the dad who beat me
>   This one's for the woman who left me

This one's for the world ripped asunder
And this one's for this desert
of exile

Black suns red pain
The mouth a tongue of sand
till scarlet flowers
burst over the ground
over the text
laid out
at the window pane of time

———∞———

The desert winds blow
in the night of Fort Cafarelli
they have crumbled the walls
covered the ground
And faintly the red sands cry:
    I am Heimatlov Heimatlov Heimatlov
    My words are unspoken unspoken unspoken
    Oh Look Upon Me Ye Mighty
    And Despair.

APPENDIX: SITES OF LABOR CAMPS IN TUNISIA, ALGERIA, AND MOROCCO

THE FOLLOWING is a comprehensive list of sites of 104 German, French, and Italian labor camps in Tunisia, Algeria, and Morocco, which includes 93 already recognized by the German Ministry of Finance and 11 for which the Claims Conference is still seeking recognition. In negotiations in 2002, Germany accepted responsibility for Jews interned at six camps in Libya: Sidi Azaz, Bug Bug, Giado, Gharyan, Jefren, and Tigrinna.

TUNISIA
Ain-Zammit
Bir M'Cherga
Bizerte (Biserta)
Bordj Fredj
Boucha
Cap Serrat (Kap Serrat)
Cheylus
Djebel-Chembi*
Djebibinia (Jebibinah)
Djelloula (Djalloula)
Djougar (Djouggar)
Drija, Oued Drija
Dumergue-Frethia
El-Guettar
Enfindaville (Enfidaville)
Gafsa Gare
Goubellat
Jefna (Djefna)

Kasserine
Katach-Baya
Kondas (Kondar)
Ksar-Tyr
Le Kef, Kef
Maa-Abiod
Massicault
Mateur
Michaud
Mohamedia
  (Mohammedia)
Rossignol
Saf-Saf
Saouaf
Sbikha
Sedjenane
Sfax
Sidi-Ahmed Gare
  (SidiAhmed)

Sousse (Ardent au Pic,
  Ardent de Piq)
Sainte Marie du Zit
  (St.-Marie-du-Zit)
Zaghouran (Zaghouan)

ALGERIA
Abdala, Abadla
Aïn-Sefra
Al-Arisha; El Arisha*
Bechar, Clomb-Beachar
Bedeau
Ben-Chicao
Beni Abbes
Berreoaghia,
  Berrouaghia
Boghari, Boghar
Boussuet, Bossuet
Carnot

Cheragas
Cherchel
Constantine
Crampas*
Crampel
Djebel-Felten
Djelfa
Djenin-Bou-Rezk,
Djenin-Bouergh
El-Aricha
El-Guerre, El-Guerrah
Fort Cafarelli
Géryville
Hadjerat-M'Guil
Kenadzan, Kenadsa
Kersas*
Khenchela
Laghouat
Le Kreider
Magenta
Méchéria
Meridija, El Meridj
Qued-Djerch, Qued
Djer
Quargla*

Rezaline, Relizane*
Saïda

MOROCCO
Agdz (Agdt)
Aïn al Quraq (Ain el
Ousak; Ain el Quarak;
Aïn-el-Ourak)
Ain Guenfounda
Aït Amar (bei Qued
Zem)
Azemmour (Sidi-El-
Ayachi)
Berguent
Bou Arfa (Bour-Afra;
Baouârfa)
Bou Denib (Boudnib)
Casablanca
D'Immouzer*
Djérada
El Karib (El Karit)
Erfoud
Foum el Flah
(Foum Defla)
Fqih ben Salh (Fquih

ben Salh) (bei Settat)
In Fout (Im Fout;
Infoud; Imfout;
Qujda-Imfout)
Kanadasa, Kenadsa
Kasbah Tadla*
Mengoub
Midelt*
Missour (Misur)
Moulay Bou Azza*
Oued Akrouch (Oured
Aktesch ; Oued
Akreuch; Oued
Ankrench)
Oued Monod; Monod*
Oued Zem
Settat (Stetat)
Sidi el Ayachi
(Sidi al Ayyashi;
Ayachi bei
Azemmour)
Skhirat
Tamanar
Tendarra (Tandara;
Tendrara)

*Recognition being sought from the German Ministry of Finance, January 18, 2006.

**This appendix is based on http://www.claimscon.org/forms/N_Africa.pdf as of May 31, 2006. It replicates the sometimes idiosyncratic spelling of geographic sites found on the claims conference list.

ACKNOWLEDGMENTS

I STARTED THE RESEARCH for this book nearly five years ago, in the basement of my home in Washington, D.C. In April 2003, my wife, two sons, and I moved to Rabat, Morocco, which became headquarters for the collection of archival files, personal testimonies, and obscure memoirs, as well as the launching pad for our journey into the fringe of the Sahara, in pursuit of labor camps forgotten long ago. I wrote most of the manuscript looking out at the most pristine beach on Morocco's Atlantic shore, leaning uncomfortably over a coffee table in room 34 of the magical Hotel Mirage, on the outskirts of Tangiers. I finally completed the book in a less exotic place, in our new home in Chevy Chase, Maryland. By the time I finished, dozens of people had contributed to this effort. Thanking them, individually, is one of the greatest joys of this entire experience.

From the start, I understood that I needed the advice and counsel of scholars with expertise on the history of World War II, the history of the Holocaust, the history of Jewish communities in Arab lands, and the history of anti-Semitism, especially in the Middle East. I turned to the following people (listed in alphabetical order), all of whom gave generously of their time and insights: Michel Abitbol, Irit Abramski, Lisa Anderson, Rick Atkinson, Robert Attal, Amatzia Baram, Ofra Bengio, Michael Berenbaum, Daniel Brumberg, Eliot A. Cohen, Miriam Cooke, Michael Curtis, Naim Dangoor, Sarah Farmer, Abdou Filali-Ansary, Layton Funk, Israel Gershoni, Sir Martin Gilbert, Harvey Goldberg, the late Gerhard Höpp, Abbas Kelidar, Gudrun Krämer, Michael Laskier, Christine Levisse-Touzé, Bernard Lewis, David Littman, Meir Litwak, Yaacov Lozowick, Léon

Masliah, Albert Memmi, Susan Gilson Miller, Shmuel Moreh, Timothy J. Naftali, Claude Nataf, Mordechai Paldiel, Robert O. Paxton, Denis Peschanski, Renee Poznanski, Walter Reich, Jacob Rosen, Jacques Roumani, Maurice Roumani, Vivienne Roumani-Denn, Claire Rubinstein, Haim Saadoun, Jonathan Sarna, Daniel Schroeter, the late Paul Sebag, Edith Shaked, Claude Sitbon, Kenneth W. Stein, Norman Stillman, Mark Tessler, Yaron Tsur, Seth Ward, Esther Webman, and Peter Wien.

The research for this book extended to a dozen countries on four continents. I am grateful to the many people—both professional researchers and volunteers—upon whom I relied to conduct interviews, translate numerous testimonies and documents into English, and track down obscure records, books, and memoirs. I consider all of them integral parts of my research team. They include: in France, Daniel Catan and Pauline Peretz; in Israel, Daniel Zisenswine, Tomer Zaksenberg, and Elie Furhmann; in the United States, Jeffrey Goldberg (New York and Philadelphia) and Karen Stiller (California); in Germany, Frank Drauschke and his colleagues at Facts and Files; in Britain, Robert W. O'Hara; in Tunisia, Narjes Ben Yeddar; in Morocco, Sylvie Moulin; and in Montreal, interviewer *par excellence*, Naomi Litvack. Zepporah Glass, who interviewed Anny Boukris for me, was fantastic.

Officials, archivists, and historians at many institutions went out of their way to assist me. I am grateful to all for their courtesies. They include (in alphabetical order of their institution): Lyn Slome, American Jewish Historical Society, New York; Jack Sutters, American Friends Service Committee, Philadelphia; Robert Attal and Michael Glatzer, Ben-Zvi Institute, Jerusalem; Karen Taieb, Marcel Meslati, Aurélie Audeval, and Cecile Fontaine, Centre de Documentation Juive Contemporaine, Paris; Jane Yates, The Citadel Archives and Museum, Charleston, SC; Wesley A. Fisher, Mark Masurovski, Warren Green, and the staff of the Claims Conference, New York; Eric Gillespie and Andrew Woods, Colonel Robert R. McCormick Research Center, First Division Museum, Wheaton, IL; Daniel Matignon, Dépôt Central d'Archives de la Justice Militaire, Le Blanc, France; Elena Danielson, Carole Leadenham, and Ronald M. Bulatoff, Hoover Institution, Stanford, CA; Simon Levy, Jewish Museum, Casablanca; Herb Rosenbleeth, Jewish War Veterans, Washington; Amir

Shaviv and Sherry Hyman, American Jewish Joint Distribution Committee, New York; Tish Newland, Karl Marx Museum, London; Mohamed Lotfi Chaibi, director, L'Institut Supérieure d'Histoire du Mouvement National, Tunis; Clifford Chanin, The Legacy Project, Brooklyn, NY; Jim Miller, Le Centre d'Études Maghrébines à Tunis (CEMAT); Colonel Frédéric Guelton, Service Historique de l'Armée de Terre (SHAT), Vincennes, France; Lisa Goodgame, Shoah Foundation, Los Angeles; Claire Rubinstein, Société d'Histoire des Juifs de Tunisie, Paris; Hsouna Mzabi, director of the Tunisian National Library, Tunis; Colonel Chebbi, director of the Tunisian National Military Museum, Ksar Ouerda, Tunis; John Brinsfield and Teri Newsome, U.S. Army Chaplains School; Sara Bloomfield, Arthur Berger, Severin Hochberg, Radu Ioanid, Geoff Megargee, Judy Cohen, Megan Lewis, Laura Green, and Rebecca Erbelding, U.S. Holocaust Memorial Museum; and Mordechai Paldiel, Irit Abramski, and Yaacov Lozowick, Yad Vashem (The Holocaust Martyrs' and Heroes' Remembrance Authority), Jerusalem.

I thank the many people who helped me understand the origin and operation of the Trans-Sahara Railway project. They include Michel Bergeyre, Marie Bruneau, James H. Lide, Meredith Hindley, High Rockoff, and Martin C. Thomas, as well as Jean-Marie Tardy, Christian Biard, and David Menestrier of the French national railway, SNCF; Mohamed Khlie and Mohamed Hajjoubi of the Moroccan national railway, ONCF; and Nicole Thaxton, Caterpillar Corporation. Jim Carmody and Norman Brown offered insights into the non-Jewish internees at Vichy labor camps in North Africa, especially Spanish Republicans. Paul Greenberg helped me connect with his late grandfather, the incomparable Morice Tondowski.

Also, I thank the many Egyptians who assisted me in my search for an "Arab Wallenberg." They include Khairi Abaza, Gehad Auda, Tarek Heggy, Mohamed Hakki, Hussein Hassouna, Samir Rafaat, Omar Sirry, and Carmen Weinstein.

In the course of my work, U.S. diplomats were unfailingly helpful. I would especially like to mention the kindness of C. David Welch, Marc Sievers, Phil Breeden, Magda Siekert, and Michael Koplovsky.

Everywhere I went, I benefited from the intellectual, personal, and material generosity of many people. In Tunisia, I could not have found what I was looking for without the help of André Abitbol, Corinne Boukobza-Hakmoun, Fayçal Cherif, Jacob Halfon, Habib Kazdaghli, Bochra Malki, Oussama Romdhani, Kamal Sakkat, Ahmed Smaoui, and Larbi Snoussi. In Morocco, I appreciated the openness and candor of André Azoulay, Jamaa Baida, Serge Berdugo, Simon Levy, Albert Sasson, Rachid Slimi, and Najat Yamouri. In Paris, Gilles Andréani, Ali Sakkat, Pierre Thénard, Olivier Roy, and Yechiel Bar Chaim went out of their way to help me. In Israel, I am grateful for the kindness, hospitality, and sage advice of many friends, including Dagmar and Ehud Yaari, Sarah and Zeev Schiff, Tami and Guy Frenkel, Shmuel Zaksenberg, and Yaelle Goldschmidt. Along the way, a long list of other friends, acquaintances, and kind strangers offered information and advice, including José Aboulker, Roger Amgot, Bernard Belhassen, Hacène Belkacem, Mario Faivre, Deborah Isser, Charles Lane, André Nahum, Bernard Pauphilet, Catherine Tihanyi, Emile Tubiana, Lionel Uzzan, and W. Howard Wriggins. Many others who helped me asked to remain anonymous and I respect their wishes.

Four women—in Paris, Diane Afoumado; in Tel Aviv, Shira (Chantal) Simhony; and in Tunis, Hayet Laouani and Danielle Laguillon Hentati—stand out for their warm friendship and selfless contribution to this research project. Special thanks to Frédéric Gasquet, one of the kindest souls I have ever met.

I owe a special debt of gratitude to the institution I have called home for the past two decades—The Washington Institute for Near East Policy. My late father-in-law, David Litvack, often told me I had the best job in the world and, as usual, he was right. When I made the presumptuous request to move to Morocco and telecommute to Washington, the Institute's Executive Committee and Board of Trustees acceded magnanimously and supported me every step of the way. I would especially like to thank Fred S. Lafer, president during my time abroad, as well as our two past presidents, Barbi Weinberg and Mike Stein, and our current president, Howard Berkowitz, for their confidence and encouragement. Despite the ocean that separated us, my colleagues at the Institute were absolutely wonderful about maintaining the organization's vibrancy, rhythm, and intellectual productivity. I am particularly grateful to Dennis Ross, who served with distinction as director during my absence; Patrick Clawson, who rose to the challenge of directing our research staff; Nina Bisgyer, who managed the Institute's operations; and Laura Hannah, my friend and co-worker for almost two decades. Throughout, I was lucky to have Marguerite Hellwich and Rebecca Saxton as loyal and efficient executive assistants.

I extend a special thanks to the many Washington Institute research assistants, interns, and staff members who helped me with various aspects of this project since its inception, including Jeff Cary, Ben Fishman, Lauren Gottlieb, Nathan Hodson, Evan Langenhahn, Mark Nakhla, Jason O'Connor, Todd Orenstein, Eric Trager, Robyn Weinstein, Kate Weitz, and Neri Zilber. They are our best and brightest.

Parts or themes of this book appeared previously in articles in *Commentary, Ha'aretz,* and the *Baltimore Sun*, for which I thank, respectively, Neal Kozodoy, Shmuel Rosner, and Richard Gross. I had the opportunity to hone the message of this book in speeches to the Auschwitz Jewish Center Foundation, the Museum of Jewish Heritage, the Center for Strategic Studies at the University of Jordan, and the Institute for the Study of Global Anti-Semitism and Policy at Yale University, for which I thank, respectively, the incomparable Fred Schwartz, Elissa Schein, Mustafa Hamarneh, and Charles Small.

Early on, I decided not to approach Holocaust-related institutions for funding to support the research and travel for this book. The only grant I received was a small but important sum from the Founders Association, Inc., for which I am grateful. Otherwise, this work was totally self-financed, which gives new meaning to the term "labor of love."

Transforming research into a book is no simple task. Dennis Ross, Judith Miller, Jeffrey Goldberg, and Thomas L. Friedman were invaluable sources of advice and access into the world of publishing. My agent, Gail Ross, was helpful and supportive throughout. Peter Osnos, Susan Weinberg, Clive Priddle, and the entire team at PublicAffairs believed in this project and went out of their way to keep a headstrong author happy. Nancy Hechinger, my wonderfully benevolent editor, taught me the value of simplicity. Thanks to her, the passive voice has been banished from this book.

I imposed on Walter Reich, Dennis Ross, Martin Kramer, and Yaacov Lozowick to read drafts of this book, either in whole or in part; their comments, critiques, and suggestions improved the final product immensely. The handsome timeline—researched by R. Scott Rogers and designed by

Dan Kohan—helps readers make sense of what actually transpired and when.

This book, a story of past, present and, perhaps, a more hopeful future, is dedicated to three generations of my family: my parents, Morris and Beverly; my children, Benjamin and William; and my wife, Jennie. From field research to photo credits to copyediting, this book is really a Satloff/Litvack co-production, which has happily described my life for more than twenty years. Jennie, Benji and William, Mom and Dad—I love you all.

NOTES

Introduction

1. For American Jewish historical societies, see http://ajhs.org/academic/ other.cfm; for American Jewish genealogical societies, see http://www.iajgs.org /Member-Index.htm.

2. For museums in Israel, see http://www.ilmuseums.com/; for museums in Arab countries, see links from http://pearlinkonline.pearlinksoftware.com/ arabiclinks/museumspage.htm.

3. Bernard Lewis, "The Revolt of Islam," *New Yorker*, November 19, 2001.

4. See http://arabsat.com/default/fleet/inorbit/26degeast/3A.aspx.

5. Sadiq al-Azm, the world-renowned Syrian philosopher and winner of the Erasmus Prize, Europe's highest award for cultural achievement, offered an additional interpretation that places blame on the power of tribal links. When asked whether it is true that Arab intellectuals can be "bought" easily, he replied: "A critical intellectual might have brothers who are members of the intelligence services, the army or the government, simply because they all originated from a certain privileged village. Family ties are still very important in the Arab World." See http://www.qantara.de/webcom/show_article.php/_c–476/_nr-ël/_p–2/i.html.

6. See Robert Satloff, "Devising a Public Diplomacy Campaign Toward the Middle East: Part II—Core Elements," Policy Watch Number 580, October 31, 2001. See http://www.washingtoninstitute.org/templateC05.php?CID=1458.

7. Based on a review of official records of the U.S. Holocaust Memorial Museum. As museum officials point out, it is possible that other Arab leaders visited the museum, privately or incommunicado, and left no record.

8. In an essay published six weeks after the attacks, I proposed a series of measures for the U.S. government's ideological battle against Islamic extremists. A

special initiative on Holocaust education for Arab students was on my list. See Note 6 above.

9. Email communication from professor Norman Stillman, author of *The Jews of Arab Lands in Modern Times*, June 7, 2002.

Chapter 1

1. Quotations and details of the Scemla-Ferjani story are taken from a pre-publication manuscript of Frédéric Gasquet's new book, *La lettre de mon père: Une famille de Tunis dans l'enfer nazi* (Éditions du Félin, 2006); interview with Gasquet, Paris, October 27, 2005; quotations and details of Ferjani's life are taken from an interview with Mustapha Ferjani, Tunis, May 19, 2004.

2. Cited in Rick Atkinson, *An Army at Dawn: The War in North Africa, 1942–1943* (Henry Holt, 2002), p. 164.

3. "Perhaps no passage written during the war better captured the agony of France and the moral gyrations to which her sons were subject," Atkinson wrote, ibid., p. 165.

4. Ibid., p. 164.

5. According to the Wannsee list, there were 165,000 Jews in occupied France, that portion of the country governed directly by the Germans.

6. See Irit Abramski, Yad Vashem's expert on the Holocaust experience in Arab countries, quoted in *Yehudai tsafon afrikiya b'tkufat ha-shoah* (The Jews of North Africa During the Holocaust Era), an educational curriculum issued by Yad Vashem, 2006, pp. 81–82. It is also the view expressed to me by Professor Robert O. Paxton, coauthor of *Vichy France and the Jews,* in an e-mail correspondence, October 8, 2003. For further on Wannsee and the Jews of North Africa, see Edith Shaked, "The Holocaust: Reexamining the Wannsee Conference, Himmler's Appointments Book, and Tunisian Jews," The Nizkor Project, http://www.nizkor.org/hweb/people/s/shaked-edith/re-examining-wannsee.html.

7. For a breakdown of monthly rations allotted to Europeans, Muslims, and Jews in Morocco in 1942, see Michael Laskier, *North African Jewry in the Twentieth Century* (NYU Press, 1994), p. 65.

8. Gaon and Serels cite a figure of 2,575 for the number of wartime Jewish deaths in Tunisia. Added to this are several hundred Jews who died in Libyan concentration camps, Jews who died in forced labor in Morocco and Algeria, Jews deported to death camps in Europe, and North African Jews stranded in Europe who joined in the fate of European Jews. See the chapters on Morocco and Tunisia in Solomon Gaon and M. Mitchell Serels, eds., *Sephardim and the Holocaust* (Yeshiva University, 1987).

9. On Morocco, see ibid., pp. 95–100; on Algeria, see Jean Laloum, "La déportation des juifs natifs d'Algérie," *Le monde juif* 129 (January–March 1988), pp. 33–48; on Tunisia, see Claude Nataf, "Les juifs de Tunisie face à Vichy et aux persécutions allemandes," *Pardes* 16 (1992), pp. 224–226.

Chapter 2

1. For references to these assessments of student knowledge of World War II, see http://www.ericdigests.org/1992–2/war.htm.

2. Harris Poll, number 31, July 11, 2001.

3. See the U.S. History National Assessment of Education Progress testing results at www.nces.ed.gov/nationsreportcard/ushistory/results, cited at http://www.wethepeople.gov/newsroom/amnesia.html.

4. Bruce Cole, "How to Combat 'American Amnesia,'" *Wall Street Journal*, November 24, 2003.

5. "Thinking about the Holocaust 60 Years Later: A Multinational Public Opinion Survey," March–April 2005, conducted for the American Jewish Committee. For details, see http://www.ajc.org/site/apps/nl/content3.asp?c=ijTI2PHKoG&b=846741&ct=1025513.

6. Norman Stillman, *The Jews of Arab Lands in Modern Times* (Jewish Publication Society, 1991), p. 115.

7. Ibid., p. 119.

8. "Despite the tensions and periodic harassment during the final months of the Rashid Ali regime, the Jewish community of Baghdad experienced no real misfortune," writes Stillman, ibid., p. 117. For a personal account of the *farhud,* see Nissim Rejwan, *The Last Jews of Baghdad* (University of Texas Press, 2004), pp. 126–138. For the opinion that the *farhud* should be viewed as an elemental event of the Holocaust, see the works of Edwin Black, most notably *Banking on Baghdad* (John Wiley and Sons, 2004).

9. No option was ever made available for Moroccan Jews to acquire French citizenship en masse. According to historian Michel Abitbol, the French administration took shelter behind the Madrid Convention of 1880, which established the principle of perpetual allegiance to the sultan. See Michel Abitbol, *The Jews of North Africa During the Second World War* (Wayne State University Press, 1989), p. 9.

10. Cited in ibid., p. 41. On military decorations of Algerian Jews, see Sarah Taieb-Carlen, "The Jews of North Africa," *Canadian Jewish News*, September 25, 2003.

11. By 1941, Xavier Vallat had become head of Vichy France's Commissariat-Général aux Questions Juives, in charge of implementing state-sanctioned

anti-Jewish laws. Quotation cited in Michael Curtis, *Verdict on Vichy* (Arcade, 2003), p. 54.

12. Ibid., p. 45.

13. There are an increasing number of excellent, English-language accounts of the rise of Vichy and its adoption of anti-Semitism as official policy, such as Curtis's 2002 book *Verdict on Vichy*. Michael R. Marrus and Robert O. Paxton's *Vichy France and the Jews* (Basic Books, 1981) remains the gold standard.

14. Of the 106,986 Algerian Jews who enjoyed French citizenship in 1940, only 1,310—just 1.22 percent—retained the privilege after the abrogation of the Crémieux decree; those who remained French citizens usually owed their status to exemptions for wartime valor or injury. See Henri Msellati, *Les juifs d'Algérie sous le régime de Vichy* (L'Harmattan, 1999), p. 70.

15. During the Vichy era, two classes of Moroccan Jews suffered under a sort of legal limbo. First, Moroccan Jews outside of Morocco were declared stateless. Vichy refused to accept them as protected persons, and because Morocco was not functionally independent, it could not act on their behalf. Second, Jews in the Spanish zone were stuck in an undefined legal status, as Spain did not issue passports to them. See Gaon and Serels, *Sephardim and the Holocaust*, p. 95.

16. Marrus and Paxton, *Vichy France and the Jews*, p. 193.

17. Henri du Moulin de la Barthète, October 26, 1946, cited in Curtis, *Verdict on Vichy,* p. 111.

18. Stillman, *The Jews of Arab Lands in Modern Times*, p. 126; Abitbol, *The Jews of North Africa,* p. 63.

19. For details, see Nataf, "Les juifs de Tunisie," pp. 209–210.

20. Abitbol, *The Jews of North Africa,* p. 64.

21. The law extended exemptions only to decorated war veterans, war victims, or those who received special commendation by the state. In Tunisia, where Jews were also prominent in this profession, the 2 percent quota on doctors was amended to 5 percent. For details on the quotas, see ibid., pp. 66–68.

22. Msellati, *Les juifs d'Algérie,* p. 76. According to U.S. diplomats in Algiers, the imposition of a quota on Jewish doctors was "violently criticized by the natives for, in the past, Jewish doctors were about the only ones who were willing to take care of the native sick, particularly in the towns. The situation is especially acute in the Kasbah quarter of Algiers." See the report prepared by the Office of Native Affairs for May 1942, American Consulate-General, Algiers, June 22, 1942, in U.S. National Archives, Record Group (RG) 84/350/48/11/01, 1942:840.1.

23. For the 1941–1942 school year, Jewish enrollment was restricted to a maximum of 14 percent. For the 1942–1943 school year, the limit was then cut in half,

to just 7 percent. This was an especially damaging blow, because Jews constituted 14 percent of the total student population of Algeria, compared to less than 1 percent of students in metropolitan France. See Stillman, *The Jews of Arab Lands in Modern Times*, pp. 126–127. According to statistics compiled by the chief rabbi of Algiers, the rigid quota system forced more than 19,000 Jewish children out of school, including more than 16,000 from elementary school. More than 80 percent of Jewish students—542 out of 652—were expelled from university. See Eisenbeth, 1945, p. 41, cited in Abitbol, *The Jews of North Africa*, p. 71.

24. Abitbol, *The Jews of North Africa*, p. 72; Msellati, *Les juifs d'Algérie*, p. 78, citing Michel Ansky, p. 168.

25. Of 2,638 Jewish civil servants in Algeria, the government fired 2,169. Abitbol, *The Jews of North Africa*, p. 66.

26. Marrus and Paxton, *Vichy France and the Jews*, p. 106. At one point, French officials apparently contemplated a massive expropriation of Jewish bank accounts. In November 1941, Estéva received a "very secret" request from Vichy asking, "as quickly as possible and as secretly as possible, to know how much Jews have in current accounts in banks throughout Tunisia ... Absolute secrecy." See Bonat to Estéva, November 8, 1941, French Foreign Ministry Archives, Guerre 1939–1945 Vichy/Tunisia Series P.

27. Christine Levisse-Touzé, *L'Afrique du Nord dans la guerre, 1939–1945* (A. Michel, 1998), p. 154. See also the case of lawyers in Tunisia. In Tunis, the large majority of lawyers—184 out of 286—were Jews. (Indeed, eleven out of fifteen members of the governing body of the bar association were Jews.) Application of the Vichy quota would have cut the number of Jewish lawyers in Tunis to just six. The French resident-general convinced his superiors to fix a quota of 5 percent, instead of 2 percent, promising to compensate by suspending exemptions for wounded or decorated war veterans. See Estéva to Foreign Minister, October 7, 1941. Also, in Tunisia, Vichy restrictions were never placed on architects, pharmacists, dentists, and midwives. Nataf, "Les juifs de Tunisie," p. 215.

28. Ibid., pp. 215–216. Another example of Estéva's efforts on behalf of Jews was when he urged his Vichy superiors not to abrogate the French citizenship acquired by Tunisian Jews, along the Algerian model. See memo from Estéva to Laval, September 15, 1942, in French Foreign Ministry Archives, Guerre 1939–1945 Vichy/Tunisia Series P. Also, see Abitbol, *The Jews of North Africa*, p. 76.

29. See Doris Bensimon-Donath, *Évolution du judaisme marocain sous le protectorat français* (Mouton, 1968), p. 109; and the report by Dr. Joseph Schwartz, July 1943, American Jewish Joint Distribution Committee Archives (hereafter JDC), Collection 33144, File 434; and Laskier, *North African Jewry in the Twentieth*

Century, p. 63. As a nod to Muslim sensibilities, the forced relocation of Jews was evidently limited to those who had acquired their homes in European neighborhoods after September 1, 1939. See Mohammed Kenbib, *Juifs et musulmans au Maroc, 1859–1948* (Faculté des lettres et des sciences humaines-Rabat, 1994), p. 628.

30. Bensimon-Donath, *Évolution du judaisme marocain sous le protectorat français,* pp. 108–109; Kenbib, *Juifs et musulmans au Maroc,* p. 606, citing Hirschberg, p. 322.

31. Nataf, "Les juifs de Tunisie," p. 204.

32. Laskier, *North African Jewry in the Twentieth Century,* p. 65.

33. A. J. Liebling, *The Road Back to Paris* (Doubleday, 1944), p. 217.

34. Statistics derived from the list of individuals interned or placed under house arrest in the period from July 1, 1940, to November 8, 1942, Tunisian National Archives, Series MN Carton 52–1/1.

35. Marrus and Paxton, *Vichy France and the Jews,* p. 194; on Châtel, see Abitbol, *The Jews of North Africa,* p. 51, and Gitta Amipaz-Silber, *The Role of the Jewish Underground in the American Landing in Algiers, 1940–1942* (Gefen Books, 1992), pp. 145–146.

36. Darlan was Pétain's loyal aide and designated successor. Darlan happened to be traveling through Algiers the night of the invasion, visiting his polio-stricken son. As a result, he was the senior Vichy official to negotiate with Murphy, who was already in Algiers, and Major General Charles W. Ryder, commander of the force that captured the city, the U.S. Army's Thirty-fourth Division.

37. Quoted in Levisse-Touzé, *L'Afrique du Nord dans la guerre,* p. 269.

38. Abitbol, *The Jews of North Africa,* p. 115.

39. Kenbib, *Juifs et musulmans au Maroc,* p. 632.

40. Ibid.

41. For preceding two sentences, see Laskier, *North African Jewry in the Twentieth Century,* pp. 71–72. Also, see the confidential report of the American vice consul in Casablanca, April 17, 1943: "[I]t seems indubitable that there is a systematic persecution of the Jews by the Pasha of Beni-Mellal." U.S. National Archives, Casablanca consulate, confidential files, 1942–1943, 84/350/65/12/7, Box 1.

42. See the file, "The Case of Peter Winkler," in American Friends Service Committee archives, FS/RS/C-NA-Refugees (Information, Reports on Individuals).

43. For a detailed account of the Jewish underground, see Amipaz-Silber, *The Role of the Jewish Underground,* passim. Also, see José Aboulker, "Témoignage: Alger, 8 Novembre 1942," *Le Monde Juif* 152 (September–December 1994), pp. 146–153.

44. Vichy police arrested a dozen of the group's leaders, promptly released the five non-Jews and kept the seven Jews in jail. In early January 1943, British authorities intercepted a letter from Aboulker's daughter, Colette, to a correspondent in London, found in the Public Record Office (hereafter PRO) FO 371/36244.

45. Liebling, *The Road Back to Paris,* p. 228.

46. Ibid., p. 230. In her letter to a correspondent in London, Colette Aboulker wrote: "If the Allies were able to enter Algiers without striking a blow, it was thanks to the heroic action of the hundreds of young patriots who, on 8th November, paralysed the anti-Allied authorities . . . And this is what their reward has been: my father and my brother arrested, chained like criminals and carried off to a concentration camp . . . ." See PRO FO 371/36244.

47. For text of the December decree, see Tunisian National Archives, Series MN Carton 53–1.

48. Balbo-Mussolini correspondence cited in Renzo De Felice, *Jews in an Arab Land: Libya, 1835–1970* (University of Texas Press, 1985), pp. 171–173.

49. From Arbib's unpublished memoir, cited in ibid., p. 359.

50. For details, see ibid., p. 182.

51. Quotations from a series of films on the Holocaust in North Africa that aired on Israeli television in 2005. For details on the films, see *Ha'aretz*, May 4, 2005. Statistics cited in Stillman, *The Jews of Arab Lands in Modern Times*, p. 122.

52. Abitbol, *The Jews of North Africa,* pp. 116–117.

53. As historian Jacques Sabille noted, this was "the method of persecution established by Heydrich in the Polish campaign in 1939." See his *Les juifs de Tunisie sous Vichy et l'occupation* (Édition du Centre, 1954), p. 31.

54. For details, see "Nazis Planned Holocaust for Palestine: Historians," *Boston Globe,* April 7, 2006. The story cites details from new research by German historians Klaus-Michael Mallman and Martin Cueppers.

55. For the text of Estéva's November 24, 1942, note to Rudolf Rahn, German minister plenipotentiary in Tunis, see File 387–35, Centre de Documentation Juive Contemporaine Archives (hereafter CDJC Archives).

56. Nehring's order to furnish Jewish laborers, cited in the files of the Office of the Chief of Counsel for War Crimes, U.S. Army, June 19, 1947, located in File 124–7, CDJC Archives; Rauff quotation cited in Abitbol, *The Jews of North Africa,* p. 122. Also, see the book by Robert Borgel, son of the head of the Tunisian Jewish community, *Étoile jaune et croix gammée: Récit d'une servitude* (Éditions Artypo, 1944), pp. 33–36.

57. Ibid., 39–40.

58. Paul Ghez, *Six mois sous la botte* (Tunis and Paris: SAPI, 1943), pp. 17–18.

59. Borgel, *Étoile jaune et croix gammée,* p. 43.

60. Ghez, *Six mois sous la botte*, p. 16.

61. Ibid., p. 20.

62. Borgel, *Étoile jaune et croix gammée,* pp. 45–53, 61; Ghez, *Six mois sous la botte*, p. 31; Abitbol, *The Jews of North Africa,* p. 124; interview with Professor André Abitbol, Tunis, May 2004.

63. Borgel, *Étoile jaune et croix gammée,* p. 54; Sabille, *Les juifs de Tunisie sous Vichy et l'occupation,* p. 47.

64. Ghez, *Six mois sous la botte*, pp. 114–115, 87–89.

65. Ibid., p. 42.

66. Sabille, *Les juifs de Tunisie sous Vichy et l'occupation,* p. 77; Abitbol, *The Jews of North Africa,* p. 127.

67. Borgel, *Étoile jaune et croix gammée,* pp. 93–95.

68. Sabille, *Les juifs de Tunisie sous Vichy et l'occupation,* pp. 83–89.

69. Ibid., pp. 94–95.

70. Until late in the occupation, Italian Jews themselves were exempt from forced labor, their government having successfully made representations to the Germans to that effect. In the last days of the occupation, when even Frenchmen were ordered to perform labor, the Italian Jews joined in, too. See Daniel Carpi, *Between Mussolini and Hitler: The Jews and the Italian Authorities in France and Tunisia* (Brandeis University Press, 1994), pp. 235–236.

71. Sabille, *Les juifs de Tunisie sous Vichy et l'occupation,* p. 111.

72. Ghez, *Six mois sous la botte*, p. 98; see statistics in Abitbol, *The Jews of North Africa,* p. 134.

73. Eugène Boretz, *Tunis sous le croix gammée* (Algiers: Office Francais d'Edition, 1944), p. 74; Ghez, *Six mois sous la botte*, pp. 102, 126–127, 141; Sabille, *Les juifs de Tunisie sous Vichy et l'occupation,* p. 122.

74. See Rahn's December 22, 1942, description to the German foreign ministry of the fine levied on Jews, cited in Office of the Chief of Counsel for War Crimes, U.S. Army, October 2, 1947, located in File 125–23, CDJC Archives.

75. Sabille, *Les juifs de Tunisie sous Vichy et l'occupation,* pp. 115–119; on the amounts, see Ghez, *Six mois sous la botte*, p. 141.

76. Ibid., p. 151; Abitbol, *The Jews of North Africa,* p. 135.

77. Sabille, *Les juifs de Tunisie sous Vichy et l'occupation,* p. 150.

78. Ibid., p. 126.

79. Ibid., p. 124; Abitbol, *The Jews of North Africa,* p. 135.

80. Ghez, *Six mois sous la botte*, p. 141.

81. On the number of Italian Jews, see Nataf, "Les juifs de Tunisie," p. 204; Sabille, *Les juifs de Tunisie sous Vichy et l'occupation,* pp. 127–129; and Carpi, *Between Mussolini and Hitler,* pp. 198–199.

82. Sabille, *Les juifs de Tunisie sous Vichy et l'occupation,* pp. 145–149. Also, see the fascinating testimony of Abdallah Abassi, a young engineer in Sousse, who supervised 500 Jewish workers tasked with digging ditches to install telephone lines. All 2,000 Jewish laborers at Sousse's Montauzan barracks, he said, wore the yellow star. Interview by Danielle Hentati, April 23, 2005, cited in her private research paper, "Camp d'internement de Sousse, 1942–1943," July 2005.

83. Nataf, "Les juifs de Tunisie," p. 224.

84. Elie Cohen-Hadria, *Du protectorat français à l'indépendance tunisienne* (Cahiers de la Méditerranée, 1976), p. 168; Nataf, "Les juifs de Tunisie," p. 222; interviews with Claude Nataf, Paris, January 2003, and André Abitbol, Tunis, May 2004; Michel Abitbol, *The Jews of North Africa,* pp. 138–140.

85. Nataf, "Les juifs de Tunisie," p. 222.

86. In 2003, I hired the Berlin-based research firm Facts and Files to search German public archives for documents relating to the German occupation of Tunisia. In the voluminous file of documents sent to me, there was no reference to a crematorium. More generally, "it was only possible to find traces about [Rauff's operations] and forced labor camps for Jews in Tunisia," wrote the research company's Frank Drauschke. He cited the "overall problem of scattered and/or totally lost records of the Nazi security and intelligence agencies." See Facts and Files's report to me on research in German archives, October 16, 2003.

87. See, for example, testimony of Léon Bessis, *L'occupation de l'armée allemande à Sousse,* CDJC/SHJT, n.d. Quotation from Charles Sarfati, of Ariana, interviewed in Paris, October 27, 2005. On the Djebel Djeloud debate, see Laskier, *North African Jewry in the Twentieth Century*, pp. 75–76.

88. In the words of a visiting JDC delegate, Dr. Joseph Schwartz, Bizerte "has been bombed out of existence." See his July 19, 1943, report in Collection 33144, File 434, JDC Archives; also, for a total number, see Gaon and Serels, *Sephardim and the Holocaust*, p. 125.

89. Philip Jordan, *Jordan's Tunis Diary* (Collins, 1943), p. 226.

Chapter 3

1. Marrus and Paxton, *Vichy France and the Jews*, p. 68.
2. Ibid.

3. On the origin and development of the Trans-Sahara Railway, see Christian Bachelier, *La SNCF sous l'occupation allemande, 1940–1944* (Paris: Centre Nationale de la Recherche Scientifique, 1996), vol. 1, pp. 171–176; *La Vie du Rail*, February/March/April, 1986; Pascal Bejui, Luc Raynaud, and Jean-Pierre Vergez-Larrouy, *Les chemins de fer de la France d'Outre-Mer. Vol. 2: L'Afrique du Nord—Le Transsaharien* (La Regordane, 1992), pp. 230–245; and Napoleon Ney, "The Proposed Trans-Saharian Railway," *Scribner's Magazine*, vol. 10, July–December 1891, pp. 630–644.

4. Details of Vichy labor camps in eastern Morocco and western Algeria are gleaned from the voluminous documents available in British and American government archives, the archives of the American Friends Service Committee, the archives of the Joint Distribution Committee, and numerous secondary sources. On the fate of Jews in the Foreign Legion sent to these camps, see Zosa Szajkowski, *Jews and the French Foreign Legion* (Ktav, 1975), pp. 83–118, passim.

5. For pictures and testimonies, see PRO file FO 371/36244, March 4, 1943.

6. Golski, *Un Buchenwald français sous le règne du Maréchal* (Éditions Pierre Fanlac, 1945). The author survived a notoriously brutal camp in western Algeria called Hadjerat M'Guil.

7. Oral history interview of Harry Alexander, February 11, 1992, U.S. Holocaust Memorial Museum Library.

8. This number was accepted in 2004 as a basis for restitution by the German government and the Conference on Jewish Material Claims Against Germany. See http://www.claimscon.org.

9. "Barbaric Treatment of Jews and Aliens Interned in Morocco," March 4, 1943, PRO FO 371/36244.

10. Report of Edouard Wyss-Dunant's visit to Berguent, July 29, 1942, JDC Archives, Collection 33144 File 435.

11. See the Morocco page of the International Association of Jewish Genealogical Societies—Cemetery Project, http://www.jewishgen.org/cemetery/africa/morocco.html.

12. Martin Gilbert, *The Routledge Atlas of the Holocaust*, 3rd edition (London: Routledge, 2002), p. 56.

13. André Labry, *Les chemins de fer du Maroc: Histoire et évolution* (Office National des Chemins de Fer, 1998), p. 78. Reference to the "Tandara" labor camp can be found, for example, in *Le martyre des antifascistes dans les camps de concentration de l'Afrique du Nord*, a wartime pamphlet of the left-wing Secours Populaire Algérien, p. 21.

14. Report of Wyss-Dunant's visit to Bou Arfa, July 30, 1942, JDC Archives, Collection 33144, File 435.

15. Report of Wyss-Dunant's visit to Foum Deflah, July 30, 1942, American Friends Service Committee archives, General Files 1942, Refugee Services—ICRC Reports of Refugee Camp Conditions.

16. Quotations from confidential report by Major Kenneth Younger, early 1943, found among North Africa refugee camp reports, in the archives of the American Friends Service Committee, Philadelphia. Younger eventually went on to serve as a Conservative Member of Parliament.

Chapter 4

1. André Nahum, *Le roi des briks* (L'Harmattan, 1992), p. 50.

2. Sabille, *Les juifs de Tunisie sous Vichy et l'occupation,* p. 137.

3. Abraham Tzarfati oral history, Yad Vashem interview no. 3555067.

4. The lyrics—"Allez, allez, je souhaiterais être avec toi, Hitler"—are cited in Yves-Claude Aouate, "Les Algériens musulmans et les mesures antijuives du gouvernement de Vichy," *Pardes* 16 (1992), p. 199.

5. Quotation cited in ibid., p. 199.

6. See, for example, Msellati, *Les juifs d'Algérie,* pp. 91, 97; Sabille, *Les juifs de Tunisie sous Vichy et l'occupation,* pp. 18–21, 137, 140; Levisse-Touzé, *L'Afrique du Nord dans la guerre,* pp. 107, 110.

7. Interview with Gad Shahar, conducted by Shira Simhony and relayed to me by e-mail correspondence, July 30, 2003.

8. Yehoshua Duweib interview, recorded September 13, 1964, in Avraham Harman Institute of Contemporary Jewish History, Hebrew University.

9. Victor Cohen oral history, Yad Vashem interview no. 3562862.

10. Yehuda Chachmon oral history, Yad Vashem interview no. 3562945.

11. Ernest-Yehoshua Ozan interview, recorded September 22, 1964, in Avraham Harman Institute of Contemporary Jewish History, Hebrew University.

12. Quotations cited in Aouate, pp. 193–194.

13. Miriam Levy oral history, Yad Vashem interview no. 3558527.

14. Isaac Jacques Smadja oral history, Yad Vashem interview no. 3760202.

15. Victor Cohen oral history, Yad Vashem interview no. 3562862.

16. E-mail correspondence from Corinne Boukobza-Hakmoun, March 12–14, 2004.

17. Yaacov Zrivy oral history, Yad Vashem interview no. 3562517.

18. Baudouin was impressed by this "charming lesson." See the excerpt from Baudouin's memoirs cited in Robert Assaraf, *Mohammed V et les juifs du Maroc à l'époque de Vichy* (Plon, 1997), p. 140.

19. Kenbib, *Juifs et musulmans au Maroc,* p. 607.

20. Laskier, *North African Jewry in the Twentieth Century,* pp. 71–72; confidential report of the American vice consul in Casablanca, April 17, 1943, U.S. National Archives, Casablanca consulate, 1942–1943, RG 84/350/65/12/7, Box 1.

21. Monthly report of the provisional commander of the Tunis gendarmerie for July 1941, to Vichy, August 7, 1941, French Foreign Ministry Archives, Series P, Tunisia, Quai D'Orsay, Paris.

22. Yehoshua Duweib interview, September 13, 1964, Avraham Harman Institute of Contemporary Jewish History, Hebrew University.

23. Tzvi Haddad oral history, Yad Vashem interview no. 3563297.

24. "Conditions in the North African Prison Camps—Told by Those Released," press release of the International Brigade Association, London, March 3, 1943 (Karl Marx Library file).

25. Testimony on this episode was delivered to the Algiers military tribunal in early 1944. Secours Populaire Algérien. *Le martyre des antifascistes dans les camps de concentration de l'Afrique du Nord,* pp. 7–8.

26. Ibid., p. 12.

27. For reference to Caboche's Arab adjutant Ahmed, see the April 1943 report on Djelfa, CDJC file 385–9, p. 9 (provenance uncertain).

28. Secours Populaire Algérien, p. 15.

29. In a daring ruse, the resourceful local delegate of the central Jewish community, a pharmacist named Maurice Taieb, was eventually able to arrange the prisoners' transfer by claiming a (nonexistent) agreement with German field marshal von Nehring for improved treatment of Jewish workers. See Sabille, *Les juifs de Tunisie sous Vichy et l'occupation*, p. 90.

30. Quotations from a confidential report by Major Kenneth Younger, early 1943, found among North Africa refugee camp reports, in the archives of the American Friends Service Committee, Philadelphia.

31. PRO FO 371/36244, March 4, 1943.

32. After liberation in 1943, Harry was eager to get into the fight against his tormentors. Rather than give him a rifle and send him into battle, British military intelligence had a more important task for him: to hunt down Axis war criminals and bring them to justice. All quotations in this section are from the transcript of Harry Alexander's videotaped oral history interview, recorded February 11, 1992, U.S. Holocaust Memorial Museum.

33. PRO FO 443/43, letter to British authorities, dated February 19, 1943; letter to American authorities, dated December 20, 1942.

34. Abitbol, *The Jews of North Africa,* pp. 145–146. Kenbib presents a similar account in *Juifs et musulmans au Maroc,* p. 632.

35. Annie Rey-Goldzeiguer, "L'opinion publique tunisienne, 1940–1944," in *La Tunisie de 1939 à 1945: Actes du Quatrième Séminaire sur l'Histoire du Mouvement National* (Tunisian Ministry of Education, 1989), p. 141.

36. Estéva to Vichy, August 5, 1940, Quai d'Orsay Archives.

37. Estéva to Vichy, August 9, 1940, Quai d'Orsay Archives.

38. Baudouin to Estéva, August 10, 1940, Quai d'Orsay Archives; Estéva to Vichy, September 27, 1940, Quai d'Orsay Archives.

39. Levisse-Touzé, *L'Afrique du Nord dans la guerre,* p. 145.

40. Tzvi Haddad oral history, Yad Vashem interview no. 3563297.

41. Interview of Yosef Huri, conducted by Tomer Zaksenberg, September 1, 2003.

42. Youssef Mimoun oral history, Yad Vashem interview no. 3564847.

43. Tzvi Haddad oral history, Yad Vashem interview no. 3563297.

44. Estéva to Vichy, May 23, 1941, Secret, Quai d'Orsey Archives.

45. Rey-Goldzeiguer, "L'opinion publique tunisienne," p. 142. The legacy of the 1940–1941 rioting lingered for years, well past war's end. Though the Tunisian government agreed in 1941 to pay financial compensation for the losses incurred by some of the victims, not until 1948 did it reach final agreement with claimants, who by and large accepted settlements amounting to half their original claims. See Tunisian National Archives, Series SG/9–121–125.

46. For details of Mohamed al-Madi, see François de Lannoy, "De la cagoule à la brigade nord-africaine: L'itineraire de Mohamed el Maadi alias 'SS Mohamed,'" *39/45 Magazine* (Bayeux) 80 (1993), pp. 34–38.

47. Very few sources quantify Arab participation in Axis armies. For details of these Arab volunteers, see the work of self-styled historian Antonio J. Munoz, "Lions of the Desert: Arab Volunteers in the German Army, 1941–1945," *The East Came West: Muslim, Hindu and Buddhist Volunteers in the German Armed Forces, 1941–1945* (Axis Europa Books, 2001), pp. 203–238, from which this section is largely derived. The only other substantial study of the topic I ever found was a Spanish work by Carlos Caballero Jurado, *La espada del Islam: Voluntarios árabes en el ejército alemán, 1941–1945* (Garcia Espan, 1990).

48. For Arabs who hosted Gestapo officers in their homes, see Tunisian National Archives, Series MN 13–09/11.

49. Tunisian National Archives, Series MN 13–9/368.

50. The official cited was named A. Blili, secretary to the prefect of the Securité-Général, in Tunisian National Archives, Series MN Carton 13–09/37.

51. Amos Shofan interview, conducted by Tomer Zaksenberg, August 2003, Beersheva, Israel.

52. Jordan, *Jordan's Tunis Diary*, p. 208. German military archives point the finger at the Italians and tell the story of German military police who confiscated money that Arab looters and Italian soldiers stole from Jews in Gafsa and handed it over to a local Arab charity. See Military Archive (Freiburg), RH–26–90, Afrika Division, file no. 61.

53. Ghez, *Six mois sous la botte*, pp. 60–61.

54. Tzvi Haddad oral history, Yad Vashem interview no. 3563297.

55. Maurice Yaish oral history, Yad Vashem interview no. 3558900.

56. Haim Mazuz oral history, Yad Vashem interview no. 3564868.

57. Abraham Sarfati oral history, Yad Vashem interview no. 3555067.

58. Ghez, *Six mois sous la botte*, p. 72.

59. For the file on the case of Victor Nataf, see Tunisian National Archives, Series MN Carton 13–09/68; also, details from interview with former Ariana resident Charles Sarfati, Paris, October 27, 2005.

60. Interview of Amos Shofan, August 2003, Beersheva, Israel.

61. When Cherif el-Okby was killed in an Allied air raid, his death was even announced on Radio Berlin. See Rey-Goldzeiguer, "L'opinion publique tunisienne," p. 148.

62. On Driss and Boujemaa, see a note dated August 31, 1944, in Tunisian National Archives, Series MN Carton 53–2/106; on the shaykh of Oulad Akrim, see the report of the chief of the Gouballat branch of the gendarmerie, June 17, 1943, Tunisian National Archives, Series MN Carton 13/09/141; on leaving from Gabès, see Boretz, *Tunis sous le croix gammée,* p. 72.

63. In Algiers, a man named Mohamed Bouras, president of the Federation of Muslim Scouts and a typist at the French internal security office, was shot for having given documents to a German agent. See Levisse-Touzé, *L'Afrique du Nord dans la guerre*, p. 108. For details of Tunisian collaborators, see Tunisian National Archives, Series MN 52/1/102, MN 52/1/16, MN 13–09/8, MN 13–09/61.

64. See, for example, a January 1943 police report recounting the extortion of 1,500 francs from a Tunisian Jew, Hellal Moumou, by what the officer in charge described as a group of "destouriens," the French-Arabic term for "constitutionalists," meaning Tunisian nationalists. Tunisian National Archives, MN 13–09/47.

65. For the list of persons accused of collaboration with Axis forces in Bizerte, prepared by the chief of the gendarmerie's legal bureau, June 4, 1943, see Tunisian National Archives, MN 13–09/61.

66. See document titled "État les condamnés proposés pour une commutation ou réduction de peine," in Ministry of Foreign Affairs, Maroc-Tunisie, Tunisia series, no. 196, pp. 135–152.

67. Tunisian National Archives, MN 13–09/8.

68. Interview with Mustapha Ferjani, in the Ben Arrous neighborhood of Tunis, May 19, 2004. Includes details from a pre-publication manuscript of Frédéric Gasquet's new book, *La Lettre de mon père;* Félix Chiche, *Livre d'or et de sang: Les juifs au combat, citations 1939–1945, de Bir-Hakeim au Rhin et Danube* (Édition Brith Israël, 1947), pp. 39–40; and Gaon and Serels, *Sephardim and the Holocaust,* p. 125.

Chapter 5

1. For a firsthand account of the Murphy-Weygand Agreement, as the accord was commonly called, see Robert Murphy's memoirs, *Diplomat Among Warriors* (Doubleday, 1964), chaps. 5 and 6; for the official British history of this episode, see W. N. Medlicott, *The Economic Blockade*, vol. 1 (His Majesty's Stationery Office, 1952), chap. 16; more generally, see James J. Dougherty, *The Politics of Wartime Aid: American Economic Assistance to France and French Northwest Africa, 1940–1946* (Greenwood, 1978).

2. E-mail correspondence with Mirella Hassan, May 22, 2003.

3. David Guez interview, January 12, 1965, in the archives of the Avraham Harman Institute of Contemporary Jewry, Hebrew University, Jerusalem.

4. Abraham Cohen interview, Yad Vashem oral history no. 3558528.

5. Ezra Yosef interview, Yad Vashem oral history no. 3558537.

6. Emile Tubiana, unpublished memoir, 2004, p. 19.

7. Victor Cohen interview, Yad Vashem oral history no 3562862.

8. Yaacov Zrivy interview, Yad Vashem oral history no. 3562517.

9. Tzvi Haddad interview, Yad Vashem oral history no. 3563297. Regrettably, Haddad did not name the Arab do-gooder.

10. Interview with André Abitbol, Tunis, May 2004.

11. Victor Kanaf interview, Yad Vashem oral history no. 3564406.

12. Stillman, *The Jews of Arab Lands in Modern Times*, p. 122.

13. Yehuda Chachmon interview, Yad Vashem oral history no. 3562945.

14. "Barbaric Treatment of Jews and Aliens Interned in Morocco," PRO FO 371/36244, March 4, 1943.

15. Jacob André Guez, *Au Camp de Bizerte* (L'Harmattan, 2001), pp. 136–141.

16. See the report on Cheragas-Meridja, July 1943, CDJC 385–387. For more on this, see Jean-Dominique Merchet, "Quand Vichy internait ses soldats juifs d'Algérie," *Libération* (Paris), December 30, 1997.

17. Secours Populaire Algérien, *Le martyre des antifascistes dans les camps de concentration de l'Afrique du Nord*, pp. 11–14. For more on Arabs and Jews at Djenien Bou-Rezg, see André Moine, *La déportation et la résistance en Afrique du Nord, 1939–1944* (Éditions Sociales, 1972), pp. 184, 214–215.

18. "Conditions in the North African Prison Camps—Told by Those Released," press release of the International Brigade Association, London, March 3, 1943 (Karl Marx Library file).

19. The small number of Jews who retained citizenship usually owed this to their extraordinary service to France, such as having been a decorated war veteran. For a breakdown of Jewish citizenship, before and after the abrogation of the Crémieux decree, see Msellati, *Les juifs d'Algérie sous le régime de Vichy,* pp. 70–71.

20. Levisse-Touzé, *L'Afrique du Nord dans la guerre*, p. 107.

21. The 90,000 Arab POWs included 60,000 Algerians, 18,000 Moroccans, and 12,000 Tunisians. On prisoner releases, see Msellati, *Les juifs d'Algérie sous le régime de Vichy,* p. 91; on the POWs, see Levisse-Touzé, *L'Afrique du Nord dans la guerre*, pp. 109–110; on the radio stations, see ibid., p. 107.

22. Quotation cited in Msellati, *Les juifs d'Algérie sous le régime de Vichy,* p. 99. Msellati also noted that when the Crémieux decree was reinstated in 1943, there were no protests by Algerian Arabs. To the contrary, nationalist leaders had confirmed to de Gaulle that the Arabs did not oppose the restoration of French citizenship to the Jews. See pp. 248 and 252.

23. Quotation cited in Aouate, "Les Algériens musulmans et les measures antijuives du gouvernement de Vichy," p. 190. In November 1940, one Arab member of the Algiers municipal council was even courageous enough to protest publicly against Vichy's exclusion of a Jewish colleague from the annual Armistice Day commemoration—one of the most sacred days on the Pétainist calendar—by pointedly refusing to participate (p. 192). For more about Arab attitudes on the cancellation of the Crémieux decree, see Mahfoud Kaddache, "L'opinion politique musulman en Algérie et l'administration française (1939–1942)," *Revue d'Histoire de la Seconde Guerre Mondiale* 114 (1979), pp. 95–115.

24. Testimonials about el-Okbi's efforts on behalf of Jews were offered by Ferhat Abbas and the son of the leader of the Algiers Jewish community. For details discussed in this paragraph, see Aouate, "Les Algériens musulmans," pp. 195–198. Also see Marrus and Paxton, *Vichy France and the Jews,* pp. 194–195.

25. Msellati, *Les juifs d'Algérie sous le régime de Vichy,* p. 79.

26. See, for example, Levisse-Touzé, *L'Afrique du Nord dans la guerre*, pp. 154–155.

27. José Aboulker, "Témoignage: Alger, 8 Novembre 1942," *France 1940–1945: Des juifs en résistance, Le Monde Juif* 152 (September–December 1994), pp. 146–147. Also, one of Aboulker's co-conspirators in the Algiers resistance confirmed to me that two Algerian Berbers—Mohamed Sayah and his cousin Moamar—led another subgroup of saboteurs, the Orleansville cell. Private correspondence from Mario Faivre, handwritten, n.d. They are not listed in the detailed roster compiled by Msellati, *Les juifs d'Algérie sous le régime de Vichy,* pp. 276–281. For further details, see Gitta Amipaz-Silber, *The Role of the Jewish Underground in the American Landing in Algiers, 1940–1942* (Gefen, 1992).

28. The Spanish permitted the rise of even more virulent anti-Jewish and pro-Nazi sentiment in the area of northern Morocco under their control, although at times Franco expressed sympathy with the plight of Sephardic Jews under French control as a way to tweak the French. See Assaraf, *Mohammed V et les juifs du Maroc à l'époque de Vichy*, pp. 141–144, and Abitbol, *The Jews of North Africa During the Second World War,* pp. 79–80.

29. Some ascribe this to a shrewd policy of the French resident-general, Noguès, who thought it wiser to keep Jews in Jewish schools than to have Jewish students expelled from state schools roaming the streets making mischief. See, for example, Laskier, *North African Jewry in the Twentieth Century,* p. 64.

30. Assaraf, *Mohammed V et les juifs du Maroc à l'époque de Vichy,* p. 161. Also, private discussion with Serge Berdugo, head of the Jewish community of Morocco, whose father, also head of the Jewish community, participated in the secret meeting with the sultan, April 12, 2006.

31. For a sympathetic account, see Assaraf, *Mohammed V et les juifs du Maroc à l'époque de Vichy,* pp. 129–133, 161.

32. In one story, a variation on the celebrated but equally apocryphal stand attributed to Denmark's King Christian X, the French resident-general announced that all Moroccan Jews had to wear the yellow Star of David. The sultan replied that the French had better order twenty extra, for him and all the members of the royal family. In another, the Germans informed the sultan that they planned to deport Moroccan Jews to death camps in Europe. According to the story, the sultan

brashly came to the Jews' defense, declaring that none would be deported because all Moroccans are his children. There is no historical basis to these legends. (Regarding the latter, there is no evidence the Germans ever sought the deportation of Moroccan Jews.) See, for example, ibid., p. 161.

33. Michel Abitbol goes even further: "To our knowledge, no anti-Jewish measure was ever suppressed or slowed down as a result of the Sultan's intervention." Abitbol, *The Jews of North Africa During the Second World War,* p. 187. Ironically, the sultan's reputation among certain Muslims has also taken on legendary proportions. See, for example, Eqbal Ahmed, "Questions of Rights," *Dawn* (Pakistan), September 27, 1992.

34. Cited in Abitbol, *The Jews of North Africa During the Second World War,* p. 76; emphasis added.

35. Habib Bourghuiba was an exception. Despite offers of support from the Axis, he never wavered in expressing sympathy for the Allies. See, for example, Levisse-Touzé, *L'Afrique du Nord dans la guerre*, pp. 361–364.

36. For a sympathetic account of Moncef Bey, see Said Mestiri, *Moncef Bey: Tome 1, le règne* (Arcs Éditions, 1998).

37. See Boretz, *Tunis sous le croix gammée*, p. 65.

38. Quotation from Rey-Goldzeiguer, "L'opinion publique tunisienne." Also see Nataf, "Les juifs de Tunisie," pp. 207–208, 225; and Juliette Bessis, "Les États-Unis et le protectorat tunisien dans la Deuxième Guerre Mondiale," *La Tunisie de 1939 à 1945: Actes du Quatrième Séminaire sur l'Histoire du Mouvement National* (Tunisian Ministry of Education, 1989), p. 204; Sabille, *Les juifs de Tunisie sous Vichy et l'occupation*, p. 137; and interview with Nataf, Paris, January 2003.

39. Mordechai Cohen interview, Yad Vashem oral history no. 3543755.

40. Shlomo Barad interview, Yad Vashem oral history no. 3543756.

41. Mathilde Guez interview, Yad Vashem oral history no. 3559094.

42. Gasquet manuscript, p. 21.

43. For example, interviews with Claude Nataf, Paris, January 2003, and André Abitbol, Tunis, May 2004.

44. "Si Ali Sakkat, former beylical minister, lodged sixty Jewish workers at his property in Zaghouan at a critical moment of the battle," wrote Sabille, *Les juifs de Tunisie sous Vichy et l'occupation*, p. 137. A similar account can be found in a book written by the son of the wartime head of Tunisia's Jewish community. See Borgel, *Étoile jaune et croix gammée*, p. 192.

45. Regrettably, no source states precisely when the Jewish escapees arrived at Si Ali's farm so it is unclear how long they remained under his care.

46. Ibid., p. 120.

47. Despite my best efforts, I had no luck finding corroborating evidence in the form of personal testimonies from any of the sixty Jewish escapees.

Chapter 6

1. According to Anny, one of the other Jewish laborers was a man named Zuily, whose son, she said, is Nissim Zvili, former Israeli member of the Knesset who, at the time of this writing, was Israel's ambassador to France. I contacted Zvili in 2003, and he told me that family lore had it that an Arab in Mahdia had helped his family survive the German occupation. When Tunisia and Israel were still on speaking terms, in the mid–1990s, he had tried to find more about his own "Arab hero," but without success.

2. Interview with Dr. Hsouna Mzabi, director of the Tunisian National Library, February 2003.

3. In her interview, Anny even remembered the name of one of the girls who she said committed suicide, which I have refrained from including in this retelling.

4. Anny married a man named Rémy Bijaoui, with whom she had three children before they were divorced. Anny moved to the United States in 1971; Rémy moved to Israel, where he still lives today. In a brief January 2004 interview with my colleague Shira Simhony, he said he had no knowledge of the Boukris family's wartime rescue to the Abdelwahhab farm.

5. See http://www1.yadvashem.org/righteous/index_righteous.html.

6. *Lonely Planet* guide to Tunisia, second edition, 2001, p. 200.

Chapter 7

1. For details, see Levisse-Touzé, "L'Afrique du Nord dans la guerre," pp. 109–110; also, Annette Herskovits, "The Mosque That Sheltered Jews," *Street Spirit* (February 2005), http://www.thestreetspirit.org/Feb2005/mosque.htm. More generally, on German propaganda strategy toward Arabs in North Africa, see the secret telegram from Rudolf Rahn, German minister in Tunis, to Berlin, December 24, 1942, Yad Vashem Archives TR2\N11\1009\E. NG 4882, http://www1.yadvashem.org/odot_pdf/Microsoft%20word%20-%205217.pdf.

2. For details, see Chap. 1, Note 9.

3. Benghabrit's official biography can be found on the Mosque of Paris Web site at http://www.mosquee-de-paris.net/cat_index_41.html. These paragraphs

are drawn also from personal interviews with a knowledgable historian who prefers to remain anonymous.

4. In 1908, for example, the French ambassador in Tangiers praised Benghabrit's "particularly valuable" service and recommended that the foreign minister promote him to vice consul. Letter from Tangiers to Foreign Minister Stephen Pichon, September 28, 1908, Foreign Ministry Archives.

5. Albert Assouline, "Une vocation ignorée de la mosquée de Paris," *Almanach du Combattant*, 1983, pp. 123–124.

6. The communal organization of French Jews (the Conseil Représentatif des Institutions Juives de France, or CRIF) posted a summary of Berkani's film on the organization's Web site, including a reference to Benghabrit's alleged rescue of Jewish children, implicitly endorsing the film's central claim. See http://www.crif.org/?page=articles_display/detail&aid=6185&artyd=5. Also, see "Ces musulmans qui ont aidé des juifs," *Memoires Vives* (magazine of a journalism school in Lille), February 2004, p. 37.

7. See, for example, *al-Watan* (Algeria), November 26, 2005; also, *Libération* (France), July 13, 2005; *La Gazette du Maroc* (Morocco), July 18, 2005; *La Tribune* (Algeria), July 14, 2005.

8. See Chirac's quote in Christopher Caldwell's excellent article "Liberté, Égalité, Judéophobie: Why Le Pen Is the Least of France's Problems," *Weekly Standard,* May 6, 2002. More generally, see Chirac's lengthy comment in an interview with the *New York Times,* September 8, 2002, http://www.elysee.fr/elysee/elysee.fr/anglais/speeches_and_documents/2002–2001/interview_of_president_jacques_chirac_by_the_new_york_times-ellysee_palace-sunday_september_8_2002.14617.html. For a firsthand account by the editor of a Jewish newspaper, whom Chirac scolded for writing about anti-Semitism in France, see the interview with *Tribune Juive* editor Olivier Guland, "Chirac: There Are No Anti-Semites in France," *Arutz-Sheva,* January 13, 2002, http://www.israelnationalnews.com/news.php3?id=16240.

9. Comments by British chief rabbi Jonathan Sacks, delivered to the Washington Institute for Near East Policy, November 28, 2005. For the full transcript, see the PDF linked to http://www.washingtoninstitute.org/html/pdf/sacks–20051128.pdf.

10. Interestingly, Benzouaou is also cited by Assouline as the person who took "considerable risks" by providing Jews with Muslim identity papers. See his article, "Une vocation ignorée," p. 124.

11. E-mail correspondence with Mordechai Paldiel, February 7, 2006.

12. The Germans issued their first explicitly anti-Jewish ordinance in the occupied zone on September 27, 1940, requiring *inter alia* all Jews in the zone to register with the sous-prefecture of their principal residence. See Marrus and Paxton, *Vichy France and the Jews*, pp. 6–7.

13. See http://www.mosquee-de-paris.net/cat_index_41.html.

14. E-mail correspondence with Mordechai Paldiel, February 7, 2006.

15. One person who is as eager as I am to learn more about this story is Karim Sean Ben-Ghabrit Anstey, a descendant of Si Kaddour Benghabrit, who posted a query on a Francophone Web site on Berber culture in June 2006, asking for more information on his famous forebear's role on behalf of Jews during World War II. His message triggered a flurry of responses but, alas, no firsthand testimony from someone who benefited directly from the mosque's protection. See http://zighcult2.canalblog.com/archives/chanteurs__films/index.html, June 2, 2006.

Chapter 8

1. "Righteous Among the Nations" statistics are as of January 2006. See http://www1.yadvashem.org/righteous/index_righteous.html.

2. See http://www1.yadvashem.org/righteous/index_righteous.html. For details, see Martin Gilbert, *The Righteous: The Unsung Heroes of the Holocaust* (Henry Holt, 2003).

3. Rami was eventually forced off the air in Sweden, following his conviction on charges of inciting racial hatred. He still maintains an extensive Web presence. For details of Rami, see his Web site at http://rami.tv. See reference to his call for a "new Hitler" in Robert S. Wistrich, "Muslim Anti-Semitism: A Clear and Present Danger," report to the American Jewish Committee, April 2002. Also see the Anti-Defamation League, "Holocaust Denial in the Middle East: The Latest Anti-Israel Propaganda Theme," 2001.

4. *al-Akhbar*, April 18, 2001.

5. Fatma Abdallah Mahmoud, "Accursed Forever and Ever," *al-Akhbar* (Egypt), April 29, 2002. Translated by Middle East Media Research Institute (MEMRI), May 3, 2002, Special Dispatch Series, no. 375.

6. *National Zeitung*, May 1, 1964, cited in Meir Litvak and Esther Webman, "The Representation of the Holocaust in the Arab World," *Journal of Israeli History* (Spring 2004).

7. Excerpts taken from MEMRI, Inquiry and Analysis Series No. 95 [Archives], May 30, 2002, no. 95.

8. *Ha'aretz*, May 28, 2003.

9. al-*Risala*, August 21, 2003, translated by MEMRI, Special Dispatch— Palestinian/Arab Antisemitism, August 27, 2003, no. 558.

10. al-Jazeera, August 23, 2005. Translated by MEMRI, Special Dispatch— Palestinian Authority/Antisemitism Documentation Project, August 31, 2005, no. 976. 'Alloush's full plan for spreading "historical revisionism" among Arabs and Muslims can be found in an interview with the *Journal for Historical Review,* http://www.ihr.org/jhr/v20/v20n3p–7_alloush.html.

11. Letter from Ibrahim Nafie to David Makovsky, February 26, 2003; courtesy of Mr. Makovsky.

12. al-Jazeera, May 15, 2001, translated by MEMRI, Special Dispatch Series, June 6, 2001, no. 225.

13. For further details on Chenik, see Lisa Anderson, *The State and Social Transformation in Tunisia and Libya, 1830–1980* (Princeton University Press, 1986); Said Mestiri, *Le Ministre Chenik à la poursuite de l'autonomie interne* (Arcs Éditions, 2000), and *Moncef Bey: Tome 1, le règne*; Pierre Rondot, "M'hamed Chenik, pionnier de l'indépendence tunisienne (1889–1976)," *L'Afrique et l'Asie* 111 (1976), pp. 37–40; e-mail correspondence with André Nahum, January 30, 2004; and interviews with Claude Nataf, January 2003, and André Abitbol, May 2004 and October 2005.

14. Originally cached at http://egypt.usembassy.gov/AMBASSADor/qa102003.htm.

15. *Jerusalem Report*, May 31, 2004, p. 10.

16. *Ha'aretz*, April 17, 2004.

17. The full Ukeles report can be found at http://www.claimscon.org/forms/allocations/ An%20Estimate%20of%20the_Ukeles%20ICHEIC_.pdf; the full DellaPergola report can be found at http://www.claimscon.org/forms/allocations/ Review_Della%20Pergola%20ICHEIC_.pdf; also *Ha'aretz,* November 28, 2003.

18. *Yehudai tsafon afrikia b'tkufat ha-shoah* [The Jews of North Africa During the Holocaust Era], Yad Vashem publication, 2006 (in Hebrew); see *Ha'aretz*, April 24, 2006.

19. It may be difficult, however, for any Tunisian camp survivors to meet the six-month requirement, since the Germans only began setting up camps one month into their six-month occupation. As of this writing, eleven camps (five in Algeria, five in Morocco, and one in Tunisia) are still awaiting recognition. A full list of camps in French North Africa is included in the Appendix. Germany had previously accepted responsibility for Jews interned at six camps in Libya: Sidi Azaz, Bug Bug, Giado, Gharyan, Jefren, and Tigrinna. For further details, see the Web site of the Claims Conference, http://www.claimscon.org; also *Ha'aretz*, May 19, 2005.

20. For details of the June 2006 agreement, see http://www.claimscon.org/
?url=article2/negotiations; also, Jewish Telegraphic Agency report, June 14, 2006,
http://www.jta.org/page_view_story.asp?intarticleid=16720&intcategoryid=2.

21. E-mail correspondence from Wesley A. Fisher, August 22, 2003, and Marc
Masurovsky, January 12, 2004.

22. On this "new approach" to Arab views of the Holocaust, see Meir Litvak
and Esther Webman, "The Representation of the Holocaust in the Arab World,"
Journal of Israeli History (Spring 2004).

23. CNN news report, September 12, 2000, cited in http://www.ajcf.org/
article.asp?fldAuto=40.

24. For the communiqué and opposition to the trip, see "An Israeli Arab Initiative
to Visit Auschwitz," MEMRI, April 25, 2003, Inquiry and Analysis Series, no. 136.

25. Associated Press, May 27, 2003.

26. See http://www.midestweb.org/myexperience.htm.

27. *Forward*, April 29, 2005. See the museum's Web site at www.alkaritha.org.
Also, the BBC report on the museum, January 28, 2006, at http://news.bbc.co.uk/
1/hi/world/middle_east/4655242.stm.

28. See ADL press release, March 20, 2005, at http://www.adl.org/PresRele/
IslME_62/4667_62.htm.

29. Associated Press, March 22, 2001; for details of the declaration signed by
Arab intellectuals, see *Le Monde*, March 16, 2001.

30. For the Legacy Project's virtual symposium on Arab views of the Holocaust, see http://www.legacy-project.org/symposium/paper.html?ID=l.

31. On the book, see Irit Abramski-Bligh, *Pinkas Hakehillot Encyclopedia of
Jewish Communities from Their Foundation Till After the Holocaust: Libya, Tunisia*
(Yad Vashem, 1997); on the movies, see *The Unknown Holocaust of North African
Jewry, From Tripoli to Bergen-Belsen* and *Shared Fate*, reviewed in *Ha'aretz*, May 4,
2005; on the curriculum, see Note 18 above.

32. Mohamed Moncef Zitouna, *Docteur Mohamed Tlatli (1890–1943)* (Centre
de Publication Universitaire, 2004), p. 43. Also, *La Presse de Tunisie*, December 25,
2004, cited in M. Pinchon-Falcone and D. Hentati, *Memoires de la Deuxième
Guerre Mondiale en Tunisie*, private publication of the History Club of the Lycée
Pierre Mendès-France, Tunis, 2005.

33. For example, the 52,000 video testimonies included in the archive of the
Shoah Visual History Foundation include just a handful of survivors from camps
in Arab countries. (One of these, coincidentally, is a fascinating discussion with
Morice Tondowski.) Apparently, no interviews have been conducted inside
Tunisia itself. See http://www.lib.umich.edu/help/svha/facts.html.

BIBLIOGRAPHY

Books

Abitbol, Michel. *The Jews of North Africa During the Second World War*. Detroit: Wayne State University Press, 1989.

Abramski-Bligh, Irit. *Pinkas Hakehillot Encyclopedia of Jewish Communities from Their Foundation Till After the Holocaust: Libya, Tunisia*. In Hebrew. Jerusalem: Yad Vashem, 1997.

Amipaz-Silber, Gitta. *The Role of the Jewish Underground in the American Landing in Algiers, 1940–1942*. Jerusalem: Gefen Publishing House, 1992.

Anderson, Lisa. *The State and Social Transformation in Tunisia and Libya, 1830–1980*. Princeton: Princeton University Press, 1986.

Ansky, Michel. *Les juifs d'Algérie du décret Crémieux à la libération*. Paris: Éditions du Centre, 1950.

Assaraf, Robert. *Mohammed V et les juifs du Maroc à l'époque de Vichy*. Paris: Plon, 1997.

Atkinson, Rick. *An Army at Dawn: The War in North Africa, 1942–1943*. New York: Henry Holt and Company, 2002.

Attal, Robert. *Mémoires d'un adolescent à Tunis sous l'occupation nazie*. Jerusalem: Private imprint, 1996.

_____. *Regards sur les juifs d'Algérie*. Paris: L'Harmattan, 1996.

Bachelier, Christian. *La SNCF sous l'occupation allemande, 1940–1944*. Paris: Centre Nationale de la Recherche Scientifique (CNRS), 1996.

Bauer, Yehuda. *American Jewry and the Holocaust: The American Jewish Joint Distribution Committee, 1939–1945*. Detroit: Wayne State University Press, 1981.

Bejui, Pascal, Luc Raynaud, and Jean-Pierre Vergez-Larrouy. *Les chemins de fer de la France d'Outre-Mer. Vol. 2: L'Afrique du Nord—Le Transsaharien*. Chanac: La Regordane, 1992.

Bensimon-Donath, Doris. *Évolution du judaisme marocain sous le protectorat français, 1912–1956*. Paris: Mouton, 1968.

Bessis, Juliette. *La Mediterranée fasciste: L'Italie mussolinienne et la Tunisie*. Paris: Karthala, 1981.

Black, Edwin. *Banking on Baghdad*. Hoboken, NJ: John Wiley and Sons, 2004.

Blumenson, Martin. *Mark Clark*. New York: St. Martin's Press, 1984.

Bortez, Eugène. *Tunis sous la croix gammée*. Algiers: Office Français d'Édition, 1944.

Borgel, Robert. *Étoile jaune et croix gammée: Récit d'une servitude*. Tunis: Éditions Artypo, 1944.

Caballero Jurado, Carlos. *La espada del Islam: Voluntarios árabes en el ejército alemán, 1941–1945*. Madrid: Garcia Espan, 1990.

Carpi, Daniel. *Between Mussolini and Hitler: The Jews and the Italian Authorities in France and Tunisia*. Hanover, MA: Brandeis University Press, 1994.

Chiche, Félix. *Livre d'or et de sang: Les juifs au combat, citations 1939–1945, de Bir-Hakeim au Rhin et Danube*. Tunis: Édition Brith Israël, 1947.

Chouraqui, André. *Between East and West: A History of the Jews of North Africa*. Philadelphia: The Jewish Publication Society of America, 1968.

Clark, Mark W. *A Calculated Risk*. New York: Harper and Brothers, 1950.

Cohen-Hadria, Elie. *Du protectorat français à l'indépendence tunisienne: Souvenirs d'un témoin socialiste*. Nice: Cahiers de la mediterranée, 1976.

Curtis, Michael. *Verdict on Vichy: Power and Prejudice in the Vichy France Regime*. New York: Arcade Publishing, 2002.

Danan, Yves Maxime. *La vie politique à Alger de 1940 à 1944*. Paris: Librairie Générale de Droit et de Jurisprudence, 1961.

De Felice, Renzo. *Jews in an Arab Land: Libya, 1835–1970*. Austin: University of Texas Press, 1985.

Dougherty, James J. *The Politics of Wartime Aid: American Economic Assistance to France and French Northwest Africa, 1940–1946*. Westport, CT: Greenwood Press, 1978.

Eisenbeth, Maurice. *Pages vécues, 1940–1943*. Algiers: Charras, 1945.

Faivre, Mario. *We Killed Darlan*. Manhattan, KS: Sunflower University Press, 1975.

———. *Notes à propos de 1944*. Cannes: Éditions Santa Maria et Gazelle, 1997.

Fellous, Sonia, ed. *Juifs et musulmans en Tunisie: Fraternité et déchirements*. Paris: Somogy and Société d'Histoire des Juifs de Tunisie, 2003.

Gaon, Solomon, and M. Mitchell Serels, eds. *Sephardim and the Holocaust*. New York: Yeshiva University, 1987.

Gasquet, Frédéric. *La lettre de mon père: Une famille de Tunis dans l'enfer nazi*. Paris: Éditions du Félin, 2006. (Citations from pre-publication manuscript.)

Ghez, Paul. *Six mois sous la botte*. Tunis and Paris: SAPI, 1943.

Gilbert, Martin. *The Routledge Atlas of the Holocaust*. Third Edition. London: Routledge, 2002.

_____. *The Righteous: The Unsung Heroes of the Holocaust*. New York: Henry Holt and Company, 2003.

Golski (no first name). *Un Buchenwald français sous le règne du Maréchal*. Paris: Éditions Pierre Fanlac, 1945.

Gosset, Renée Pierre. *Algiers, 1941–1943: A Temporary Expedient*. London: Jonathan Cape, 1945.

Gouvernement Général de l'Algérie. *Exposé de le situation générale des territoires du sud de l'Algérie*. Alger: Imprimerie Officielle, 1947.

Guez, Gaston. *Nos martyrs sous la botte allemande*. Tunis: Paginates, 1946.

Guez, Jacob André. *Au Camp de Bizerte*. Paris: L'Harmattan, 2001.

Hamza, Hassine Raouf. *Communisme et nationalisme en Tunisie de la 'libération' à l'indépendance (1943–1956)*. Tunis: Université de Tunis I, 1994.

Hirschberg, H. Z. *A History of the Jews in North Africa*. Vol. 2. Boston: E. J. Brill, 1981.

Jones, Vincent. *Operation Torch*. New York: Ballantine, 1972.

Jordan, Philip. *Jordan's Tunis Diary*. London: Collins, 1943.

Kaspi, André. *Les juifs pendant l'occupation*. Paris: Éditions du Seuil, 1991.

Kenbib, Mohammed. *Juifs et musulmans au Maroc, 1859–1948, contribution à l'histoire des relations inter-communautaires en terre d'Islam*. Rabat: Université Mohammed V, 1994.

Krämer, Gudrun. *The Jews in Modern Egypt, 1914–1952*. London: I. B. Tauris, 1989.

Labry, André. *Les chemins de fer du Maroc: Histoire et évolution*. Rabat: Office National des Chemins de Fer, 1998.

Lamb, Charles. *War in a Stringbag*. London: Arrow Books, 1977.

Laskier, Michael M. *North African Jewry in the Twentieth Century: The Jews of Morocco, Tunisia and Algeria*. New York: New York University Press, 1994.

Levisse-Touzé, Christine. *L'Afrique du Nord dans la guerre, 1939–1945*. Paris: A. Michel, 1998.

Liebling, A. J. *The Road Back to Paris*. Garden City, NY: Doubleday, Doran and Company, 1944.

Lipstadt, Deborah. *Denying the Holocaust: The Growing Assault on Truth and Memory*. New York: Plume, 1994.

Lonely Planet Guide to Tunisia. Victoria, Australia: Lonely Planet Publications, 2001.

Marrus, Michael R., and Robert O. Paxton. *Vichy France and the Jews*. New York: Basic Books, 1981.

Medlicott, W. N. *The Economic Blockade*. Vol. 1. London: H.M. Stationery Office, 1952.

Melton, George. *Darlan*. Westport, CT: Praeger, 1988.

Memmi, Albert. *Jews and Arabs*. Chicago: J. Philip O'Hara, 1975.

———. *The Pillar of Salt*. Boston: Beacon Press, 1992.

Mestiri, Said. *Moncef Bey: Tome 1, le règne*. Tunis: Arcs Éditions, 2nd ed., 1998.

———. *Moncef Bey: Tome 2, chronique des années d'exil*. Tunis: Arcs Éditions, 1990.

———. *Le Ministre Chenik à la poursuite de l'autonomie interne*. Tunis: Arcs Éditions, 2000.

Moine, André. *La déportation et la résistance en Afrique du Nord (1939–1944)*. Paris: Éditions Sociales, 1972.

Msellati, Henri. *Les juifs d'Algérie sous le régime de Vichy: 10 juillet 1940–3 Novembre 1943*. Paris: L'Harmattan, 1999.

Munoz, Antonio. *The East Came West: Muslim, Hindu and Buddhist Volunteers in the German Armed Forces, 1941–1945*. Bayside, NY: Axis Europa Books, 2001.

Murphy, Robert. *Diplomat Among Warriors*. New York: Doubleday, 1964.

Nahum, André. *Le roi de briks*. Paris: L'Harmattan, 1992.

Pendar, Kenneth. *Adventure in Diplomacy*. New York: Dodd, Mead and Company, 1945.

Rejwan, Nissim. *The Last Jews of Baghdad*. Austin: University of Texas Press, 2004.

Resner, Lawrence. *Eternal Stranger: The Plight of the Modern Jew from Baghdad to Casablanca*. Garden City, NY: Doubleday, 1951.

Sabille, Jacques. *Les juifs de Tunisie sous Vichy et l'occupation*. Paris: Édition du Centre de Documentation Juive Contemporaine, 1954.

Sebag, Paul. *Histoire des juifs de Tunisie: Des origins à nos jours*. Paris: L'Harmattan, 1991.

———. *Communistes de Tunisie, 1939–1943: Souvenirs et documents*. Paris: L'Harmattan, 2001.

_____. *Les noms des juifs de Tunisie: Origines et significations.* Paris: L'Harmattan, 2002.

Secours Populaire Algérien. *Le martyre des antifascistes dans les camps de concentration de l'Afrique du Nord.* Algiers: n.p., n.d.

Steinberg, Lucien. *The Jews Against Hitler.* London: Gordon and Cremonesi, 1974.

Stillman, Norman A. *The Jews of Arab Lands: A History and Source Book.* Philadelphia: Jewish Publication Society of America, 1979.

_____. *The Jews of Arab Lands in Modern Times.* Philadelpha: Jewish Publication Society, 1991.

Szajkowski, Zosa. *Jews and the French Foreign Legion.* New York: Ktav Publishing House, 1975.

Verrier, Anthony. *Assassination in Algiers: Churchill, Roosevelt, De Gaulle, and the Murder of Admiral Darlan.* New York: W. W. Norton and Company, 1990.

Zanuck, Darryl F. *Tunis Expedition.* New York: Random House, 1943.

Zitouna, Mohamed Moncef. *Docteur Mohamed Tlatli (1890–1943).* Tunis: Centre de Publication Universitaire, 2004.

Articles

Aboulker, José. "La part de la résistance française dans les événements de l'Afrique du Nord." *Les Cahiers Français* 47 (August 1943): 3–45.

_____. "Témoignage: Alger, 8 Novembre 1942," *France 1940–1945: Des juifs en résistance. Le Monde Juif* 152 (September–December 1994): 146–153.

Ahmed, Eqbal. "Questions of Rights." *Dawn,* September 27, 1992.

'Alloush, Ibrahim. "A Conversation with Dr. Ibrahim 'Alloush." *Journal for Historical Review* 20 (3) (May–June 2001): 7. Available on-line at http://www.ihr.org/jhr/v20/v20n3p-7_alloush.html.

Amipaz-Silber, Gitta. "Relations Between Jews and Arabs in Vichy Algeria." *Massuah* 15 (1987): 140–150.

Aouate, Yves-Claude. "Les Algériens musulmans et les mesures antijuives du gouvernement de Vichy (1940–1942)." *Pardes* 16 (1992): 189–202.

Armati, Lucas, and Meriem Amellal. "Ces musulmans qui ont aidé des juifs." *Memoires Vives* (February 2004): 37.

Assouline, Albert. "Une vocation ignorée de la mosquée de Paris." *Almanach du Combattant* (1983): 123–124.

Avrahami, Yitzhak. "The Jews of Tunisia Under the Vichy Authority and the German Occupation, October 1940–May 1943." *Shorashim ba-Mizrach* (1989): 403–440.

Bessis, Juliette. "Les États-Unis et le protectorat tunisien dans la Deuxième Guerre Mondiale." In *La Tunisie de 1939 à 1945: Actes du Quatrième Séminaire sur l'Histoire du Mouvement National*. Tunis: Tunisian Ministry of Education, 1989.

Caldwell, Christopher. "Liberté, Égalité, Judéophobie: Why Le Pen Is the Least of France's Problems." *Weekly Standard*, May 6, 2002.

Chaibi, Mohamed Lotfi. "Éléments pour l'étude de quelques comportements inter-ethniques en Tunisie durant l'occupation germano-italienne." In Charles-Robert Ageron, ed., *Mélanges*, vol. 1, pp. 135–172. Tunis: Fondation Temimi, 1996.

Cherif, Mohamed-Hedi. "Mouvement national et occupation germano-italienne de la Tunisie (Novembre 1942–Mai 1943)." In *La Tunisie de 1939 à 1945: Actes du Quatrième Séminaire sur l'Histoire du Mouvement National*. Tunis: Ministry of Education, 1989.

Chouraqui, Sidney. "Le camp de juifs français de Badeau ou Vichy après Vichy." *Revue d'Histoire de la Shoah* 161 (September–December 1997): 217–245.

Cohen, David. "Le roi Mohammed V et les juifs du Maroc." *Information Juive* (Paris) 59 (October 1986): 12.

Cole, Bruce. "How to Combat 'American Amnesia.'" *Wall Street Journal*, November 24, 2003.

de Lannoy, François. "De la cagoule à la brigade nord-africaine: L'itinéraire de Mohamed el Maadi, alias 'SS Mohamed.'" *39/45 Magazine* (Bayeux) 80 (1993): 34–38.

———. "Hitler et les nationalismes arabes." *39/45 Magazine* 80 (1993): 18–23.

Friedman, Matti. "End of Story." *Jerusalem Report*, May 31, 2004.

Habibi, Emil. "Your Holocaust, Our Catastrophe." *Tel Aviv Review* 1 (1988): 332–336.

Herskovits, Annette. "The Mosque That Sheltered Jews." *Street Spirit* (February 2005). Available on-line at http://www.thestreetspirit.org/Feb2005/mosque.htm.

Jancu, Robert. "Wanted by the Arabs—'A Holocaust.'" *Judaism* 38 (2) (Spring 1989): 135–142.

Kaddache, Mahfoud. "L'opinion politique musulman en Algérie et l'administration française (1939–1942)." *Revue d'Histoire de la Seconde Guerre Mondiale* 114 (1979): 95–115.

Laloum, Jean. "La déportation des juifs natifs d'Algérie." *Le Monde Juif* 129 (January–March 1988): 33–48.

Laskier, Michael M. "Between Vichy Antisemitism and German Harassment: The Jews of North Africa During the Early 1940s." *Modern Judaism* 11 (3) (October 1991): 343–369.

Levisse-Touzé, Christine. "Les camps d'internement en Afrique du Nord pendant la Seconde Guerre Mondiale." In Charles-Robert Ageron, ed., *Mélanges*, vol. 2, pp. 601–608. Tunis: Fondation Temimi, 1996.

Lewis, Bernard. "The Revolt of Islam." *New Yorker*, November 19, 2001.

Litvak, Meir, and Esther Webman. "The Representation of the Holocaust in the Arab World." *Journal of Israeli History* (Spring 2004): 100–115.

Merchet, Jean-Dominique. "Quand Vichy internait ses soldats juifs d'Algérie." *Libération* (Paris), December 30, 1997.

Milles, François. "Première revanche: Rommel: 'Les Juifs dans le desert.'" In Jerôme Tharaud, ed, *Le Chemin d'Israel*. Paris: Plon, 1973.

Nataf, Claude. "Les juifs de Tunisie face à Vichy et aux persécutions allemandes." *Pardes* 16 (1992): 203–231.

"Nazis Planned Holocaust for Palestine: Historians." *Boston Globe,* April 7, 2006.

Ney, Napoleon. "The Proposed Trans-Saharian Railway." *Scribner's Magazine* 10 (July–December 1891): 632–644.

Rainero, R. "La politique fasciste à l'égard de l'Afrique du Nord: L'épée de l'Islam et la revendification sur la Tunisie." *Revue Française d'Histoire d'Outre-Mer* 64 (237) (1977): 498–515.

Raphael, Lois A. C. "Dakar and the Desert Road." *Political Science Quarterly* 59 (1) (March 1944): 15–29.

Rey-Goldzeiguer, Annie. "L'opinion publique tunisienne, 1940–1944." In *La Tunisie de 1939 à 1945: Actes du Quatrième Séminaire sur l'Histoire du Mouvement National*. Tunis: Ministry of Education, 1989.

Rondot, Pierre. "M'Hamed Chenik: Pionnier de l'indépendance tunisienne (1889–1976)." *L'Afrique et l'Asie* 111 (1976): 37–40.

Saadoun, Haim. "The Effect of the Palestinian Issue on Muslim-Jewish Relations in the Arab World: The Case of Tunisia (1929–1939)." In *Israel and Ishmael: Studies in Muslim-Jewish Relations,* pp. 105–123. London: Curzon, 2000.

Smith, Kingsbury. "Unrevealed Facts About Robert Murphy." *American Mercury* 59 (251) (November 1944): 528.

Snoussi, Mohamed Larbi. "Tolérance et intolérance en Tunisie au début de la colonisation: Le cas des juifs tunisiens (1881–1914)." *Revue d'Histoire Maghrébine* 109 (January 2003): 79–107.

Taieb-Carlen, Sarah. "The Jews of North Africa." *Canadian Jewish News,* September 25, 2003.

Tarnopolsky, Noga. "The Arab Institute for Holocaust Research and Education." *Forward,* April 29, 2005.

Miscellany

This section includes manuscripts, reports, speeches, films, video testimonies, special translations, and other citations.

Abdallah Mahmoud, Fatima. "Accursed Forever and Ever." *Al-Akhbar* (Egypt), April 29, 2002. Translated by Middle East Media Research Institute (hereafter MEMRI), May 3, 2002, Special Dispatch Series, no. 375.

Alexander, Harry. Videotaped oral history interview, U.S. Holocaust Memorial Museum Library, February 11, 1992.

'Alloush, Ibrahim. Interview by al-Jazeera, August 23, 2005. Translated by MEMRI, Special Dispatch—Palestinian Authority/Antisemitism Documentation Project, August 31, 2005, no. 976.

Anti-Defamation League."Holocaust Denial in the Middle East: The Latest Anti-Israel Propaganda Theme." 2001.

_____. "First Arab Museum on Holocaust: Anti-Israel Theme Undermines Educational Message." Press release, March 20, 2005. Available on-line at http://www.adl.org/PresRele/IslME_62/4667_62.htm.

Azm, Sadiq Jalal al-. "Democratisation Is a Gradual Process." Interview in *Qantara*, May 27, 2003. Available on-line at http://www.qantara.de/webcom/show_article.php/_c-476/_nr-1/_p-1/i.html?PHPSESSID=586932399788bbaf8.

Berkani, Derri, producer/director. *Une résistance oubliée: La mosquée de Paris.* 1991.

Chemseddine, Anwar, "The Arabs' View of the Holocaust Is Indeed Troubled." Internet essay, The Legacy Project. Available on-line at http://www.legacy-project.org/index.php?page=comment_detail&commentID=1&sympID=1.

Curtiz, Michael, director; Julius J. Epstein, Philip G. Epstein, and Howard Koch, screenwriters. *Casablanca.* 1942.

Filaly-Ansari, Abdou. "The Holocaust Creates a Real Uneasiness Within Informed Opinion." Internet essay, The Legacy Project. Available on-line at http://www.legacy-project.org/index.php?page=comment_detail&commentID=11&sympID=1.

Guland, Olivier. "Chirac: There Are No Anti-Semites in France." *Arutz-Sheva* (radio station), January 13, 2002. Available on-line at http://www.israelnationalnews.com/php3?id=16240.

Hentati, Danielle. "Camp d'internement de Sousse, 1942–1943." Private research paper, July 2005.

"An Israeli Arab Initiative to Visit Auschwitz." MEMRI, April 25, 2003, Inquiry and Analysis Series, no. 136.

Khouri, Rami G. "The Holocaust, Seen from the Arab World." Internet essay, The Legacy Project, 2001. Available on-line at http://www.legacy-project.org/index.php?page=symp_detail&sympID=1.

Levisse-Touzé, Christine. "L'épuration à Alger." Presentation at a colloquium titled, "Du nazisme à la purification ethnique: Évolution du crime contre l'humanité," December 10, 2001. Available on-line at www.memoresist.org/10-12-2001.php.

Middle East Media Research Institute (MEMRI). Inquiry and Analysis Series No. 95 (Archives), May 30, 2002, no. 95.

Pinchon-Falcone, M., and D. Hentati. *Mémoires de la Deuxième Guerre Mondiale en Tunisie.* Private publication of the History Club of the Lycée Pierre Mendès-France. Tunis, 2005.

Qasim, Faisal al-. al-Jazeera, May 15, 2001. Translated by MEMRI, Special Dispatch Series, June 6, 2001, no. 225.

Rantisi, Abd al-Aziz. *al-Risala*, August 23, 2005. Translated by MEMRI, Special Dispatch—Palestinian/Arab Antisemitism, August 27, 2003, no. 558.

Sacks, Jonathan. "Muslims and Jews in Europe Today." Presentation to The Washington Institute for Near East Policy, Washington, DC, November 28, 2005. Available on-line at http://www.washingtoninstitute.org/html/pdf/sacks-20051128.pdf.

Satloff, Robert. "Devising a Public Diplomacy Campaign Toward the Middle East: Part II—Core Elements." Policy Watch no. 580, October 31, 2001. Available on-line at http://washingtoninstitute.org/templateC05.php?CID=1458.

Shaked, Edith. "The Holocaust: Reexamining the Wannsee Conference, Himmler's Appointments Book, and Tunisian Jews." The Nizkor Project. Available on-line at http://www.nizkor.org/hweb/people/s/shaked-edith/re-examining -wannsee.html.

Société d'Histoire des Juifs de Tunisie. Photo exhibition on "Les juifs de Tunisie pendant la Seconde Guerre Mondiale," Paris, December 2002–January 2003.

"Thinking About the Holocaust 60 Years Later: A Multinational Public Opinion Survey," March–April 2005, conducted for the American Jewish Committee. Available on-line at http://www.ajc.org/site/apps/nl/content3 .asp?c=ijTI2PHKoG&b=846741&ct=1025513.

Tondowski, Morice. Videotaped oral history, Shoah Visual History Foundation.

Trenner, Maximilian. "La croix gammée s'aventure en Tunisie." Unpublished manuscript: Centre de Documentation Juive Contemporaine Archives, 380- 8-1, n.d.

Tubiana, Emile. Unpublished memoir of childhood, 2004.

U.S. History National Assessment of Education Progress. Available on-line at http://www.nces.ed.gov/nationsreportcard/ushistory/results.

Wistrich, Robert S. "Muslim Anti-Semitism: A Clear and Present Danger." Report to the American Jewish Committee, April 2002.

World Jewish Congress. *Collection of Reports and Documents Pertaining to the Jewish Situation in French North Africa.* June 1943.

Yad Vashem. *Yehudai tsafon afrikiya b'tkufat ha-shoah* (The Jews of North Africa During the Holocaust Era). Educational curriculum issued 2006.

Archives Researched

American Friends Service Committee, Philadelphia

American Jewish Historical Society, New York

American Jewish Joint Distribution Committee, New York

Avraham Harman Institute of Contemporary Jewry, Hebrew University, Jerusalem

Centre de Documentation Juive Contemporaine, Paris

The Citadel, South Carolina (Papers of Mark Clark)

Colonel Robert R. McCormack Research Center, First Division Museum, Wheaton, Illinois

French government archives (Paris, Le Mans, Nantes)

German federal archives (Berlin, Freiburg)

Hoover Institution, Stanford University (Papers of Robert Murphy)

Institut Supérieure de la Mouvement Nationale, Tunis
Institute Ben Zvi, Jerusalem
Jewish Welfare Board, New York
Karl Marx Library, London (Records of International Brigade Association)
U.S. National Archives, Washington, DC
Public Record Office, British Foreign Office Archives
Service Historique de l'Armée de Terre, Vincennes, France
Shoah Visual History Foundation, Los Angeles
Tunisian National Archives, Tunis
Tunisian National Military Museum, Ksar Ouerda, Tunis
U.S. Holocaust Memorial Museum, Washington, DC
Yad Vashem (Holocaust Martyrs' and Heroes' Remembrance Authority), Jerusalem

INDEX

THE INDEX includes references to people, places, institutions and specialized terms cited in this book. For the sake of brevity, only selected references to terms cited repeatedly in the text (e.g., Jews, Arabs, Algeria) are included. Persons mentioned only by their first name in the text are not included. As noted in the introduction, with a few exceptions, I have used the spelling most closely associated with the person in question. While this can sometimes produce idiosyncrasies, it provides a more accurate reflection of how names were actually spelled and used.

PublicAffairs is a publishing house founded in 1997. It is a tribute to the standards, values, and flair of three persons who have served as mentors to countless reporters, writers, editors, and book people of all kinds, including me.

I.F. Stone, proprietor of *I. F. Stone's Weekly*, combined a commitment to the First Amendment with entrepreneurial zeal and reporting skill and became one of the great independent journalists in American history. At the age of eighty, Izzy published *The Trial of Socrates*, which was a national bestseller. He wrote the book after he taught himself ancient Greek.

Benjamin C. Bradlee was for nearly thirty years the charismatic editorial leader of *The Washington Post*. It was Ben who gave the *Post* the range and courage to pursue such historic issues as Watergate. He supported his reporters with a tenacity that made them fearless and it is no accident that so many became authors of influential, best-selling books.

Robert L. Bernstein, the chief executive of Random House for more than a quarter century, guided one of the nation's premier publishing houses. Bob was personally responsible for many books of political dissent and argument that challenged tyranny around the globe. He is also the founder and longtime chair of Human Rights Watch, one of the most respected human rights organizations in the world.

For fifty years, the banner of Public Affairs Press was carried by its owner Morris B. Schnapper, who published Gandhi, Nasser, Toynbee, Truman, and about 1,500 other authors. In 1983, Schnapper was described by *The Washington Post* as "a redoubtable gadfly." His legacy will endure in the books to come.

Peter Osnos, *Founder and Editor-at-Large*